PERFORMANCE AND ACCOUNTABILITY REPORT

FY 2008

U.S.NRC

United States Nuclear Regulatory Commission

Protecting People and the Environment

MISSION

License and regulate the Nation's civilian use of byproduct, source,

and special nuclear materials to ensure adequate protection of

public health and safety, promote the common defense and security,

and protect the environment.

VISION

Excellence in regulating the safe and secure use and management

of radioactive materials for the public good.

TABLE OF CONTENTS

United States Nuclear Regulatory Commission

Protecting People and the Environment

From left to right, Commissioner Kristine L. Svinicki, Commissioner Gregory B. Jaczko, Chairman Dale E. Klein, and Commissioner Peter B. Lyons.

A MESSAGE FROM THE CHAIRMAN

I am pleased to present the U.S. Nuclear Regulatory Commission's (NRC's) Performance and Accountability Report for fiscal year (FY) 2008. The report highlights our achievements in meeting the two strategic goals—safety and security—while adhering to the principles of good regulation—independence, openness, efficiency, clarity, and reliability. Continuing with our trend of excellence in reporting, the NRC received a seventh consecutive Certificate of Excellence in Accountability Reporting from the Association of Government Accountants (AGA) for the FY 2007 Performance and Accountability Report.

In 2008, the NRC continued to provide effective and efficient regulatory oversight of the nuclear industry as it embarks upon a period of significant growth and development. The agency is currently reviewing 17 combined license applications to build and operate 26 new nuclear power plants. These proposed nuclear power plants, if approved and constructed, would be the first new plants to be built in over 30 years, and are of critical importance to the industry and the Nation. The NRC has streamlined its application process to ensure that nuclear power plants are able to contribute safely to meeting the growing demand for electricity while minimizing the cost and time required to receive regulatory approval for new plants, consistent with safety and security requirements.

In FY 2008, the NRC received the U.S. Department of Energy's application for construction of the Nation's first geologic repository for high-level nuclear waste at Yucca Mountain, NV. The NRC has found that the application is sufficiently complete for the agency to begin its full technical review.

Commensurate with NRC's programmatic achievements is a commitment to prudently manage the resources entrusted to it by the American public. The NRC continues to position its resources and infrastructure to support our mission to "License and regulate the Nation's civilian use of byproduct, source, and special nuclear materials to ensure adequate protection of public health and safety, promote the common defense and security, and protect the environment." The NRC is proud to have obtained an unqualified opinion on the agency's financial statements for the fifth consecutive year. This report provides information that demonstrates that the agency's financial and performance data are reliable and complete.

The NRC has also made significant strides in improving its financial systems and business operations. A material weakness related to the Federal Information Security Management Act (FISMA) audit from FY 2007 has now been removed. The NRC continues to evaluate its internal controls and to implement internal control improvements, including those related to financial reporting and financial management systems, as required by the Federal Managers Financial Integrity Act (FMFIA). Based on these FISMA and FMFIA assessments, I have concluded that there is reasonable assurance that the NRC is in substantial compliance with the FMFIA. In support of the President's Management Agenda, the NRC is currently cross-servicing its human resources, payroll, e-Travel, and accounting services. The agency is also in the process of integrating and modernizing its financial systems to enhance internal controls, reporting, and decisionmaking.

The Commission is proud of this year's performance in achieving the agency's safety and security goals and looks forward to continuing its high-quality service to the American public in FY 2009 and beyond.

Dale E. Klein
November 14, 2008

iii

ᴍAGA.

CERTIFICATE OF EXCELLENCE IN ACCOUNTABILITY REPORTING®

Presented to the

U.S. Nuclear Regulatory Commission

In recognition of your outstanding efforts preparing NRC's Performance and Accountability Report for the fiscal year ended September 30, 2007.

A *Certificate of Excellence in Accountability Reporting* is presented by AGA to federal government agencies whose annual Performance and Accountability Reports achieve the highest standards demonstrating accountability and communicating results.

John H. Hummel, CGFM
Chair, Certificate of Excellence
in Accountability Reporting Board

Relmond P. Van Daniker, DBA, CPA
Executive Director, AGA

This Certificate of Excellence was presented by the Association of Government Accountants to the U.S. Nuclear Regulatory Commission for fiscal year 2007 accountability reporting.

CHAPTER 1
MANAGEMENT'S DISCUSSION
AND ANALYSIS

Photo Courtesy of NRC Photo Library.

11555

UNITED STATES
NUCLEAR REGULATORY
COMMISSION

WWW.NRC.GOV

U.S. Nuclear Regulatory Commission headquarters in Rockville, MD.

INTRODUCTION

The U.S. Nuclear Regulatory Commission (NRC) Performance and Accountability Report presents the agency's program performance and financial management information during fiscal year (FY) 2008. The annual report provides an opportunity for the public to assess how effectively the NRC uses its funds to achieve results. When preparing this report, the NRC staff followed the requirements of the Chief Financial Officers Act, as amended by the Reports Consolidation Act, Government Management Reform Act of 1994, and Government Performance Results Act of 1993. This Performance and Accountability Report covers activities from October 1, 2007, to September 30, 2008.

The NRC emphasizes keeping the public informed of its activities. Visit our Web site at http://www.nrc.gov to access this report and to learn more about who we are and what we do to serve the American public.

Chapter 1, "Management's Discussion and Analysis," provides an overview of the NRC and its accomplishments during FY 2008. Chapter 1 consists of the following seven sections: "About the NRC" describes the agency's mission, organizational structure, and regulatory responsibility; "Program Performance Overview" summarizes the agency's success in achieving its strategic goals, which are further described in Chapter 2; "Program Performance Results" shows the agency's program performance results; "Future Challenges" includes forward-looking information; "President's Management Agenda" describes the agency progress in five management initiatives; "Financial Performance Overview" highlights the NRC's financial position and audit results contained in Chapter 3; and "Systems, Controls, and Legal Compliance" describes the agency's compliance with key legal and regulatory requirements.

ABOUT THE NRC

The U.S. Congress established the NRC on January 19, 1975, as an independent Federal agency regulating the commercial and institutional uses of nuclear materials. The Atomic Energy Act, as amended, and the Energy Reorganization Act, as amended, define the NRC's purpose. These acts provide the foundation for the NRC's mission to regulate the Nation's civilian use of byproduct, source, and special nuclear materials to ensure adequate protection of public health and safety, to promote the common defense and security, and to protect the environment.

To fulfill its responsibility to protect public health and safety, the NRC performs the following three principal regulatory functions:

(1) Establishes standards and regulations.

(2) Issues licenses for nuclear facilities and users of nuclear materials.

(3) Inspects facilities and users of nuclear materials to ensure compliance with regulatory requirements.

The agency regulates civilian nuclear power plants, other nuclear facilities, as well as other uses of nuclear materials. These other uses include nuclear medicine programs at hospitals; academic activities at educational institutions; research work; industrial applications, such as gauges and testing equipment; and the transport, storage, and disposal of nuclear materials and wastes.

ORGANIZATION

The NRC is headed by a Commission composed of five members, with one member designated by the President to serve as Chairman. With the advice and consent of the Senate, the President appoints each member to serve a 5-year term. The Chairman is the principal executive officer and official spokesman for the Commission. The Executive Director for Operations carries out program policies and decisions made by the Commission.

The NRC's headquarters is located in Rockville, MD. Four regional offices are located in King of Prussia, PA; Atlanta, GA; Lisle, IL; and Arlington, TX. The NRC's technical training center is located in Chattanooga, TN. The NRC also employs at least two resident inspectors at each of the Nation's nuclear power reactor sites. The NRC's Operations Center, located at the headquarters building in Rockville, MD, is the focal point for the agency's communications with its licensees, State agencies, and other Federal agencies concerning operating events in the commercial nuclear sector. NRC operations officers staff the Operations Center 24 hours a day. Appendix F to this report presents the NRC organization chart.

The NRC's budget for FY 2008 was $926.1 million (see Figure 1) with 3,707 full-time equivalent staff (see Figure 2). The NRC recovers approximately 90% of its appropriations from fees paid by NRC licensees.

Figure 1
NRC BUDGETARY AUTHORITY, FY 2003–2008
(Dollars in Millions)

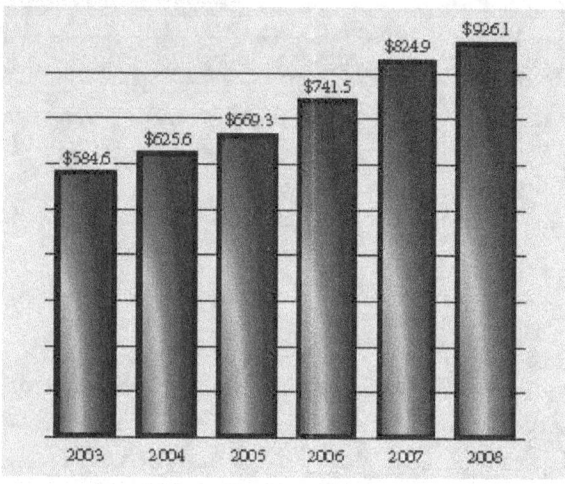

Figure 2
NRC PERSONNEL CEILING, FY 2003–2008
(Staff)

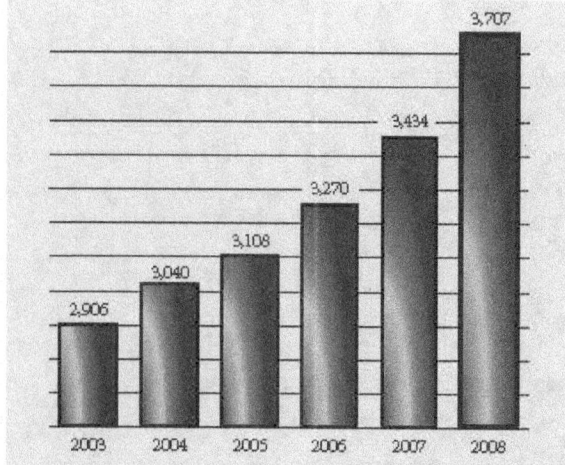

THE NUCLEAR INDUSTRY

The NRC regulates the commercial use of radioactive materials. The nuclear material cycle begins with the mining and production of nuclear fuel, continues with the use of nuclear fuel to power the Nation's 104 nuclear power plants, and ends with the safe transportation and storage of spent nuclear fuel and other nuclear waste. The NRC's regulatory programs ensure that radioactive materials are used safely and securely at every stage in the nuclear material cycle. Under the NRC's Agreement State program, 35 States have assumed primary regulatory responsibility over the industrial, medical, and other smaller users of nuclear materials in their States. The NRC works closely with these States to ensure that they maintain public safety. To address safety and security issues, the NRC has developed regulatory practices, knowledge, and expertise specific to each activity in the nuclear material cycle.

Approximately 20 percent of the Nation's electricity is generated by the 104 NRC-licensed commercial nuclear reactors operating in 31 States (see Figure 3). Since 1996, nuclear electric generation has increased by approximately 20 percent. The NRC oversees 3,738 licenses for medical, academic, industrial, and general uses of nuclear materials (see Figure 4). The agency conducts approximately 1,287 health and safety inspections of its nuclear material licensees annually. In addition, the 35 Agreement States oversee 18,700 licenses.

Figure 3
U.S. COMMERCIAL NUCLEAR POWER REACTORS

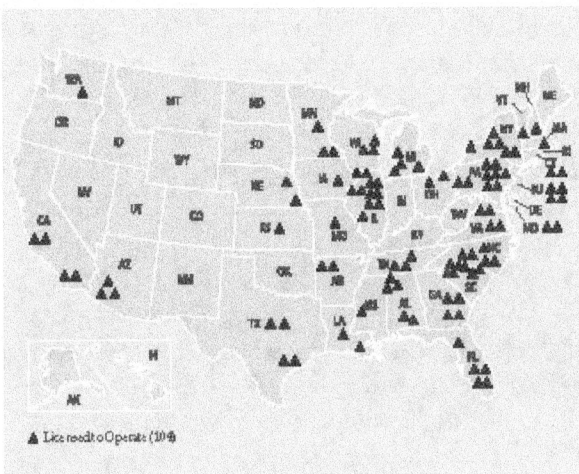

▲ Licensed to Operate (104)

Figure 4
U.S. MATERIALS LICENSEES

☐ NRC ■ Agreement States

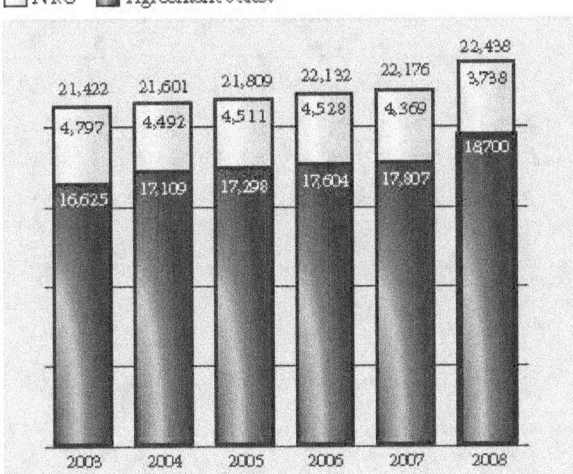

The NRC, Agreement States, and their licensees share a common responsibility to protect public health and safety.

FUEL FACILITIES

The production of nuclear fuel begins at uranium mines where milled uranium ore is used to produce a uranium concentrate called "yellow cake." At a special facility, the yellow cake is converted into uranium hexafluoride gas and loaded into cylinders. The cylinders are sent to a gaseous diffusion plant, where uranium is enriched for use as reactor fuel. The enriched uranium is then converted into oxide powder, fabricated into fuel pellets (each about the size of a fingertip), loaded into metal fuel rods about 3.5 meters long, and bundled into reactor fuel assemblies at a fuel fabrication facility. Assemblies are then transported to nuclear power plants, nonpower research reactor facilities, and naval propulsion reactors for use as fuel. The NRC licenses eight major fuel fabrication and production facilities and three enrichment facilities in the United States. Because they handle extremely hazardous material, these facilities take special precautions to prevent theft, diversion by terrorists, and dangerous exposures to workers and the public from this nuclear material.

REACTORS

Power plants change one form of energy into another. Electrical generating plants convert heat energy, the kinetic energy of wind or falling water, or solar energy, into electricity. A nuclear power plant converts heat energy into electricity. Other types of heat-conversion plants burn coal, oil, or gas to produce heat energy that is then used to produce electricity. Nuclear energy cannot be seen. There is no burning of fuel in the usual sense. Rather, energy is given off by the nuclear fuel as certain types of atoms split in a process called nuclear fission. This energy is in the form of fast-moving particles and invisible radiation. As the particles and radiation move through the fuel and surrounding water, the energy is converted into heat. The radiation energy can be hazardous, and facilities take special precautions to protect people and the environment from these hazards.

Because the fission reaction produces potentially hazardous radioactive materials, nuclear power plants are equipped with safety systems to protect workers, the public, and the environment. Radioactive materials require careful use because they produce radiation, a form of energy that can damage human cells. Depending on the amount and duration of the exposure, radiation can potentially cause cancer. In

a nuclear reactor, most hazardous radioactive substances, called fission byproducts, are trapped in the fuel pellets or in the sealed metal tubes holding the fuel. However, small amounts of these radioactive fission byproducts, principally gases, become mixed with the water passing through the reactor. Other impurities in the water also become radioactive as they pass through the reactor. The facility processes and filters the water to remove these radioactive impurities and then returns the water to the reactor cooling system.

Figure 5
SCHEMATIC OF A NUCLEAR POWER REACTOR

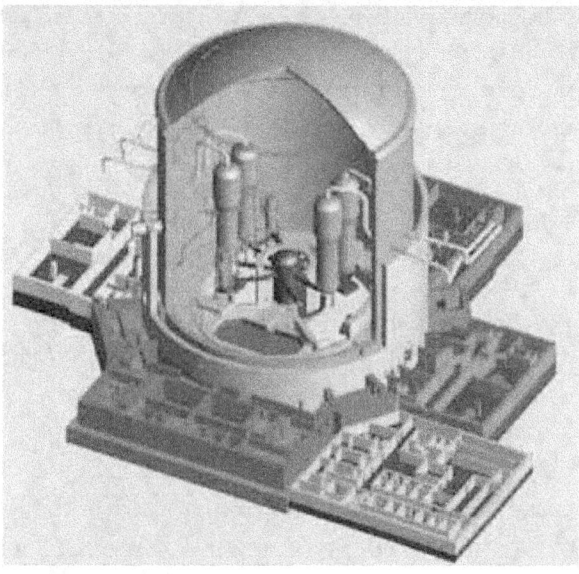

MATERIALS USERS

The medical, academic, and industrial fields all use nuclear materials. For example, about one-third of all patients admitted to U.S. hospitals are diagnosed or treated using radioisotopes. Most major hospitals have specific departments dedicated to nuclear medicine. In all, about 112 million nuclear medicine or radiation therapy procedures are performed annually, with the vast majority used in diagnoses. Radioactive materials used as a diagnostic tool can identify the status of a disease and minimize the need for surgery. Radioisotopes give doctors the ability to look inside the body and observe soft tissues and organs, in a manner similar to the way X-rays provide images of bones. Radioisotopes carried in the blood also allow doctors to detect clogged arteries or check the functioning of the circulatory system.

The same property that makes radiation hazardous can also make it useful in treating certain diseases like cancer. When living tissue is exposed to high levels of radiation, cells can be destroyed or damaged. Doctors can selectively expose cancerous cells (cells that are dividing uncontrollably) to radiation to either destroy these cells or damage them so they can no longer reproduce.

Many of today's industrial processes also use nuclear materials. High-tech methods that ensure the quality of manufactured products often rely on radiation generated by radioisotopes. To determine whether a well drilled deep into the ground has the potential for producing oil, geologists use nuclear well-logging, a technique that employs radiation from a radioisotope inside the well to detect the presence of different materials. Radioisotopes are also used to sterilize instruments; find flaws in critical steel parts and welds that go into automobiles and modern buildings; authenticate valuable works of art; and solve crimes by spotting trace elements of poison. Radioisotopes can also eliminate dust from film and compact discs and reduce static electricity (which may create a fire hazard) from can labels. In manufacturing, radiation can change the characteristics of materials, often giving them features that are highly desirable. For example, wood and plastic composites treated with gamma radiation resist abrasion and require low maintenance. As a result, they are used for some flooring in high-traffic areas of department stores, airports, hotels, and churches.

WASTE DISPOSAL

During normal operations, a nuclear power plant generates the following two types of radioactive waste: high-level waste, which consists of used fuel (usually called spent fuel), and low-level waste, which includes contaminated equipment, filters, maintenance materials, and resins used in purifying water for the reactor cooling system. Other users of radioactive materials also generate low-level waste.

Nuclear power plants handle each type of radioactive waste differently. They must use special procedures in the handling of the spent fuel because it contains the highly radioactive fission byproducts created while the reactor was operating. Typically, the spent fuel from nuclear power plants is stored in water-filled pools at each reactor site or at a storage facility in Illinois. The water in the spent fuel storage pool provides cooling and adequately shields and protects workers from the radiation. Several nuclear power plants have also begun using dry casks to store spent fuel. These heavy metal or concrete casks rest on concrete pads adjacent to the reactor facility. The thick layers of concrete and steel in these casks shield workers and the public from radiation.

Currently most spent fuel in the United States remains stored at individual plants. Permanent disposal of spent fuel from nuclear power plants requires a disposal facility that can provide reasonable assurance that the waste will remain isolated for thousands of years. The U.S. Department of Energy submitted an application for a permanent disposal facility at Yucca Mountain, NV, for spent fuel, which is docketed and under review.

Licensees often store low-level waste onsite until its radioactivity has decayed and the waste can be disposed of as ordinary trash, or until amounts are large enough for shipment to a low-level waste disposal site in containers approved by the U.S. Department of Transportation. The NRC has developed a waste classification system for low-level radioactive waste based on its potential hazards, and has specified disposal and waste form requirements for each of the following general classes of waste: Class A, Class B, and Class C waste. Generally, Class A waste contains lower concentrations of radioactive material than Class B and Class C wastes. There are two low-level disposal facilities that accept a broad range of low-level wastes. They are located in Barnwell, SC, and Richland, WA.

PROGRAM PERFORMANCE OVERVIEW

The NRC's FY 2008–2013 Strategic Plan determines the agency's long-term goals and strategic direction. The agency has two strategic goals: safety and security. To achieve its goals, the agency is organized into two major programs: the Nuclear Reactor Safety Program, and Nuclear Materials and Waste Safety Program.

NUCLEAR REACTOR SAFETY PROGRAM

The Nuclear Reactor Safety Program encompasses all NRC efforts to ensure that civilian nuclear power reactor facilities and research and test reactors are licensed and operated in a manner that adequately protects the public health and safety, preserves the environment, and protects against radiological sabotage and theft or diversion of special nuclear materials.

NUCLEAR MATERIALS AND WASTE SAFETY PROGRAM

The Nuclear Materials and Waste Safety Program focuses on the safe and secure use of remaining radioactive materials. The Nuclear Materials and Waste Safety Program regulates fuel facilities, medical and industrial nuclear materials users, the disposal of both high-level and low-level waste, the decommissioning of power plants, and the storage and transportation of spent nuclear fuel.

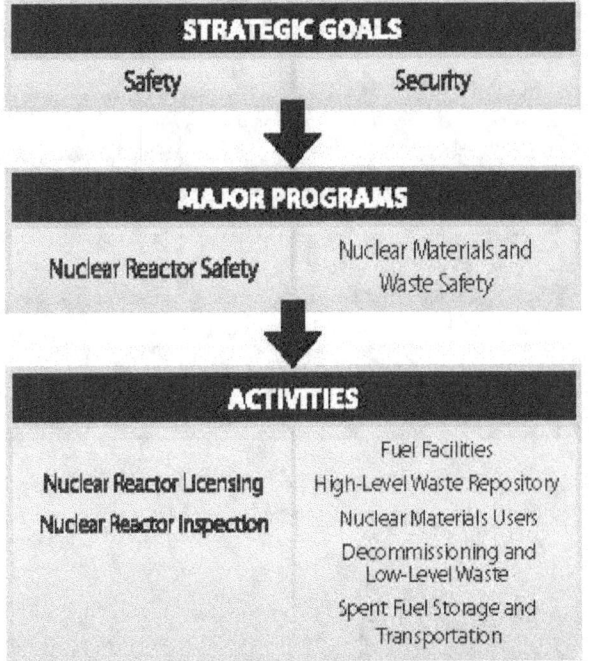

NRC PERFORMANCE MEASURE RESULTS

FY 2008 Safety Goal

Performance Measures	2003	2004	2005	2006	2007	2008
1. Number of new conditions evaluated as red by the Reactor Oversight Process is ≤3.	1	1	0	0	0	0
2. Number of significant accident sequence precursors of a nuclear reactor accident is zero.	0	0	0	0	0	0
3. Number of operating reactors with integrated performance that entered the Manual Chapter 0350 process, or the multiple/repetitive degraded cornerstone column, or the unacceptable performance column of the Reactor Oversight Process Action Matrix, with no performance exceeding Abnormal Occurrence Criterion I.D.4 is ≤4.	2	1	0	0	1	0
4. Number of significant adverse trends in industry safety performance with no trend exceeding the Abnormal Occurrence Criterion I.D.4 is ≤1.	0	0	0	0	0	0
5. Number of events with radiation exposures to the public and occupational workers that exceed Abnormal Occurrence Criterion I.A is:						
Reactors: 0	0	0	0	0	0	0
Materials: ≤3	0	0	1	0	0	0
Waste: 0	0	0	0	0	0	0
6. Number of radiological releases to the environment that exceed applicable regulatory limits is:						
Reactor: ≤3	0	0	0	0	0	0
Materials: ≤2	0	1	0	0	0	0
Waste: 0	0	0	0	0	0	0

FY 2008 Security Goal

Performance Measures	2003	2004	2005	2006	2007	2008
1. Number of Unrecovered losses or thefts of risk-significant radioactive sources is zero.	0	0	0	0	0	0
2. Number of substantiated cases of theft or diversion of licensed, risk-significant radioactive sources or formula quantities of special nuclear material, or number of attacks that result in radiological sabotage, is zero.	0	0	0	0	0	0
3. Number of substantiated losses of formula quantities of special nuclear material or substantiated inventory discrepancies of formula quantities of special nuclear material that are caused by theft or diversion or by substantial breakdown of the accountability system sabotage is zero.	0	0	0	0	0	0
4. Number of substantial breakdowns of physical security or material control that significantly weaken the protection against theft, diversion, or sabotage is less than one.	0	0	0	0	0	0
5. Number of significant, unauthorized disclosures of classified and/or safeguards information is zero.	0	0	0	0	0	0

FY 2008 Organizational Excellence Objectives and Associated Measures

Measure	2003	2004	2005	2006	2007	2008
Organizational Excellence Objective 1: Openness						
1 Eighty-eight percent of selected openness output measures achieve performance targets.				50%	66%	80%
a. Ninety percent of stakeholder formal requests for information receive an NRC response within 60 days of receipt.				100%	100%	100%
b. Ninety percent of non-sensitive, unclassified regulatory documents generated by the NRC and sent to the agency's Document Processing Center are released to the public by the 6th working day after the date of the document.				63%	75%	82%
c. Ninety percent of non-sensitive, unclassified regulatory documents received by the NRC that are released to the public by the 6th working day after the document is added to the ADAMS main library.				77%	87%	66%
d. The NRC achieves a 71% user satisfaction score for the agency's public Web site greater than or equal to the Federal Agency Mean score based on results of the yearly American Customer Satisfaction Index for Federal Web sites.				70%	71%	71%
e. Complete 50% of Freedom of Information Act requests in 20 days (median).				61%	67%	71%
f. Issue 90% of Director's Decisions under 10 CFR 2.206 within 120 days.				100%	100%	100%
g. Make 90% of Final Significance Determination Process determinations within 90 days for all potentially greater-than-green findings.				92%	100%	100%
h. Ninety percent of stakeholders believe they were given sufficient opportunity to ask questions or express their views.				90%	96%	97%
i. At least 90% of Category 2 and 3 meetings on regulatory issues for which public notices are issued at least 10 days in advance of the meeting.				92%	93%	90%
j. Complete all of the key stakeholder and public interactions for the reactor performance assessment cycle.						Met
Organizational Excellence Objective 2: Effectiveness						
1. Ninety percent of selected processes deliver efficiency improvements.				25%	60%	80%
a. Reduce the average age at closure for licensing actions by 2.5%.						Not Met
b. At the rate of one per year, Category III license renewal applications will be considered for a 40-year license.				Not Met	Not Met	Met
c. Improve the timeliness of the review process for nuclear power reactor License Termination Plans by at least 30 percent over 3 years (FY 2006-FY 2008) as compared to the historical average.						38%
d. Implement process enhancements to permit improvement for the reactor rulemaking petition timeliness by 2.5%.					5%	Met
f. Reduce the staff cost for letters to DOE by 5%.						40%
2. No more than one instance per program where licensing or regulatory activities unnecessarily impede the safe and beneficial uses of radioactive materials.				0	0	0
Organizational Excellence Objective 3: Operational Excellence						
1. Ninety percent of selected support processes deliver efficiency improvements.				50%	0%	0%
a. Five percent reduction of agency FTE used to develop and submit the FY 2008 and FY 2009 performance budgets.				0%	2%* increase	6% increase
b. Issue offer letter 80% of the time within 45 work days of the closing date of the announcement.				67%	31%	56%
2. Eighty percent of selected NRC management programs deliver intended outcomes.			60%	80%	100%	100%
a. Infrastructure management program.			100%	100%	100%	100%
b. Financial Management & Budget and Performance Integration program.			67%	67%	88%	100%
c. Expanded electronic government program.			50%	75%	75%	75%
d. Management of Human Capital program.			80%	100%	80%	100%

*FY 2007 PAR showed 12%. Data were error and recalculated to be 2%.

PROGRAM PERFORMANCE RESULTS

Ensure Adequate Protection of Public Health and Safety and the Environment

Safety is the primary goal of the NRC. The agency achieves this goal by ensuring that the performance of licensees is at or above acceptable safety levels. NRC safety programs work in conjunction with our licensees in a partnership. The NRC licensees are responsible for designing, constructing, and operating nuclear facilities safely. The NRC is responsible for regulatory oversight of the licensees. NRC safety goal activities are designed to create the following strategic outcomes.

Strategic Outcomes:
- Prevent the occurrence of any nuclear reactor accidents.
- Prevent the occurrence of any inadvertent criticality events.
- Prevent the occurrence of any acute radiation exposures resulting in fatalities.
- Prevent the occurrence of any releases of radioactive materials that result in significant radiation exposures.
- Prevent the occurrence of any releases of radioactive materials that cause significant adverse environmental impacts.

FY 2008 RESULTS

In FY 2008, the NRC achieved all five of its safety goal strategic outcomes. The NRC also uses six performance measures to determine whether it has met its safety goal. The agency met all six performance measure targets in FY 2008.

Three of the performance measures focus on performance at individual nuclear power plants. Inspection results show that all of the nuclear power plants are operating safely. The fourth measure tracks the trends of several key indicators of nuclear power plant safety. This measure is the broadest measure of the safety of nuclear power plants, incorporating

the performance results from all plants to determine industry average results. The measure results show that there were no statistically significant adverse trends in any of the indicators in FY 2008.

The last two safety performance measures track harmful radiation exposures to the public and occupational workers, and radiation exposures that harm the environment. None of these measures exceeded their targets in FY 2008.

Ensure Adequate Protection in the Secure Use and Management of Radioactive Materials

The NRC must remain vigilant in ensuring the security of nuclear facilities and materials in an elevated threat environment. The agency achieves its common defense and security goal using licensing and oversight programs similar to those employed in achieving its safety goal.

Strategic Outcome:
- Prevent any instances where licensed radioactive materials are used domestically in a manner hostile to the security of the United States.

FY 2008 RESULTS

In FY 2008, the NRC achieved its security goal strategic outcome. The NRC also uses five security goal performance measures to determine whether the agency has met its security goal. The agency met all five performance measure targets in FY 2008. The first performance measure tracks unrecovered losses or thefts of risk-significant radioactive sources. The measure ensures that those radioactive sources that the agency has determined to be risk-significant to the public health and safety are accounted for at all times. The ability to account for these sources is critical to secure the nation from "dirty bomb" attacks or other means of radiation dispersal.

The second, third, and fourth performance measures evaluate the number of significant security events and incidents that occur at NRC-licensed facilities. These measures determine whether nuclear facilities maintain adequate protective forces to prevent theft or diversion of nuclear material or sabotage; whether systems in place at licensee plants accurately account for the type and amount of materials processed, utilized, or stored; and whether the facilities account for special nuclear material at all times with no losses of this material. There were no events that met the conditions for this measure in FY 2008.

The last security measure tracks significant unauthorized disclosures of classified and/or safeguards information that may cause damage to national security or public safety. This measure focuses on whether classified information or safeguards information is stored and utilized in such a way as to prevent its disclosure to the public, terrorist organizations, other nations, or personnel without a need to know. Unauthorized disclosures can harm national security or compromise public health and safety. The measure also focuses on whether controls are in place to maintain and secure the various devices and systems (electronic or paper based) which the agency and its licensees use to store, transmit, and utilize this information. There were no documented disclosures of this type of information during FY 2008.

ORGANIZATIONAL EXCELLENCE OBJECTIVES
Openness, Effectiveness, and Operational Excellence

This FY 2008 Performance and Accountability Report reflects the agency's new FY 2008–2013 Strategic Plan. Under this new strategic plan, the former goals of openness, effectiveness, and operational excellence are now considered to be organizational excellence objectives because they support achievement of the agency's two strategic goals of safety and security. The performance measures related to these three former strategic goals remain in effect in FY 2008, as required by the Government Performance Results Act (GPRA). These measures will not be reported after this year's report.

Openness

The agency missed its openness measure target requiring that 88 percent of selected openness output measures achieve their goals. The agency achieved a score on this measure of 80 percent, missing 2 out of 10 output measure targets.

The agency missed the output measure target that called for 90 percent of nonsensitive, unclassified regulatory documents generated by the NRC and sent to the agency's Document Processing Center be released to the public by the 6th working day after the date of the document. However, the agency has improved since FY 2006, increasing from 63 percent to 75 percent in FY 2007 and 82 percent in FY 2008. The agency continues to struggle to meet this measure because of the time it takes to conduct its internal document review processes. The agency will continue to review these processes to find additional efficiencies to reduce the amount of time necessary to release documents.

The agency also missed the output measure target requiring 90 percent of nonsensitive, unclassified regulatory documents to be released by the 6th working day after the document is added to the Agencywide Documents Access and Management System (ADAMS). The results declined from 87 percent in FY 2007 to 66 percent in FY 2008. As with the previous measure, the NRC needs to find efficiencies to reduce the time to process documents. The agency is also engaging in activities to increase staff training as a means to close the gap on this measure.

Effectiveness

The agency successfully met the targets for its two performance measures for effectiveness. The effectiveness measures focus on achieving efficiencies in agency processes.

Operational Excellence

The agency achieved one of two operational excellence performance measures. The first measure, to deliver efficiency improvements for selected support processes, was not achieved. The agency set a target to reduce the agency staff hours used to develop its performance budget by 5 percent.

However, the NRC experienced a large growth in staff due to the New Reactor Program ramping up to receive applications from licensees to develop and construct new reactors. As a result, additional budget staff was hired to manage the program. The agency is developing a new budget process that is expected to generate efficiencies that will reduce budget staff hours in FY 2009. In addition the agency was unable to issue an offer letter to new employees within 45 work days of the closing date of the employment announcement 80 percent of the time. Offer letters were issued within 45 days only 56 percent of the time in FY 2008. As a result, the NRC undertook a Lean Six Sigma study, a corporate improvement methodology, during the second quarter of FY 2007 to evaluate the hiring process from the closing date of the announcement to the offer date and develop recommendations to help streamline that process. The agency is currently leading a separate effort to implement the recommendations made by the Lean Six Sigma study workgroup and to develop a plan to assess the NRC's progress towards reducing the hiring time frame to meet the 45-day target.

The second operational excellence performance measure assessed the agency's performance in delivering outcomes in four management programs: infrastructure management, financial management, information technology management, and human capital management. These programs were able to meet their intended outcomes.

DATA COMPLETENESS AND RELIABILITY

The NRC considers the data contained in this report to be complete, reliable, and relevant. The data are complete because the agency reports actual performance data for every performance goal and indicator in the report. The agency also considers the data in this report reliable and relevant, because it has been validated and verified. Appendix D, "Verification and Validation of NRC's Measures and Metrics," contains the processes the agency uses to collect, validate, and verify performance data in this report.

PROGRAM ASSESSMENT RATING TOOL RESULTS

There were no Program Assessment Rating Tool (PART) reviews conducted by the agency during FYs 2006 and 2008. The following table shows the results of the agency's PART scores from FY 2003 to FY 2007.

Program	Year	Score	Rating
Reactor Inspection and Performance Assessment	2003	89	Effective
Fuel Facilities Licensing and Inspection	2003	89	Effective
Nuclear Materials Users Licensing and Inspection	2004	93	Effective
Reactor Licensing	2005	74	Moderately Effective
Spent Fuel Storage and Transportation Licensing and Inspection	2005	89	Effective
Decommissioning and Low-Level Waste	2007	91	Effective
High-Level Waste Repository	2007	87	Effective

FUTURE CHALLENGES

The NRC ensures that the health and safety of the American public and the environment are adequately protected from any harmful effects of using nuclear materials. The industry has experienced a substantial improvement in safety at nuclear power plants over the past 20 years as both the nuclear industry and the NRC have gained substantial experience in the operation and maintenance of nuclear power facilities. Improvements in safety have occurred at a time when nuclear power generation has increased significantly from 675,000 gigawatt hours in calendar year (CY) 1996 to approximately 806,000 gigawatt hours in CY 2007. However, despite the excellent safety and security record of the industry, the agency cannot rest on its achievements. The primary challenges the agency faces are the large number of new nuclear plants expected to apply for licenses, the safe disposal of high-level nuclear waste, and the need to ensure security at nuclear facilities.

NEW NUCLEAR POWER PLANTS

With increased concerns about the continued availability and cost of oil as well as concerns over the environmental damage caused by coal-burning electrical plants, the amount of electricity supplied by nuclear power is likely to increase substantially in the future. The NRC last issued a nuclear power plant construction permit in 1977. To date, the agency has received a total of 17 Combined Operating License (COL) applications for sites across the country. The agency's primary challenge is to license new reactors to ensure that they will operate safely as they provide electricity required by the Nation for economic growth. However, before licensing any new nuclear reactor, the agency requires a detailed analysis of new reactor designs. This analysis includes a study of the reactor's vulnerability to accidents and security compromises. It also includes the development of inspection procedures, tests, analyses, and acceptable criteria for construction. The NRC is also evaluating commercial gas centrifuge facilities that utilize new methods of enriching nuclear fuel for reactors.

SAFE DISPOSAL OF HIGH-LEVEL WASTE

Safely disposing of the waste from nuclear power plants is vital to protecting public health and the environment. Lack of storage options would become a major road block for the continued growth of the industry. Earlier in FY 2008, the U.S. Department of Energy (DOE) filed a license application to establish the Nation's first repository for high-level radioactive waste at Yucca Mountain, NV. The NRC staff accepted and docketed the application. The agency has begun a review to evaluate a wide range of technical and scientific issues and will attempt to resolve regulatory concerns. In the meantime, the agency must ensure safe and secure interim storage capacity until a repository is licensed and ready to receive high-level nuclear waste. Most nuclear waste is now safely and securely stored at reactor sites. In addition to the storage of nuclear waste, safely transporting spent nuclear fuel is a significant issue for the public and the agency. More than 1,300 spent fuel shipments regulated by the NRC have been safely transported in the United States in the past 25 years. The NRC anticipates that the bulk of nuclear waste now stored at the reactor sites will eventually be moved to a permanent storage site. Therefore, the agency must be able to assure the public that all movements of nuclear waste, including those to a permanent storage site, will be safe and secure.

SECURITY AT NUCLEAR FACILITIES

In addition to safety, the security of nuclear materials is of paramount importance to the Nation. Nuclear facilities are among the most secure facilities in the Nation. The NRC, in concert with other Federal agencies, constantly monitors intelligence to determine the level of threat faced by nuclear facilities. The agency continues to improve the regulatory requirements to better ensure the security of nuclear materials and facilities. The threat faced by the Nation from those seeking to steal classified information has become more urgent in recent years. Nuclear facilities have implemented increased security measures, including "force-on-force" training exercises, to help ensure protection of this vital national infrastructure.

PRESIDENT'S MANAGEMENT AGENDA

INITIATIVE 1

Strategic Management of Human Capital

One of the agency's biggest challenges is training the more than 1,531 new staff members hired between October 2004 and October 2008. While many of these new employees come to the NRC with experience and a variety of valuable

U.S.NRC
United States Nuclear Regulatory Commission
Protecting People and the Environment

skills, many others have a solid educational background but little or no experience. This means that the agency will have to conduct extensive training for many staff members while at the same time working to orient them in the regulatory culture of the agency.

In FY 2008, the staff implemented a comprehensive knowledge management (KM) program. NRC headquarters and regional offices have developed their own KM plans. Staff have designed these KM plans to achieve the following three goals:

(1) Maintain human resource processes, policies, and practices to attract and retain knowledgeable staff.

(2) Share best practices in KM to build a culture of knowledge retention.

(3) Use information technology application to facilitate the acquisition, storage, and sharing of knowledge.

The agency has created a KM Steering Committee composed of managers and staff and chaired by senior leadership, hired a full-time KM expert from industry, designed a Web-based "KM Dashboard" to facilitate knowledge sharing about successful KM activities across the agency, and designed an expertise exchange program that formalizes the mentoring of newer employees by more experienced staff.

INITIATIVE 2
Budget and Performance Integration

The NRC continues to make progress in integrating its budget and performance management processes. This progress includes improved management of agency performance resulting from a revised agency Strategic Plan, accurate monitoring of agency program performance, and integrated performance goal and cost information.

The NRC will continue this progress by updating and improving the agency's financial systems. The agency is replacing its core accounting system, as well as its License Fee Billing System, Cost Accounting System, Allotment/Allowance Financial Plan System, and Capitalized

Property System. At the same time, the agency is aligning its budget and accounting structures. This will enable the NRC to use cost and other financial data together to evaluate agency program performance. The integration of financial, budget, and performance data will provide managers the kinds of information that can be used to drive improved agency performance.

INITIATIVE 3
Competitive Sourcing

One of the NRC's corporate management strategies is to acquire goods and services efficiently. To achieve this, the NRC established output measures associated with the competitive sourcing initiative of the President's Management Agenda, adopted a performance-based approach to contracting, and posted procurement synopses on the agency's Web site.

The NRC uploaded its Year 2008 Federal Activities Inventory Reform Act inventory spreadsheet to the Office of Management and Budget's Workforce Inventories Tracking System on June 30, 2008. In accordance with the NRC's Competitive Sourcing Plan, the agency completed four business case analyses of commercial activities that were available for competition in FY 2008.

INITIATIVE 4
Expanded Electronic Government

The NRC has aligned its IT investments with the Federal Government's Electronic Government (e-Gov) program. The NRC has transitioned to a number of e-Gov services and is in the process of transitioning to others. The agency has also institutionalized internal processes to ensure the effective use of, and compliance with, e-Gov initiatives. The NRC emphasizes enterprise architecture in its systems development lifecycle methodology. It has a project management methodology in place that provides full lifecycle guidance for the agency in terms of enterprise architecture, capital planning and investment control, infrastructure development, and lifecycle management processes. The Information Technology Senior Advisory Council, comprised of senior business managers, plays an integral role in establishing priorities and ensuring that technology investments align with the agency's mission and goals.

INITIATIVE 5

Improved Financial Management

The agency's goals for improved financial management include providing reliable, transparent, useful, and timely information for stakeholder knowledge and for management decisionmaking; maintaining effective internal controls; and implementing integrated and compliant systems to meet the agency's reporting needs. These strategies will ensure that the agency adequately protects its financial assets, consistent with risk. Over the next 2 years, the agency will be conducting a major financial systems modernization project that will impact all NRC financial systems. The project will consolidate the NRC's financial systems into a single integrated financial management system that a shared service provider will host and maintain. This single integrated system will result in more efficient transaction processing using electronic workflow, greater access to information through the use of ad hoc reporting tools, and improved overall system performance. An integrated financial management system will also improve internal controls in the following two ways: (1) It will eliminate multiple data transfers between stand-alone systems. (2) It will also eliminate the resultant manual reconciliations that staff currently perform to ensure data integrity.

FINANCIAL PERFORMANCE OVERVIEW

As of September 30, 2008, the financial condition of the NRC was sound with respect to having sufficient funds to meet program needs and adequate control of these funds in place to ensure obligations did not exceed budget authority.

The NRC prepared its financial statements in accordance with the accounting standards codified in the Statements of Federal Financial Accounting Standards (SFFAS) and Office of Management and Budget (OMB) Circular A-136, "Financial Reporting Requirements."

SOURCES OF FUNDS

The NRC has two appropriations, salaries and expenses and Office of the Inspector General. Funds for both appropriations are available until expended. The NRC's total new FY 2008 budget authority was $926.1 million. Of this amount, $917.3 million was for the salaries and expenses appropriation, and $8.7 million was for the Office of the Inspector General appropriation. This represents an increase in new budget authority of $101.2 million over FY 2007 ($100.8 million for the Salaries and Expenses appropriation and $0.4 million for the Office of the Inspector General appropriation). In addition, $87.6 million from prior-year appropriations, $6.3 million from prior-year reimbursable work, and $8.8 million for new reimbursable work to be performed for others was available to obligate in FY 2008. The sum of all funds available to obligate for FY 2008 was $1,028.8 million, which is a $117.9 million increase over the FY 2007 amount of $910.9 million.

Figure 6
SOURCES OF FUNDS
(In Millions)

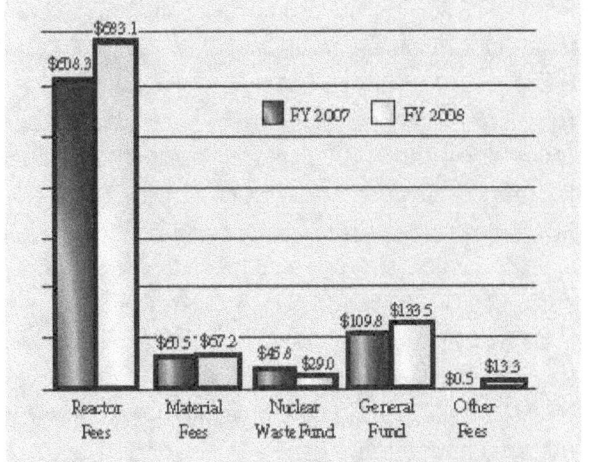

The Omnibus Budget Reconciliation Act of 1990 (OBRA-90), as amended, requires the NRC to collect fees to offset approximately 90 percent of its new budget authority, less the amount appropriated to the NRC from the Nuclear Waste Fund and amounts appropriated for waste incidental to reprocessing and generic homeland security for FY 2008. The NRC recovered $763.6 million in fees in FY 2008. This is 98 percent of the fee recovery requirement.

USES OF FUNDS BY FUNCTION

The NRC incurred obligations of $949.8 million in FY 2008, which was an increase of $111.0 million over FY 2007. Approximately 55 percent of obligations were used for salaries and benefits. The remaining 45 percent was used to obtain technical assistance for the NRC's principal regulatory programs, to conduct confirmatory safety research, to cover operating expenses, (e.g., building rentals, transportation, printing, security services, supplies, office automation, and training), staff travel, and reimbursable work. The unobligated budget authority available at the end of FY 2008 of $79.0 million, increased compared to the FY 2007 amount of $72.2 million. Of this $79.0 million, $7.3 million is for reimbursable work and $71.7 million is available to fund critical NRC needs in FY 2009.

AUDIT RESULTS

The NRC received an unqualified audit opinion on its FY 2008 financial statements. In FY 2007, the auditors identified a continuing material weakness in the agency's information systemwide security controls related to an Office of the Inspector General (OIG) independent evaluation of the NRC's implementation of the Federal Information Security Management Act (FISMA). The FISMA report identified two significant deficiencies related to a lack of contingency plan testing for information security systems, and a lack of certification and accreditation for most of the agency's major information systems. These deficiencies were also identified as a material weakness in the agency's FY 2007 Federal Managers' Financial Integrity Act (Integrity Act) assurance statement. In FY 2008, during the FISMA

Figure 7
USES OF FUNDS BY FUNCTION
(In Millions)

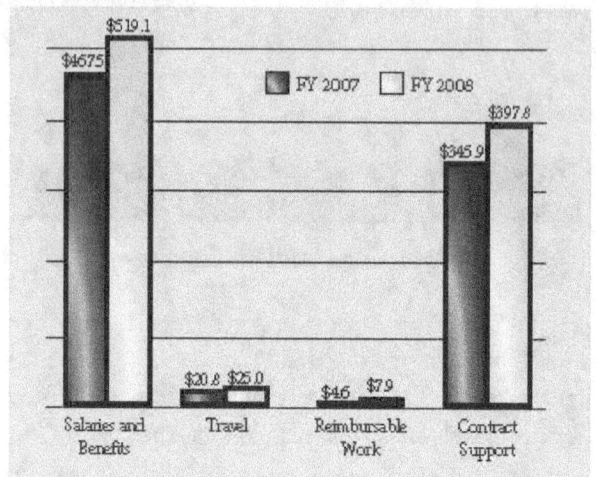

evaluation, the OIG found that improvements in contingency plan testing, and certification and accreditation had been sufficient enough to remove the significant deficiency. As a result, the NRC reported no material weaknesses for internal control in the Integrity Act assurance statement.

In FY 2004, FY 2005, and FY 2006, the auditors identified a material weakness concerning the Fee Billing System and the quality assurance process over fee billing. In FY 2007, the auditors downgraded this finding to a significant deficiency due to successful implementation of quality assurance procedures over fee billing. In FY 2008, the auditors closed this significant deficiency due to continued diligence in performing quality assurance efforts.

In FY 2008, the auditors identified a significant deficiency related to the method by which the NRC estimates the accounts payable balance which represents costs for billed and unbilled goods and services received (prior to year end) that are unpaid. Prior to FY 2008, the NRC used an algorithm that recognized accounts payable as a specific percentage of NRC's total expenses to date. Once this percentage was calculated, it was applied to an annualized expense figure. In FY 2008, the NRC implemented a revised methodology to calculate the accounts payable estimate. The new methodology involves analyzing the actual activity for the largest obligations to include in the estimate. For the remaining smaller obligations, the actual activity of a percentage of the obligations was analyzed and an algorithm was developed to estimate the total amount to include in the accounts payable balance. In FY 2009, the NRC will continue to refine this new estimation methodology to ensure accuracy.

In FY 2007, the Fee Billing System was also identified as a substantial noncompliance with the Federal Financial Management Improvement Act (Improvement Act). In FY 2008, the Fee Billing System continues to be substantially noncompliant with the Improvement Act due to a lack of current certification and accreditation. Although there may be a potential risk with security controls, there are a number of existing mitigating controls that provide NRC management reasonable assurance that the financial data resulting from financial management systems is accurate. NRC plans to complete certification and accreditation activities for the Fee Billing System in FY 2009.

A summary of the Financial Statement Audit Results is included in Appendix C.

LIMITATIONS OF THE FINANCIAL STATEMENTS

Staff have prepared principal statement to report the financial position and results of operations of the NRC, pursuant to the requirements of 31 U.S.C. 3515(b). While the statements have been prepared from the books and records of the NRC in accordance with Generally Accepted Accounting Principles (GAAP) for Federal Entities and the formats prescribed by the Office of Management and Budget (OMB), the statements are in addition to the financial reports used to monitor and control budgetary resources, which are prepared from the same books and records. The statements should be read with the realization that they are for a component of the U.S. Government, a sovereign entity.

FINANCIAL STATEMENT HIGHLIGHTS

The NRC's financial statements summarize the financial activity and financial position of the agency. The financial statements, footnotes, and required supplementary

information appear in Chapter 3, "Financial Statements and Auditors' Report." Analysis of the principal statements follows.

Analysis of the Balance Sheet

The NRC's assets were $554.5 million as of September 30, 2008. This is an increase of $69.1 million from the end of FY 2007. The assets reported in NRC's Balance Sheet are summarized in the accompanying table.

ASSET SUMMARY
(In Millions)

	FY 2008	FY 2007
Fund Balance with Treasury	$393.5	$356.4
Accounts Receivable, Net	$121.4	$93.9
Property & Equipment, Net	$35.5	$31.8
Other	$4.1	$3.3
Total Assets	$554.5	$485.4

The fund balance with the U.S. Department of the Treasury (Treasury) represents the NRC's largest asset of $393.5 million as of September 30, 2008, an increase of $37.1 million from the FY 2007 year-end balance. This balance accounts for 71 percent of Total Assets and represents appropriated funds, collected license fees, and other funds maintained at the Treasury to pay current liabilities. The increase in Fund Balance with Treasury is primarily due to $926.1 million in new budget authority and $8.3 million in reimbursable collections which are offset by $884.0 million in expenditures and a $13.3 million decrease in fee overcollections.

Accounts Receivable, Net, as of September 30, 2008, was $121.4 million, which includes an offsetting allowance for doubtful accounts of $1.7 million. This is a 29 percent increase from the FY 2007 year-end Accounts Receivable, Net, balance of $93.9 million. The increase is primarily due to fees for new reactor licensing, and materials and facilities inspections. The value of Property and Equipment, Net, was $35.5 million, representing 6 percent of Total Assets. The

majority of this balance represents information technology software and leasehold improvements.

LIABILITIES SUMMARY
(In Millions)

	FY 2008	FY 2007
Accounts Payable	$54.1	$27.7
Federal Employee Benefits	7.1	6.8
Other Liabilities	75.8	169.7
Total Liabilities	$137.0	$204.2

The NRC's liabilities were $137.0 million as of September 30, 2008. The accompanying table shows a decrease in Total Liabilities of $67.2 million from the FY 2007 year-end balance of $204.2 million. This decrease is primarily due to a decrease of $93.9 million as a result of a change in accounting for fee revenue and the corresponding transfer of fee revenue collections to Treasury. Beginning in FY 2008, this liability is no longer being recorded. The decrease is offset by an increase of $26.4 million in Accounts Payable for new reactors and existing reactor and materials licensing tasks. Of the agency's liabilities, $52.5 million were not covered by budgetary resources, which is a 12 percent increase over the balance of $46.8 million as of September 30, 2007. The liabilities not covered by budgetary resources include unfunded accrued annual leave and future workers' compensation.

NET POSITION SUMMARY
(In Millions)

	FY 2008	FY 2007
Unexpended Appropriations	$289.3	$254.0
Cumulative Results of Operations	128.2	27.2
Total Net Position	$417.5	$281.2

The difference between Total Assets and Total Liabilities, Net Position, was $417.5 million as of September 30, 2008. This is an increase of $136.3 million from the FY 2007 year-end balance. Net Position is comprised of two components: Unexpended Appropriations and Cumulative Results of Operations as shown in the accompanying table. Unexpended Appropriations is the amount of authority granted by Congress that has not been expended. The increase of Unexpended Appropriations of $35.3 million for FY 2008 is primarily due to funding for expected added volume of new reactor licensing activities. Cumulative Results of Operations represents the cumulative excess of financing sources over expenses. The increase is due primarily to a change in accounting for fee revenue and the corresponding transfer of fee revenue collections to Treasury.

Analysis of the Statement of Net Cost

The Statement of Net Cost presents the net cost of NRC's two programs as identified in the NRC Annual Performance Plan. The purpose of this statement is to link program performance to the cost of programs. The NRC's Net Cost of Operations for the year ended September 30, 2008, was $146.5 million, which is an increase of $53.1 million over the FY 2007 net cost of $93.4 million. Net costs by program are shown in the following table.

NET COST OF OPERATIONS
(In Millions)

	FY 2008	FY 2007
Nuclear Reactor Safety and Security	$(20.0)	$(30.6)
Nuclear Materials & Waste Safety and Security	166.5	124.0
Net Cost of Operations	$146.5	$93.4

Net Costs are gross costs offset by earned revenue. Gross costs increased in Nuclear Reactor Safety and Security in the areas of new reactor and existing licensing tasks and in Nuclear Materials & Waste Safety and Security due to contract support for high-level waste, nuclear materials licenses, fuel facilities, and spent fuel storage and transport. Earned revenue increased primarily because of the increase in appropriations for NRC activities, of which the NRC is required to collect 90 percent through fee billing.

Total earned revenue for the year ended September 30, 2008, was $797.6 million, which is an increase of $104.3 million from the earned revenue of $693.3 million for the year ended September 30, 2007. Earned revenue is derived from fees for reactor and materials licensing and inspections in accordance with Title 10 of the *Code of Federal Regulations* (10 CFR) Part 170, "Fees for Facilities, Materials, Import and Export Licenses, and Other Regulatory Services under the Atomic Energy Act of 1954, as Amended," and 10 CFR Part 171, "Annual Fees for Reactor Licenses and Fuel Cycle Licenses and Materials Licenses, Including Holders of Certificates of Compliance, Registrations, and Quality Assurance Program Approvals and Government Agencies Licensed by the NRC."

Analysis of Statement of Changes in Net Position

The Statement of Changes in Net Position reports the change in net position during the reporting period. Net position is affected by changes in its two components— Cumulative Results of Operations and Unexpended Appropriations. The increase in Net Position of $136.3 million from FY 2007 to FY 2008 is due primarily to an increase in the net change in Cumulative Results of Operations of $101.0 million primarily due to the change in accounting for fee revenue and the corresponding transfer of fee revenue collections to Treasury. The increase in Unexpended Appropriations of $35.3 million is primarily due to the increase in the appropriation for FY 2008 for the expected added volume of new reactor licensing activities.

Analysis of the Statement of Budgetary Resources

The Statement of Budgetary Resources reports the source and status of budgetary resources at the end of the period. It presents the relationship between budget authority and budget outlays, and the reconciliation of obligations to total outlays. For FY 2008, NRC had Total Budgetary Resources available of $1,028.8 million, the majority of which was derived from new budget authority. This represents a 13 percent increase over FY 2007 budgetary resources

available of $910.9 million. The increase provides funding for growth in new reactor licensing including costs for staffing and office space.

For FY 2008, the NRC had Obligations Incurred of $949.8 million, compared to FY 2007 Obligations Incurred of $838.8 million. This increase was due primarily to the increase of appropriations received for new and existing reactor licensing activities. Gross outlays for FY 2008 were $884.0 million, which represents a $119.6 million increase from FY 2007 total outlays of $764.4 million. The increase is primarily due to the increase in spending in the area of Nuclear Reactor Safety and Security for new reactor and existing reactor licensing programs.

SYSTEMS, CONTROLS, AND LEGAL COMPLIANCE

MANAGEMENT ASSURANCES

This section provides information on the NRC's compliance with the Federal Managers' Financial Integrity Act, the Office of Management and Budget (OMB) Circular A-123, "Management's Responsibility for Internal Control," and the Federal Financial Management Improvement Act. Appendix C, "Summary of Financial Statement Audit and Management Assurances," includes a summary of management assurances.

Federal Managers Financial Integrity Act

The Federal Managers Financial Integrity Act (Integrity Act) mandates that agencies establish controls that reasonably ensure that (1) obligations and costs comply with applicable law; (2) assets are safeguarded against waste, loss, unauthorized use, or misappropriation; and (3) revenues and expenditures are properly accounted for and recorded. The Integrity Act encompasses program, operational, and administrative areas as well as accounting and financial management. It also requires the Chairman to provide an assurance statement on the adequacy of internal controls and on the conformance of financial systems with governmentwide standards.

U.S.NRC
United States Nuclear Regulatory Commission
Protecting People and the Environment

Management Control Review Program

Managers throughout the NRC are responsible for implementing effective controls in their areas of responsibility. Each Office Director and Regional Administrator prepares an annual assurance statement that identifies any control weaknesses requiring the attention of the NRC's Executive Committee on Internal Control (ECIC). These statements are based on various sources, including management knowledge gained from the daily operation of agency programs and reviews, management reviews, program evaluations, audits of financial statements, reviews of financial systems, annual performance plans, Inspector General and U.S. Government Accountability Office reports, and reports and other information provided by the congressional committees of jurisdiction.

The NRC's ECIC includes senior executives from the offices of the Chief Financial Officer and the Executive Director of Operations, with the Office of the General Counsel and the Office of the Inspector General participating as advisors. The ECIC met and reviewed the assurance statements provided by the offices and regions. The ECIC then informed the Chairman as to whether the NRC had any internal control deficiencies serious enough to require reporting as a material weakness or material noncompliance.

The NRC's ongoing internal control program requires, among other things, that reports on internal control deficiencies be integrated into the offices' and regions' annual operating plans. The operating plan process provides for periodic updates and ensures that key issues receive senior management attention. Combined with the individual assurance statements discussed previously, the internal control information in these plans provides the framework for monitoring and improving the agency's internal controls on an ongoing basis.

U.S. NUCLEAR REGULATORY COMMISSION FEDERAL MANAGERS' FINANCIAL INTEGRITY ACT STATEMENT FOR FY 2008

The U.S. Nuclear Regulatory Commission's (NRC) management is responsible for establishing and maintaining effective internal control and financial management systems that meet the objectives of the Federal Managers Financial Integrity Act (FMFIA). The NRC conducted its assessment of internal control over the effectiveness and efficiency of operations and compliance with applicable laws and regulations, and in accordance with OMB Circular A-123, "Management's Responsibility for Internal Control." Based on the results of this evaluation, the NRC can provide reasonable assurance that its internal control over the effectiveness and efficiency of operations and compliance with applicable laws and regulations as of September 30, 2008, was operating effectively and no material weaknesses were found in the design or operation of internal control.

In addition, the NRC conducted its assessment of the effectiveness of internal control over financial reporting, which includes safeguarding of assets and compliance with applicable laws and regulations, in accordance with the requirements of Appendix A of OMB Circular A-123. Based on the results of the evaluation, the NRC can provide reasonable assurance that NRC's internal control over financial reporting as of June 30, 2008, was operating effectively, and no material weaknesses were found in the design or operation of the internal control over financial reporting.

Dale Klein

Dale E. Klein
Chairman
U.S. Nuclear Regulatory Commission
November 14, 2008

FY 2008 Integrity Act Results

The NRC evaluated its internal control systems for the fiscal year ending September 30, 2008. The

NRC is able to provide a statement of assurance, based on this evaluation, that the internal controls and financial management systems meet the objectives of the Integrity Act. The NRC has reasonable assurance that its internal controls are effective and that its financial management systems conform to governmentwide standards.

Resolution of FY 2007 Material Weakness

The FY 2007 independent evaluation of the NRC's Implementation of the Federal Information Security Management Act (FISMA) identified the following two significant deficiencies in the NRC's information technology (IT) security program:

- Only 2 of 30 operational NRC information systems have a current certification and accreditation, and only 4 out of the 11 systems used or operated by a contractor or other organization on behalf of the agency have a current certification and accreditation.
- Annual contingency plan testing is still not being performed for all of the NRC's operational information systems.

The NRC reported these two findings as one material weakness associated with the Agency's overall IT security program under the provisions of the Integrity Act.

The Office of the Inspector General performed an independent evaluation of the NRC's implementation of the Federal Information Security Management Act for FY 2008. The independent evaluator no longer considers either of these items as significant deficiencies, since one-half of the systems have a current certification and accreditation, and annual contingency plan testing was completed for all systems. As a result of this evaluation, the NRC no longer considers this a material weakness.

Office of Management and Budget Circular A-123, "Management's Responsibility for Internal Control," Including Appendix A, "Internal Control over Financial Reporting"

In FY 2006, the NRC implemented the requirements of the Office of Management and Budget revised Circular A-123, which defined and strengthened management's responsibility for internal control in Federal agencies. The revised Circular

included updated internal control standards. A new section, Appendix A, "Internal Control over Financial Reporting," required Federal agencies to assess the effectiveness of internal control over their financial reporting and to prepare a separate statement of assurance as of June 30, every year.

In FY 2008, the NRC continued its assessment of internal control over financial reporting. The scope of financial reports, materiality values, risk assessments, key processes, and key controls was reevaluated. A 3-year rotational testing plan was adopted last year in FY 2007. Three of the original nine key processes were determined to be significant enough to be included in the testing each year of the 3-year cycle. The remaining six key processes will be tested once in the 3-year cycle, two each year. Based on the results of this evaluation, the NRC can provide reasonable assurance that its internal control over financial reporting was operating effectively as of June 30, 2008, and that the evaluation found no material weaknesses in the design or operation of the internal controls over financial reporting.

Federal Financial Management Improvement Act

The Federal Financial Management Improvement Act (Improvement Act) requires each agency to implement and maintain systems that comply substantially with (1) Federal financial management system requirements, (2) applicable Federal accounting standards, and (3) the standard general ledger at the transaction level. The Improvement Act requires the Chairman to determine whether the agency's financial management systems comply with the Improvement Act and to develop remediation plans for systems that do not comply.

FY 2008 Improvement Act Results

As of September 30, 2008, the NRC evaluated its financial systems to determine if they complied with applicable Federal requirements and accounting standards required by the Improvement Act. The NRC evaluated the following eight systems: the Federal Financial System, Federal Personnel Payroll Systems, Human Resources Management System, Cost Accounting System, Advice of

Allotments/Financial Plan System, Capitalized Property System, Fee Billing System, and Controller Resource Database System.

As of September 30, 2008, the agency's financial management systems are in substantial compliance with the Improvement Act, except for one system which is in substantial noncompliance because of a FISMA finding related to a lack of current certification and accreditation. The NRC plans to complete the certification and accreditation activities by March 31, 2009, and to request an authority to operate. In making this determination, the NRC considered all the information available, including the report from the NRC ECIC on the effectiveness of internal controls, the Office of the Inspector General audit reports, and the results of the agency's financial management systems reviews. The agency also relied on the Department of the Interior National Business Center (DOI-NBC) annual reasonable assurance statement, which concluded that, for FY 2008, the cross-serviced financial systems are in substantial compliance with Federal financial management system requirements.

The Inspector General auditors identified the Fee Billing System as an Improvement Act noncompliance in the FY 2004 through FY 2006 Financial Statement Audit. The NRC took a number of additional remedial actions during FY 2007 to improve quality assurance over license fee billing processes and eliminated the noncompliance issue related to these fee billing processes. The NRC continues to define and implement compensating controls over this system, to maintain quality assurance procedures, and to reduce the risk that errors will go undetected.

PROMPT PAYMENT

The Prompt Payment Act requires Federal agencies to make timely payments to vendors for supplies and services, to pay interest penalties when payments are made after the due date, and to take cash discounts when they are economically justified. In FY 2008, the NRC paid 93 percent

Figure 8
PROMPT PAYMENT
(Percentage)

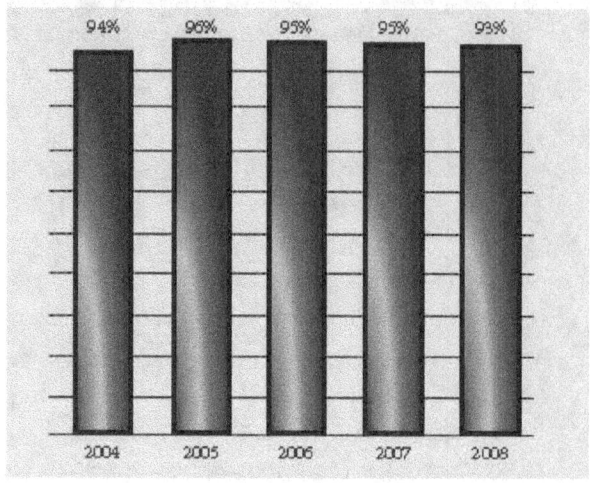

of the 10,368 invoices subject to the Prompt Payment Act on time (see Figure 8). The NRC incurred $20,852 in interest penalties during FY 2008.

IMPROPER PAYMENTS

The NRC remains at low risk of making improper payments. At the present time, the NRC's payments consist of commercial vendor, interagency, and travel reimbursements. The NRC monitors and reports improper payments within its programs and continues to evaluate internal controls guarding against improper payments. The NRC continues to perform annual risk assessments for each of these areas. Based on the FY 2008 risk assessments, the number and amount of improper payments fall below the external reporting requirement established by OMB guidance on what is considered a significant risk. The NRC awards less than $500 million in annual contracts, and, therefore, is not subject to annual reporting under the Recovery Auditing Act.

The DOI-NBC's Federal Personnel/Payroll System, as the system of record for payroll disbursements, is responsible for monitoring and reporting on any improper payroll-related payments.

DEBT COLLECTION

The Debt Collection Improvement Act enhances the ability of the Federal Government to service and collect debts. The agency's goal is to maintain the level of delinquent debt owed to the NRC at year end to less than 1 percent of its annual billings. The NRC continues to meet this goal, and at the end of FY 2008, delinquent debt was $2.0 million (Figure 9). The NRC continues to pursue the collection of

Figure 9
DELINQUENT DEBT
(In Millions)

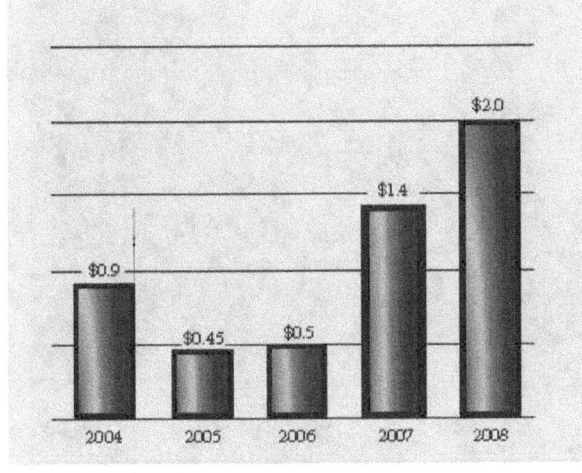

delinquent debt and refers all eligible debt over 180 days delinquent to the Treasury for collection.

BIENNIAL REVIEW OF USER FEES

The Chief Financial Officers Act requires agencies to conduct a biennial review of fees, royalties, rents, and other charges imposed by agencies, and to make revisions to cover program and administrative costs incurred. Each year, the NRC revises the hourly rates for license and inspection fees and adjusts the annual fees to meet the fee collection requirements of the Omnibus Budget Reconciliation Act of 1990, as amended. The most recent changes to the license, inspection, and annual fees are described in the *Federal Register* (73 FR 32385, June 6, 2008).

In order to more appropriately recover actual costs, the NRC revised the fees and charges for the Material Access Authorization Program, for the Information Access Authorization Program, and for administrative charges for delinquent debt. The NRC conducted no other reviews this year.

INSPECTOR GENERAL ACT

The agency has established and continues to maintain an excellent record in resolving and implementing Office of the Inspector General open audit recommendations. Appendix B includes this information, as well as data concerning disallowed costs determined through contract audits conducted by the Defense Contract Audit Agency.

NRC Chairman Dale E. Klein and University of Illinois at Urbana Champaign (UI) Head of the Department of Nuclear, Plasma, and Radiological Engineering, Professor Jim Stubbins, hold a ceremonial check representing the nearly $740,000 in grants the NRC recently provided for nuclear-related education at UI. Chairman Klein was on campus to observe a forum marking the 50th anniversary of nuclear engineering on campus.

CHAPTER 2
PROGRAM PERFORMANCE

Photo Courtesy of Florida Power and Light Company

St. Lucie Nuclear Power Plant near Ft. Pierce, FL. This facility is run by the Florida Power and Light Company.

MEASURING AND REPORTING PERFORMANCE

This chapter presents information on the U.S. Nuclear Regulatory Commission's (NRC's) performance in achieving its mission during fiscal year (FY) 2008. The agency's mission is to license and regulate the Nation's civilian use of byproduct, source, and special nuclear materials to ensure adequate protection of public health and safety, promote the common defense and security, and protect the environment.

This chapter also describes the NRC's achievements in accomplishing its two strategic goals of safety and security. The safety goal discussion addresses the NRC's key activities of reactor licensing, new reactor licensing, reactor inspection, fuel facilities, material users, high-level waste repository, decommissioning and low-level waste, and spent fuel storage and transportation. The security goal discussion addresses security activities in the Nuclear Reactor Safety and Nuclear Materials and Waste Safety Programs. Lastly, it describes information on data sources, data quality, and the completeness and reliability of performance data. The discussion focuses primarily on the NRC's methods for collecting and analyzing data, ensuring data security, and improving the agency's performance measures and the quality of its data during the current reporting period.

Chairman Dale E. Klein (center), tours Shearon Harris nuclear power plant near Raleigh, NC, with congressional staff members who represent Representative David Price, D-NC, and Senator Richard Burr, R-NC.

GOALS AND PERFORMANCE MEASURES

STRATEGIC GOAL 1: SAFETY

Ensure Adequate Protection of Public Health and Safety and the Environment

Strategic Outcomes

The NRC has five strategic outcomes associated with the safety goal that determine whether the agency has achieved its objective to ensure adequate protection of public health and safety and the environment. The following are the five strategic outcomes:

* Prevent the occurrence of any nuclear reactor accidents.
* Prevent the occurrence of any inadvertent criticality events.
* Prevent the occurrence of any acute radiation exposures resulting in fatalities.
* Prevent the occurrence of any releases of radioactive materials that result in significant radiation exposures.
* Prevent the occurrence of any releases of radioactive materials that cause significant adverse environmental impacts.

RESULTS: In FY 2008, the NRC achieved all of its safety goal strategic outcomes.

PERFORMANCE MEASURES

The table on the next page lists the agency's annual performance measures and their outcomes over the past 6 years. The NRC uses these performance measures to determine its success in achieving the safety goal.

U.S.NRC
United States Nuclear Regulatory Commission
Protecting People and the Environment

FY 2008 Safety Goal Performance Measures

Measure	2003	2004	2005	2006	2007	2008
1. Number of new conditions evaluated as red by the Reactor Oversight Process is ≤3.	1	1	0	0	0	0
2. Number of significant accident sequence precursors of a nuclear reactor accident is zero.	0	0	0	0	0	0
3. Number of operating reactors with integrated performance that entered the Manual Chapter 0350 process, or the multiple/repetitive degraded cornerstone column or the unacceptable performance column of the Reactor Oversight Process Action Matrix, with no performance exceeding Abnormal Occurrence Criterion I.D.4 is ≤4.	2	1	0	0	1	0
4. Number of significant adverse trends in industry safety performance with no trend exceeding the Abnormal Occurrence Criterion I.D.4 is ≤1.	0	0	0	0	0	0
5. Number of events with radiation exposures to the public and occupational workers that exceed Abnormal Occurrence Criterion I.A is:						
Reactors: 0	0	0	0	0	0	0
Materials: ≤3	0	0	1	0	0	0
Waste: 0	0	0	0	0	0	0
6. Number of radiological releases to the environment that exceed applicable regulatory limits is:						
Reactor: ≤3	0	0	0	0	0	0
Materials: ≤2	0	1	0	0	0	0
Waste: 0	0	0	0	0	0	0

ANALYSIS OF FY 2008 RESULTS

1. **Reactor Oversight Process:** The NRC reactor inspection program monitors nuclear power plant performance in three broad areas—reactor safety, radiation safety, and security. Plant performance is analyzed based on many performance indicators and inspection findings. Each finding is then divided into one of four categories—red, yellow, white, green. Red findings indicate a finding of high safety significance. There were no red performance indicators or findings in FY 2008.

2. **Reactor significant precursors:** The second measure tracks significant precursor events. This statistical measure of risk determines the likelihood of an event impacting safety adversely. A significant precursor is an event that has a probability of 1 in 1000 (or greater) of leading to substantial damage to the reactor fuel. Based on screening reviews, the NRC has not identified any significant precursor events in FY 2008.

3. **Reactor performance:** The conditions in this measure indicate whether the NRC finds significant performance issues in a plant during an inspection or from performance indicators under the reactor oversight process. If any of the conditions in this measure are met, the NRC will take action to ensure that plant safety is improved. There were no reactors that met the conditions in this measure in FY 2008. Palo Verde Nuclear Generation Station in Toponah, AZ, met the conditions in this measure during FY 2007. The agency applied significant oversight for that plant in FY 2008 to ensure improved performance.

4. **Reactor safety trends:** This measure tracks trends for several key indicators of industry safety performance. These indicators provide insights into major areas of reactor performance, including reactor safety, radiation safety, and emergency preparedness. Statistical analysis techniques are applied to each indicator to calculate long-term trends. These trends represent industry averages rather than individual plant performance. No statistically significant adverse trends have been identified for any of the indicators in FY 2008.

5. **Nuclear material radiation exposures:** This measure tracks the number of radiation exposures to the public and occupational workers that exceed Abnormal Occurrence Criterion I.A.3, which is defined as those events that produce unintended permanent functional damage to an organ or a physiological system, as determined by a physician. This measure tracks both nuclear reactors and other nuclear material users, such as hospitals and industrial users. No radiation exposures exceeding Abnormal Occurrence Criterion I.A.3 occurred in FY 2008.

6. **Nuclear material releases to the environment:** This measure indicates the effectiveness of the NRC's nuclear material environmental regulatory programs. Exceeding the applicable regulatory limits is defined as a total effective radiation dose equivalent to individual members of the public that is attributable to a licensed user of nuclear materials but does not exceed 0.1 rem in a year, exclusive of dose contributions from background radiation. No nuclear material releases to the environment that exceeded regulatory limits occurred in FY 2008.

THE INDUSTRY TRENDS PROGRAM

The NRC measures the effectiveness of its Nuclear Reactor Safety Program activities based on the continued safe operation of the Nation's nuclear power plants. The NRC compiles data on overall safety performance using several industry-level performance indicators, a number of which are addressed in the following pages. These indicators (except precursor occurrence rate) show significant improvement in the long-term trends for safety performance of nuclear power plants since 1988, the baseline year for the statistical analyses. Plant operating experience data have yielded a steady stream of improvements in the reliability of plant systems and components, plant operating procedures, training of power plant operators, and regulatory oversight. For ease of viewing, all the charts in this section display data since 1993.

The industry safety indicators are derived through engineering and scientific analyses by the NRC's Office of Nuclear Reactor Regulation and Office of Nuclear Regulatory

Research. The analyses of the events for FY 2008 are still ongoing. The performance indicator results are subject to minor variations as licensees submit revisions to the source data and may differ slightly from data reported in previous years as a result of refinements in data quality. The results of these analyses are reported annually both to the Commission and to Congress.

Figure 10
SIGNIFICANT EVENTS
(Per Reactor)

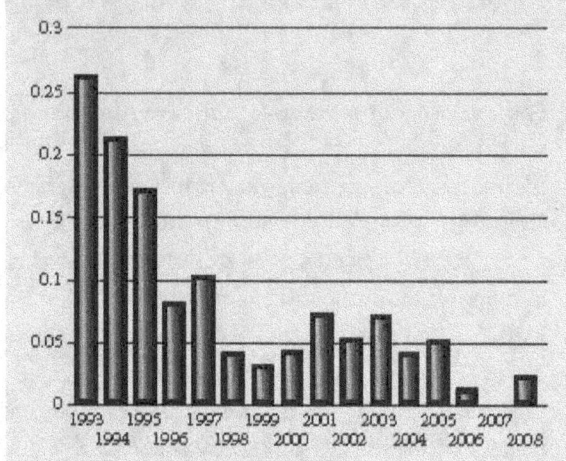

Significant events meet specific criteria such as degradation of important safety equipment. The agency reviews operating events and assesses their safety significance. The number of significant events has declined since 1993.

Figure 11
RADIATION EXPOSURE
(Exposure - Person cSv)

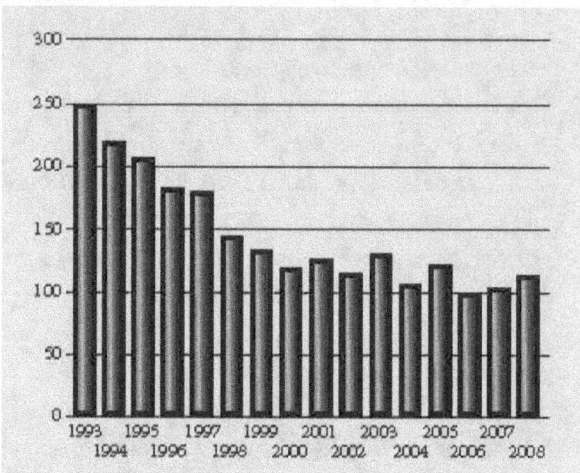

The total (collective) radiation dose received by workers is an indication of the radiological challenges of maintaining and operating nuclear power plants. The trend shows a reduction in collective dose since 1988 and demonstrates the effectiveness of the controls on radiation exposure.

Figure 12
SAFETY SYSTEM ACTUATIONS
(Per Reactor)

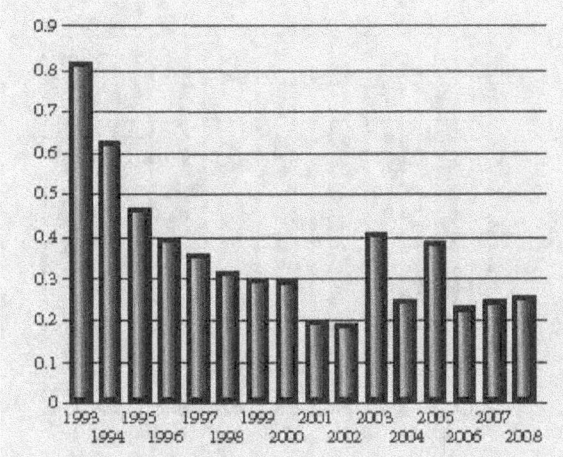

Safety systems mitigate off-normal events, such as the widespread power blackout in August 2003, by providing reactor core cooling and water addition. Actuations of safety systems that are monitored include certain emergency core cooling and emergency electrical power systems. Actuations can occur as a result of "false alarms" (such as testing errors) or in response to actual events.

Figure 14
PRECURSOR OCCURENCE RATE
(Per Reactor)

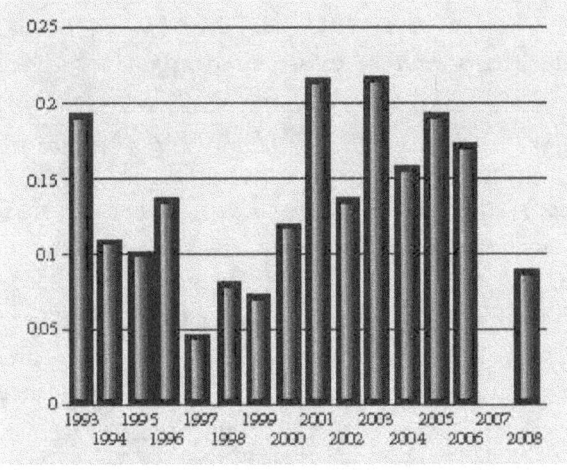

A precursor event is an event that has a probability of greater than 1 in 1 million of leading to substantial damage to the reactor fuel. There is no statistically significant adverse trend in the occurrence rate of precursor events since 1993, the baseline year for the statistical analysis. Because of the complexities associated with evaluating precursor events, the data always lag behind other indicators.

Figure 13
AUTOMATIC SCRAMS
(Per Reactor)

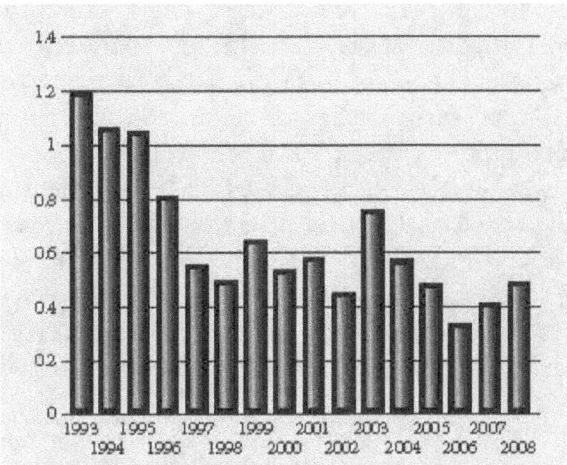

A scram is a basic reactor protection safety function that shuts down the reactor by inserting control rods into the reactor core. Scrams can result from events that range from relatively minor incidents to precursors of accidents. The massive power blackout in August 2003 accounts for most of the increase in FY 2003, but it has not affected the statistical trend for number of scrams, which has been declining steadily since 1988.

Figure 15
SAFETY SYSTEM FAILURES
(Per Reactor)

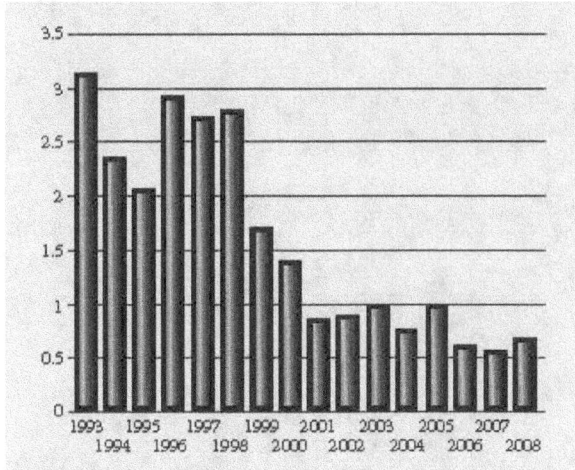

Safety system failures include any events or conditions that could prevent a safety system from fulfilling its safety function. The statistical trend for the number of safety system failures across the industry has declined since 1988.

Nuclear Reactor Licensing Activity

The agency's nuclear reactor licensing activity ensures that civilian nuclear power reactors and test and research reactors are operated in a manner that adequately protects public health and safety and the environment while safeguarding special nuclear materials used in reactors. Safety at nuclear power plants has improved substantially over the past 20 years, as both the nuclear industry and the NRC have been proactive in identifying and correcting problems to improve the operation and maintenance of nuclear power facilities. The combined efforts of the nuclear industry and the NRC led to this improvement in the safety performance of nuclear power plants.

The NRC had completed 1,054 reactor licensing actions (see Figure 16). The Office of Nuclear Reactor Regulation has experienced a significant decrease in the number of licensing action submittals in the past 2 years. The agency received only 1,270 actions in 2007, compared with an average of 1,630 submittals since 2003

The NRC continues to complete licensing actions in a timely manner. The staff completed approximately 96 percent of the licensing actions in the agency's inventory within 1 year of receipt and 100 percent within 2 years (see Figure 17).

Figure 16

LICENSING ACTIONS COMPLETED
(Number of Actions)

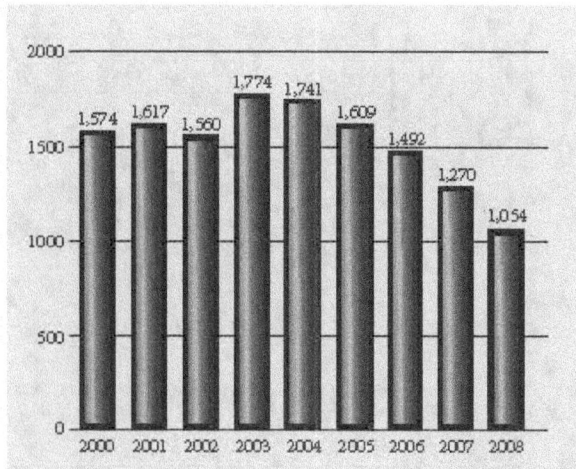

Figure 17

LICENSING ACTION AGE

■ Percent less than 1 Year Old □ Percent less than 2 Years Old

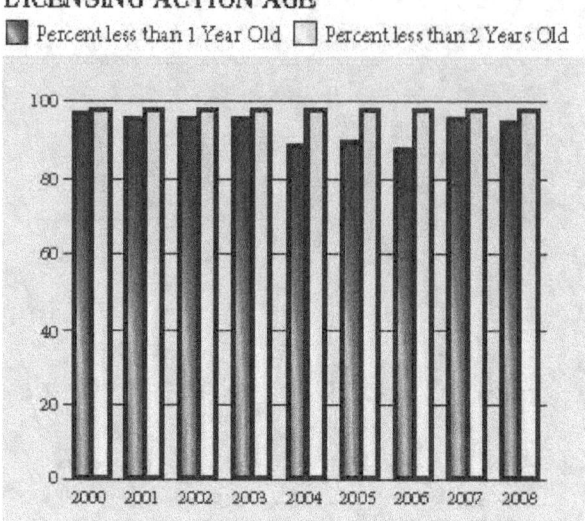

The NRC also evaluates nuclear reactor power uprate applications, which allow licensees to increase the power output of their plants. The NRC reviews focus on the potential impacts of the proposed power uprate on overall plant safety and evaluate whether plant operation at the increased power level is safe. During FY 2008, the NRC completed the reviews of 11 power uprate licensing actions, which will add about 740 megawatts electric to the grid. This brings the cumulative additional power from all power uprates approved since 1977 to about 5,640 megawatts electric. The NRC currently has five power uprates under review, which if approved, will add about 519 megawatts electric to the grid. The NRC expects to receive 23 new power uprate applications in the next 5 years, which if approved, will add about 1,712 megawatts electric to the grid.

During FY 2008, the NRC undertook several rulemaking activities to improve protection of public health and safety and the environment and to reduce unnecessary regulatory burden. The agency published a proposed rule on alternate fracture toughness requirements for protection against pressurized thermal shock events in reactor vessels using updated analysis methods. The agency also published a final rule on occupational exposure reporting and recordkeeping requirements that reduces regulatory burden to such an extent that licensees will save more than $100 million each year.

NEW REACTOR LICENSING

The NRC published a major revision to Title 10, Part 52, "Early Site Permits; Standard Design Certifications; and Combined Licenses for Nuclear Power Plants," of the *Code of Federal Regulations* (10 CFR Part 52). In addition, the NRC updated Regulatory Guide 1.206, "Combined License Applications for Nuclear Power Plants (LWR Edition)," and issued a major revision to NUREG-0800, "Standard Review Plan for the Review of Safety Analysis Reports for Nuclear Power Plants." To date, the NRC has received 17 combined license (COL) applications from the nuclear power industry for sites across the country. Of the applications received, 10 have been accepted and docketed and are currently under review. In addition, the industry has indicated that it will submit three more COL applications in CY 2009 and 2010.

The NRC is continuing to develop an effective and efficient construction inspection program for plants to be licensed under 10 CFR Part 52. These activities include (1) the creation of a working group on the closure of inspections, tests, analyses, and acceptance criteria (ITAAC) to resolve policy issues and develop resulting processes and procedures; (2) inspector development and training; (3) development of information technology systems to capture inspection results and track ITAAC closure; (4) issuance of inspection procedures; (5) development of generic inspection schedules, and (6) development of an assessment and enforcement program. Vendor inspections are already taking place to support increased fabrication activities domestically and internationally in response to new reactor construction plans. The NRC conducts these inspections to ensure the effective implementation of the high-quality standards set for components by the agency to protect the public.

On June 12, 2008, the agency issued Regulatory Guide 4.21, "Minimization of Contamination and Radioactive Waste Generation: Life-Cycle Planning," which affects both design, certification and COL application reviews. This guide provides an acceptable method for minimizing contamination and radioactive waste generation over the total life cycle of a facility, from initial facility layout and design, through procedures for operation, and concluding with final decontamination and dismantling at the time of decommissioning.

COL APPLICATIONS ACCEPTED IN FY 2008

Site Name (units)	State	Company	Date Submitted	Accepted
Calvert Cliffs (1 unit)	MD	UNISTAR	7/13/07 3/13/08	1/25/08[1] 6/3/08
South Texas Project (2 units)	TX	NRG Energy	9/20/07	11/29/07
Bellefonte (2 units)	AL	NuStart Energy	10/30/07	1/18/08
North Anna (1 unit)	VA	Dominion	11/27/07	1/28/08
William Lee Nuclear Station (2 units)	SC	Duke	12/13/07	2/25/08
Shearon Harris (2 units)	NC	Progress Energy	2/19/08	4/17/08
Grand Gulf (1 unit)	MS	NuStart Energy	2/27/08	4/17/08
Vogtle (2 units)	SC	Southern Nuclear Operating Co.	3/31/08	5/30/08
Summer (2 units)	SC	South Carolina E&G	3/31/08	7/31/08
Callaway (1 unit)	MO	AmerenUE	7/24/08	Pending
Levy County (2 units)	FL	Progress Energy	7/30/08	10/06/08
Victoria County (2 units)	TX	Exelon	9/03/08	Pending
Fermi (1 unit)	MI	Detroit Edison	09/18/08	Pending
Comanche Peak (2 units)	TX	Luminant Power	09/19/08	Pending
River Bend (1 unit)	LA	Entergy	9/25/08	Pending
Nine Mile Point (1 unit)	NY	Unistar	9/30/08	Pending
Bell Bond (1 unit)	PA	PPL Generation	10/10/08	Pending

[1] The Calvert Cliffs Combined Operating License application was received in two parts; the first part was accepted for review on January 25, 2008, and the second part was accepted on June 3, 2008.

For the licensing of new reactors, a proposed rule was published that would require applicants for new reactor designs to perform a design-specific assessment of the effect of the impact of a large commercial aircraft. Applicants would have to perform a rigorous assessment of the design to identify design features and functional capabilities that could provide additional inherent protection to avoid or mitigate the effects of an aircraft impact to the extent practicable with reduced reliance on operator actions.

New Reactor Designs

The NRC is actively reviewing several nuclear reactor designs and plans to conclude these reviews with a design certification rulemaking. By referencing a certified design, the license application review can proceed in a way that promotes safety and minimizes undue regulatory burden and delays.

The NRC is currently performing the design certification review of the General Electric Economic Simplified Boiling-Water Reactor (ESBWR), AREVA Evolutionary Power Reactor (EPR), and Mitsubishi's U.S. Advanced Pressurized-Water Reactor (USAPWR). The agency is also in the process of amending a design certification for the Westinghouse AP1000 design. In addition, vendors for four small reactors have requested preapplication discussions with the NRC. The NRC has had public preapplication meetings with these vendors to help the NRC staff understand the designs of the various reactors.

Early Site Permits

An early site permit is a permit for partial construction. Early site permits are valid for 10 to 20 years and can be renewed for an additional 10 to 20 years. The NRC review of an early site permit application addresses site safety issues, environmental protection issues, and plans for coping with emergencies, independent of the review of a specific nuclear plant design. The agency issued early site permits to the Clinton site in Illinois on March 15, 2007, the Grand Gulf site in Mississippi on April 5, 2007, and the North Anna site in Virginia on November 27, 2007. The NRC is currently reviewing the early site permit for the Vogtle site in Georgia.

LICENSE RENEWAL

Reactor operating licenses for nuclear reactors are granted for 40 years and can be renewed for an additional 20 years. The review process for renewal applications is designed to assess whether a reactor can continue to be operated safely during the extended period of operation.

To renew a license, the utility must demonstrate that the effects of aging will not adversely affect structures or

Figure 18

LICENSE RENEWAL APPLICATIONS

- Cumulative Number of License Renewals Received
- Cumulative Number of License Renewals Completed

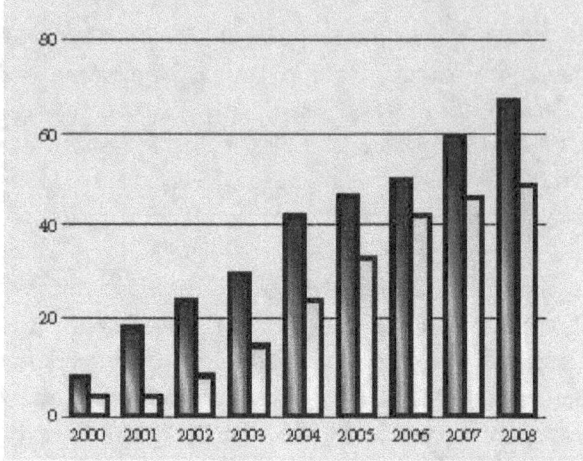

components important to safety during the renewal period. Such structures and components include the reactor vessel, piping, electrical cabling, containment structure, and steam generators. For some structures or components, additional action may be needed to ensure adequate margins of safety. Additionally, the agency assesses the potential impacts of the extended period of operation on the environment to verify that the impacts are not so great as to preclude license renewal.

The NRC has received applications to renew the licenses for 67 units at 40 sites since the license renewal program began in 2000 and has renewed licenses for 49 units at 27 sites during that time (see Figure 18). The NRC is currently reviewing applications to renew the licenses for 18 units at 13 sites. The agency expects that almost all of the licensees for currently licensed units will ultimately apply to renew their licenses.

NUCLEAR REACTOR INSPECTION

The NRC's Reactor Oversight Process outlines the agency's actions to verify that nuclear plants are being operated safely and in accordance with the NRC's rules and regulations. The NRC has full authority to demand that a licensee take immediate action for any conditions that result in excess risk to the public, including requiring a plant to shut down if necessary. The agency evaluates inspection findings and performance indicators to assess the safety performance of each operating nuclear power plant. The NRC performs a rigorous program of inspections at each plant and may perform supplemental inspections and take additional actions to ensure that the plants address significant safety issues. The results of NRC inspection findings for each plant are available to the public at http://www.nrc.gov/NRR/OVERSIGHT/ASSESS/pim_summary.html. The NRC also conducts public meetings with licensees to discuss the results of the NRC's assessments of its safety performance.

In FY 2008, all of the Nation's nuclear power plants were operated within NRC safety requirements. The safety indicators for nuclear plants as a whole showed no adverse trends, and more than 99 percent of plant safety indicators were rated green in FY 2008.

The NRC continued to improve the Reactor Oversight Process in FY 2008. Agency assessments confirm that the Reactor Oversight Process has resulted in a more objective, risk-informed, and predictable regulatory process that focuses NRC and licensee resources on aspects of plant performance that have the greatest impact on safe plant operations.

Investigations and Enforcement

Compliance with NRC requirements plays an important role in giving the agency confidence that reactor safety is being maintained. NRC policies deter noncompliance and encourage prompt identification and timely, comprehensive corrections. Licensees, contractors, and their employees who do not achieve the high standard of compliance expected by the NRC are subject to enforcement sanctions. Each enforcement action depends on the circumstances of the case. The NRC will not permit licensees to continue to conduct licensed activities if they cannot achieve and maintain adequate levels of safety. In FY 2008, there were 37 escalated enforcement actions with $1,053,000 in fines assessed. Allegations of reactor-related wrongdoing are referred to the Office of Investigation for evaluation and recommendations regarding further enforcement action.

FUEL FACILITIES

The NRC licenses and inspects all commercial nuclear fuel facilities that process and fabricate uranium ore into reactor fuel. This fuel is the manufactured material that powers the Nation's nuclear reactors. Licensing and inspection activities include detailed health, safety, safeguards, and environmental licensing reviews, as well as inspections of licensee programs, procedures, operations, and facilities to ensure safe and secure operations.

The NRC conducted several significant fuel cycle licensing reviews in FY 2008. The agency completed the process of recognizing the transfer of ownership of General Electric nuclear power plants to General Electric-Hitachi. To ensure that the fuel facilities are operating safely and securely, the agency reviewed, among other issues, safety analyses for controlling hazardous materials and the engineered and human performance barriers relied on to control hazardous materials. The NRC also conducted comprehensive reviews of fuel cycle licensees, including a review of licensees' integrated safety analyses (ISA). The ISA describes the management measures to ensure that the selected controls are available and reliable. The ISA allows a licensee to use risk information to identify hazards and to develop the engineered and human performance barriers relied on to control and mitigate hazards. The NRC completed ISA summary and environmental reviews for Areva Richland and Global Nuclear Fuels-America. The NRC also completed a review of the annual ISA updates for all fuel facilities.

The NRC received applications from the United States Enrichment Corporation (USEC) for the renewal of certificates of compliance for gaseous diffusion plants located near Paducah, KY, and Piketon, OH. Gaseous diffusion is a technology used to produce enriched uranium by forcing gaseous uranium hexafluoride through semipermeable membranes. By use of a large cascade of many stages, high separations can be achieved. Gaseous diffusion was the first economical enrichment process to be developed successfully. The gaseous diffusion plant certificates were renewed in 2003 and expire in 2008. USEC has requested renewal for a 5-year

period. The NRC held public meetings near both of the facilities to allow for public input on the certificate renewal process.

To support growing industry interest in potential recycling or reprocessing of spent nuclear fuel, the NRC began analyzing existing regulations during FY 2008 to address changes that must be made for these types of plants to ensure adequate protection of the public and the environment. The purpose of the agency's activity is to establish an effective regulatory framework for licensing a spent nuclear fuel recycling facility that considers technology-neutral regulatory approaches, innovative designs, and an advanced fuel cycle.

The Conference Report for the Consolidated Appropriations Act, 2008 directed the NRC to review the regulatory process for the U.S. Department of Energy (DOE) Hanford Waste Treatment Plant. In most cases, the regulations and requirements that DOE has in place are similar to those of the NRC. The NRC has determined that the DOE program, if properly implemented, is adequate to ensure the protection of public health and safety. Nevertheless, based on its review, the NRC made several suggestions in a report for DOE consideration. The NRC delivered the report to the Secretary of Energy and the House and Senate Committees on Appropriations in August 2008. The NRC suggested that DOE evaluate the way its requirements are implemented and consider improving the transparency of its decisions and actions regarding the plant. The NRC also suggested that DOE consider the list of issues identified in a table in the report and the specific safety and regulatory issues in an appendix to the report. Finally, the NRC suggested that DOE explore ways to gain and maintain more independence between regulatory oversight and project management functions.

Investigations and Enforcement

Compliance with NRC requirements plays an important role in giving the agency confidence that safety of fuel-cycle facilities is being maintained. NRC policies deter noncompliance and encourage prompt identification and timely, comprehensive corrections. Licensees, contractors, and their employees who do not achieve the high standard of compliance expected by the NRC are subject to enforcement sanctions. Each enforcement action depends on the circumstances of the case. The NRC will not permit licensees to continue to conduct licensed activities if they cannot achieve and maintain adequate levels of safety. In FY 2008, there were four escalated enforcement actions with $48,750 in fines assessed.

NUCLEAR MATERIALS USERS

The NRC licenses and inspects the commercial use of nuclear material for industrial, medical, and academic purposes. Commercial uses of nuclear materials include medical diagnosis and therapy, medical and biological research, academic training and research, industrial gauging and nondestructive testing, production of radiopharmaceuticals, and fabrication of commercial products (such as smoke detectors) and other radioactive sealed sources and devices. The NRC and 35 Agreement States regulate more than 22,000 specific materials licensees and 150,000 general materials licensees. The NRC currently regulates and inspects approximately 3,750 specific licensees for the use of nuclear byproduct and other radioactive materials.

Detailed health and safety reviews of license applications, as well as inspections of licensee procedures, operations, and facilities, provide reasonable assurance of safe operations and the production of safe products. The NRC routinely inspects nuclear materials licensees to ensure that they are using nuclear materials safely, maintaining accountability of those materials, and protecting public health and safety. The agency also analyzes operational experience from NRC and Agreement State licensees and regularly evaluates the safety significance of events reported by licensees and Agreement States.

In FY 2008, the NRC completed reviews of 2,952 materials licensing actions and 1,229 materials program inspections. From 2003 through 2008, the NRC maintained the timeliness of its reviews of nuclear materials license renewals and sealed source and device designs. In addition, the NRC completed 94 percent of the requests for license renewal and sealed source and device design reviews within

180 days of receipt and 98 percent of new applications and license amendments within 90 days.

The NRC worked with DOE to recover unwanted or orphaned radioactive sources. The source recovery program removes radioactive sources and aids in preventing inadvertent source melts or malevolent uses of sources. Since the inception of this program in 1997, more than 17,700 radioactive sources have been recovered from more than 690 sites within the United States.

The NRC is assisting U.S. Customs and Border Protection in fulfilling its congressional mandate to verify the legitimacy of radioactive material shipments coming into the United States through established ports of entry. The NRC regularly provides U.S. Customs and Border Protection with information on the licensing of radioactive materials, including import and export licensing data, and has established processes to provide around-the-clock technical support for the verification of the licensing status for materials in transit.

The NRC completed an update of the inventory of high-risk sources, defined as International Atomic Energy Agency (IAEA) Category 1 and Category 2 sources. The NRC also used the inventory to enhance the safety, security, and control of radioactive sources, including the issuance of increased control orders.

In addition to continuing to evaluate the need to enhance security at byproduct material licensees in FY 2008, the NRC is inspecting licensee compliance with these safety and security measures and coordinating with Agreement States to identify and resolve any implementation issues. The NRC also issued security orders to irradiator facilities, manufacturer and distributor facilities, and licensees shipping IAEA Category 1 quantities, including orders requiring this group of licensees to implement a program to fingerprint and conduct a criminal history check for access to safeguards information and access to material. The NRC and the Agreement States issued orders and legally binding agreements to licensees subject to increased controls that require fingerprinting and criminal history checks for access to material. The NRC and Agreement States will continue to inspect these licensees to ensure the proper implementation

of the increased control orders and other associated requirements. The NRC revised its screening process for new license applications to increase assurance that the material will be used as intended.

The NRC also works with international counterparts, both bilaterally and through multilateral organizations, to enhance the safety and security of radioactive sources. Examples of these activities include participating in ongoing meetings of countries implementing the IAEA Code of Conduct on the Safety and Security of Radioactive Sources to ensure harmonized national approaches, developing and implementing a memorandum of understanding with Canada for coordinated export and import licensing of sources, and bilateral work with countries of the Commonwealth of Independent States to support regulatory control over high-risk sources of concern. The section on international activities (pages 42-43) contains additional details.

Rulemaking Activities

In FY 2008, the NRC undertook several rulemaking activities to allow the use of radioactive materials while protecting public health and safety and the environment. These activities included publishing several rules that certify the safety of casks for the storage of spent nuclear fuel and implementing improvements to the licensing and distribution of byproduct materials. The agency also published a rule ensuring that its database of special nuclear materials contains the most accurate information possible for each licensee.

NRC is updating 10 CFR Part 110, "Export and Import of Nuclear Equipment and Material," to revise the definition of radioactive waste, incorporate changes to Appendix P, "Category 1 and 2 Radioactive Material," based on experience gained in 2005-2008, and rewrite or clarify Part 110.23 "General License for the Export of Byproduct Material."

Investigation and Enforcement

Out of approximately 929 inspections, 77 resulted in escalated actions, including the issuance of civil penalties. Violations included exporting licensed material in nonconforming packages, failing to maintain a minimum of two independent controls to secure a portable gauging device, transferring a portable gauging device containing radioactive

material to a company not licensed to receive the material, and failing to secure licensed material from unauthorized access. The NRC issued associated civil penalties in the amount of $124,000. Allegations of materials-related wrongdoing are referred to the Office of Investigation for evaluation and recommendation regarding further enforcement action.

HIGH-LEVEL WASTE REPOSITORY

The NRC formally docketed the U.S. Department of Energy (DOE) license application for the proposed high-level nuclear waste repository at Yucca Mountain, NV. The decision to docket the application follows the NRC staff's determination that the application, submitted June 3, 2008, is sufficiently complete for the staff to begin its full technical review. Docketing the application triggers a 3-year deadline, with a possible 1-year extension, set by Congress for the NRC to decide whether to grant a construction authorization.

After reviewing the DOE environmental impact statement and its supplements, the NRC staff determined that it would be practicable for the agency to adopt the DOE report. However, the staff is requesting that DOE supplement some aspects of its ground water analyses.

The U.S. Department of Energy's license application for the proposed Yucca Mountain high-level waste repository is formally presented by DOE's Edward Sproat (front, right), Director of the Office of Civilian Radioactive Waste Management, to Michael F. Weber (front, left), Director of NRC's Office of Nuclear Material Safety and Safeguards.

A subsequent *Federal Register* notice, to be published in early FY 2009, will provide an opportunity for interested parties to seek an adjudicatory hearing before the NRC's Atomic Safety and Licensing Board regarding the NRC's adoption of the environmental impact statement or the substance of the license application. This will include allegation processing, investigations of wrongdoing, and inspections and field reviews. The NRC also conducted public outreach activities and meetings during FY 2008 to make the regulatory process accessible to interested stakeholders.

The NRC continued to interact with DOE to assess technical and regulatory issues related to its spent fuel management program, which will use standardized transportation, aging, and disposal (TAD) canisters. In June 2007, DOE issued final performance specifications for the disposal canister, and in May 2008, DOE awarded two contracts for the design, licensing, and demonstration of the TAD canister system. The TAD canister will be the primary means for packaging spent nuclear fuel for interim storage and for transportation to and disposal in the proposed repository at Yucca Mountain, NV.

DECOMMISSIONING AND LOW-LEVEL WASTE

The NRC oversaw decommissioning activities at 15 power and early demonstration reactors, 11 research and test reactors, 32 uranium recovery sites, and 28 complex material and fuel cycle facilities that are undergoing decommissioning in FY 2008. Decommissioning removes radioactive contamination from buildings, equipment, ground water, and soil, achieving levels that permit the release of the property, with or without restrictions on its future use by the public. The NRC terminates the licenses for decommissioned facilities after the licensees demonstrate that the residual onsite radioactivity is within regulatory limits and sufficiently low to protect the health and safety of the public and the environment. In addition to the uranium recovery sites undergoing decommissioning, the NRC conducts regulatory oversight at five operational uranium recovery sites.

In FY 2008, the NRC reviewed the applications for seven new, expanding, or restarting uranium recovery facilities, including initiating four environmental reviews. The NRC also reviewed the DOE remedial action plan for the Moab uranium tailings pile. Additionally, the NRC conducted a number of regulatory activities to help ensure the safe management and disposal of the low-level radioactive waste generated by users of radioactive materials, nuclear power plants, and other NRC licensees.

The NRC has overseen decommissioning activities at numerous complex materials sites and power reactor sites. In FY 2008, the NRC terminated the licenses or completed regulatory oversight activities at one power reactor, one research and test reactor, and six complex materials sites. Completion of decommissioning, environmental, and performance assessment activities enables sites to return to productive use while ensuring that residual radioactivity does not pose an unacceptable risk to the public. The agency completed NUREG-1888, "Environmental Impact Statement for the Reclamation of the Sequoyah Fuels Corporation Site in Gore, Oklahoma."

In FY 2008, the NRC initiated an Annual Waste Incidental to Reprocessing Monitoring Report. The agency performed the first Savannah River Site (SRS) Saltstone facility monitoring visit and issued an SRS monitoring report. The NRC also worked with DOE, the U.S. Department of State, and the U.S. Environmental Protection Agency (EPA) to develop an enhanced consultation process for future waste determinations at SRS. In FY 2008, the staff issued the Commission paper on the low-level waste strategic assessment.

SPENT FUEL STORAGE AND TRANSPORTATION

The NRC ensures that reactor spent fuel is safely stored to support continued reactor operations and is safely transported when necessary. The NRC conducts licensing and certification reviews to ensure (1) the compliance of storage designs with NRC regulations for the storage of reactor spent fuel and (2) the safe transport of domestic and international shipments of nuclear reactor spent fuel and other risk-significant radioactive materials.

Shipments of radioactive materials are safely and securely transported each year within the United States. Several Federal agencies share responsibility for regulating the safety and security of those shipments. The NRC closely coordinates its transportation-related activities with those of the U.S. Department of Transportation (DOT) and, as appropriate, DOE. To help ensure the safety and security of both spent fuel storage and transportation, the NRC inspects vendors, fabricators, and licensees using transport container packages, spent fuel storage casks, and interim storage of spent fuel both at and away from reactor sites.

In FY 2008, the NRC completed 78 transport package design reviews and 11 storage container and installation design reviews. The NRC review of transportation and interim storage licensing requests ensures that shipments are made in NRC-approved packages that meet rigorous performance requirements and verifies that spent fuel is safely stored, thereby enabling continued reactor and decommissioning operations. The NRC also conducted 18 inspections of activities related to material package certificate holders, spent

Figure 19
STORAGE AND TRANSPORTATION DESIGN REVIEWS COMPLETED

■ Transportation Container Design Reviews
☐ Storage Container/Installation Design Reviews

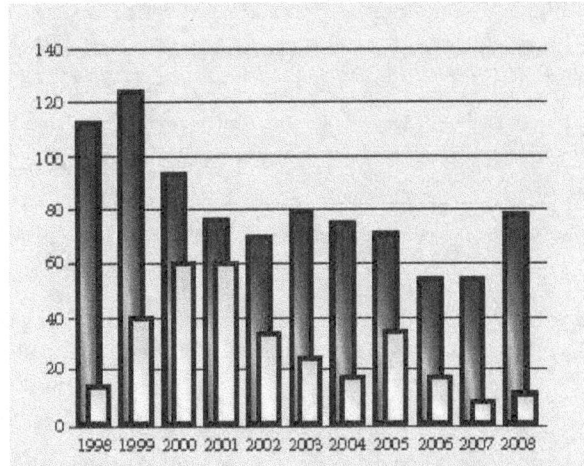

fuel storage container certificate holders, and preoperational activities and initial operations at independent spent fuel storage facilities to ensure that casks are being fabricated according to approved safety requirements.

The NRC, DOE, and DOT cosponsored the 15th International Symposium on Packaging and Transportation of Radioactive Materials (PATRAM) in October 2007. PATRAM is an international symposium held to exchange information on all aspects of the packaging and transportation of radioactive materials. This conference brought together representatives of the domestically and internationally regulated communities.

In addition, the NRC will broaden the scope of the license term rulemaking related to 10 CFR Part 72, "Licensing Requirements for the Independent Storage of Spent Nuclear Fuel and High-Level Radioactive Waste, and Reactor-Related Greater Than Class C Waste."

This expanded-scope of this rulemaking will provide a streamlined process to resolve noncompliance issues for general licensees who have implemented new procedures for casks already in service.

In February 2008, the NRC staff from several offices presented topics and participated in discussions as part of an internal workshop on burnup credit. Burnup credit is the use of the reduced reactivity of spent fuel in criticality safety analyses. At the February workshop, the following was discussed: (1) criticality and isotopic validation, including examining available data to support the validation, (2) alternatives to burnup measurements for spent nuclear fuel, and (3) the risk related to the transport of spent nuclear fuel. In March 2008, the staff briefed the Advisory Committee on Nuclear Waste and Materials (ACNW&M) on the status of burnup credit. Additionally, the staff updated the Commission on its activities to expand the technical basis for burnup credit in spent fuel transportation packages in July 2008.

RESEARCH ACTIVITIES

The NRC's safety research program evaluates and resolves safety issues for nuclear power plants and other facilities regulated by the NRC; provides the basis for regulatory changes and improvements; develops technical bases and tools to address emerging issues and new and advanced reactor designs; coordinates NRC activities related to consensus and voluntary standards for agency use; and assesses operational events to identify accident precursors. The agency conducts its research program to evaluate existing and potential safety issues; supply independent expertise, information, and technical judgments to support timely and realistic regulatory decisions; reduce uncertainties in risk assessments; and develop technical regulations and standards. When possible, the NRC engages in cooperative research with other Government agencies, the nuclear industry, universities, and international partners.

During the past year, the NRC research program has addressed key areas that support the agency's safety mission, including verification and validation of fire safety models for nuclear power plant applications, completion of the development of a licensing strategy for the next generation nuclear plant, a proactive material degradation assessment of reactor system and pressure boundary components and their susceptibility to known and potential degradation mechanisms, research to support the licensing of new digital instrumentation and control systems, and research on seismic hazard issues to support the evaluation of new reactor sites and of the seismic safety of existing nuclear facilities.

Fire Safety

The NRC's fire safety research program supports regulatory activities related to fire protection and fire risk analysis. During FY 2008, this program focused on risk-informed fire protection activities such as the fire protection rule, 10 CFR 50.48(c), "National Fire Protection Association Standard NFPA 805," and the fire protection inspection significance determination process. Work has also continued on fire modeling activities, including a fire modeling phenomena identification and ranking table issued in the summer of 2008 and a fire modeling users' guide for nuclear power plant applications, scheduled to be released in FY 2009. The NRC also issued the final NUREG/CR-6931,

"Cable Response to Live Fire (CAROLFIRE)," which provides research results on cable configurations that were identified as needing further study and gives the necessary data to develop a cable response model to reduce the uncertainty in predicting electrical cable damage in the performance of fire modeling analyses. The NRC, in partnership with Electric Power Research Institute, has been developing human reliability analysis methodology to determine operator performance during fire events. The NRC's fire safety research in FY 2008 has also focused on fuel cycle issues, including potential "red oil" fire hazards in the proposed mixed-oxide facility, and the performance of spent nuclear fuel transportation cask seals in beyond-design-basis fires, such as the Harbor Tunnel fire in Baltimore, MD.

Licensing of the Next Generation Nuclear Plant

The Energy Policy Act of 2005 (EPAct) specifies that the Secretary of DOE and the NRC Chairman must jointly submit a licensing strategy for the next generation nuclear plant (NGNP) project within 3 years of enactment of the EPAct. The NGNP project consists of research, development, design, construction, licensing, and operation of a very-high-temperature prototype nuclear plant, which can be used to generate electricity, hydrogen, or both. In addition, the EPAct provides that the NRC shall have licensing and regulatory authority for any reactor authorized under the EPAct.

The jointly developed Report to Congress, submitted in August 2008, summarizes the licensing strategy developed by DOE and the NRC for the NGNP.

Materials Degradation

The NRC continues to conduct research on materials degradation to identify susceptible materials and components in light-water reactors. The NRC developed advanced fracture mechanics tools to demonstrate the adequate structural integrity of reactor coolant system pressure boundary components. The NRC performed extensive nondestructive and destructive examination of some examination of some of these components in decommissioned nuclear reactors to assess the progression of stress-corrosion damage mechanisms and to validate the advanced fracture mechanics models. The

research was directly applied to demonstrate adequate safety margins in operating plants.

Digital Instrumentation and Control

The NRC's research supports the licensing of new digital instrumentation and control systems planned for retrofits in operating reactors and for use in new reactors. The NRC is also actively engaged in ongoing cyber research to ultimately provide regulatory guidance and tools for evaluating digital systems for cyber vulnerabilities, including potential vulnerabilities in digital electrical protection relaying that may affect the electrical grid.

Seismic Research (Earth Sciences)

The NRC is conducting research on seismic hazard issues to support the siting of new reactors and the evaluation of the seismic safety of existing nuclear facilities. The agency is performing research to develop the next generation of probabilistic seismic hazard assessment methods for the central and eastern United States. In cooperation with academic institutions, other Federal and State agencies, and industry, the NRC has initiated a program to develop ground motion propagation and earthquake source zone models. The NRC has also undertaken a study of the potential tsunami hazards for the east and gulf coasts, in cooperation with the U.S. Geological Survey and the National Oceanographic and Atmospheric Administration.

State-of-the-Art Reactor Consequence Analysis

The NRC is developing a method to estimate more accurately the offsite consequences from hypothetical severe accidents for operating commercial nuclear power plants in order to provide the public with more realistic information regarding the risk associated with commercial nuclear power plants.

The NRC, the U.S. nuclear industry, and the international nuclear community have performed extensive severe accident research to improve their understanding of the phenomena of severe accidents; the performance of the plants' systems and components under these conditions; the timing, magnitude,

and composition of the fission product release; and the effectiveness of different design and mitigative measures, including emergency preparedness.

The Commission directed the staff to produce a policy paper for a Commission decision regarding how guidance from the EPA's Protection Action Guides manual could be incorporated into an improved economic consequence model. The Commission directed staff to use the Commission decision resulting from this policy paper to update a computer code with an improved economic consequence model. The resulting economic consequence model may be applied to the State-of-the-Art Reactor Consequence Analyses (SOARCA) results if so directed by the Commission.

EMERGENCY PREPAREDNESS AND INCIDENT RESPONSE

The NRC emergency preparedness and incident response activities ensure that the agency can respond effectively to events at its licensees' sites and that adequate protective measures can be taken to mitigate plant damage and to minimize possible radiation doses to members of the public. The agency is currently engaged in a rulemaking effort that will update 11 areas in the emergency preparedness regulations.

In FY 2008, the NRC worked with States to address replenishment of potassium iodide supplies as a supplement to public protective action plans within the 16 kilometers (10-miles) emergency planning zones around nuclear power plants.

In FY 2008, the NRC completed the first phase of the Emergency Response Data System modernization effort. This phase involved conversion from proprietary server and client software to a commercial off-the-shelf system that can be accessed using a Web browser. The agency worked with affected States to ensure that the modernization effort did not adversely affect their ability to access data from facilities for which they have responsibility. The agency is currently negotiating memoranda of understanding to provide additional interested States with access to the Emergency Response Data System.

The agency completed numerous improvements to its Headquarters Operations Center, including installation of additional audiovisual equipment and the replacement of all computer workstations. The agency continues to pursue a strategy of modernization that incorporates lessons learned from use of the facility, as well as best practices from other agencies.

In FY 2008, NRC emergency responders participated in 14 exercises with licensee sites, 6 of which involved the NRC Headquarters response team, including 1 fuel cycle facility exercise and 1 unannounced exercise. In addition, the NRC participated in two Governmentwide interagency exercises and one intraagency tabletop drill. The NRC has also attended six hostile-action-based emergency preparedness drills hosted voluntarily by nuclear power plants to demonstrate responses to the unique challenges posed by security-based events.

INTERNATIONAL ACTIVITIES

The NRC's international responsibilities involve participation in activities that support U.S. Government compliance with international treaties and agreements; export and import licensing of nuclear facilities, equipment and materials; programs of bilateral nuclear cooperation and assistance; and support for multinational nuclear safety organizations such as the IAEA and the Organization for Economic Cooperation and Development's Nuclear Energy Agency (NEA).

Notable accomplishments in FY 2008 in the area of international treaties and agreements include high-level NRC participation in the April 2008 Review Meeting of Contracting Parties to the Convention on Nuclear Safety, preparations for the April 2009 Review Meeting of Contracting Parties to the Joint Convention on the Safety of Spent Fuel Management and the Safety of Radioactive Waste Management, and Commission review of U.S. Government agreements for peaceful uses of nuclear energy with Turkey, Russia, India, and the United Emirates. The Commission also approved the proposed adherence of the United States to the Protocol Additional to the Agreement between the

United States of America and the IAEA and is working with NRC licensees and through rulemaking to prepare for new reporting requirements.

In the area of export and import licensing, the NRC continued to work both domestically and internationally to enhance nuclear safety and security through the regulatory oversight of radioactive sources (see the section on nuclear materials users for specific examples). In May 2008, the NRC attended an IAEA open-ended meeting of technical and legal experts for sharing of information on lessons learned from States' implementation of the Supplementary Guidance on Import and Export of Radioactive Sources. The United States and 36 other States provided papers and six States provided presentations on their experiences at this meeting, which was attended by 167 experts from 88 IAEA member states.

Accomplishments in the area of bilateral activities during FY 2008 include an information exchange agreement that the NRC concluded with the National Nuclear Safety Administration of China. This arrangement is the first to include provisions with the Intellectual Property Rights (IPR) with China. The NRC also concluded an information exchange arrangement with the Vietnam Agency for Radiation and Nuclear Safety and Control (VARANSAC). Under this arrangement, the NRC will help VARANSAC develop its regulatory structure, exchange nuclear safety information, and assist in training technical staff. Additionally, the NRC signed a memorandum of cooperation (MOC) with the Canadian Nuclear Safety Commission (CNSC) for the Import and Export of Certain Radioactive Sources. This MOC was the first of its kind for both the United States and Canada. It resolves regulatory differences between the NRC and the CNSC regarding the implementation of the IAEA Code of Conduct. The MOC is expected to be used as a model for other countries interested in entering into an agreement with the NRC regarding the import and export of certain radioactive sources. The NRC developed pilot reactor licensing-related assistance projects that focus on helping select countries of the Commonwealth of Independent States establish the nuclear safety and security regulatory infrastructure needed for the design, construction, and operation of new nuclear

power plants. The NRC supported State Department-led efforts to discuss their intentions and plans for developing nuclear power programs with countries of the Middle East.

The NRC continues to support the development and implementation of programs focused on leveraging the knowledge and resources within the international regulatory community in the licensing of new reactor designs. In the multilateral context, the NRC continues its leadership role in the Multinational Design Evaluation Program (MDEP), through which regulatory authorities in over a dozen countries share expertise and resources in reviewing new and future reactor designs. The Nuclear Energy Agency (NEA) serves as secretariat for the multilateral MDEP activities. At its meeting in March 2008, the MDEP Policy Group approved continuation of the program, merging the current three stages into a single program. Some key accomplishments over the year include: the performance of the first joint vendor inspection; initiation of a project with the code organizations to compare the pressure boundary codes of four member countries; and the establishment of the MDEP library to collect and share regulatory documents of common interest that describe design requirements and guidance, review process and inspection program of new reactors.

The NRC has worked both domestically and internationally to enhance nuclear safety and security through the regulatory oversight of radioactive sources. For FY 2008, the NRC received a significant budget increase from Congress to support these efforts, which enabled the NRC to expand ongoing or planned radioactive-source-related assistance efforts for the regulatory authorities of the Commonwealth of Independent States, expand assistance provided to the Iraqi Radioactive Source Regulatory Authority, establish initial assistance efforts for select regulatory authorities in Africa, and enhance support for and coordination with sources-related assistance activities conducted by the IAEA. The NRC has also worked with the Executive Branch agencies and the IAEA to develop international security guidance documents for materials control, accounting, and physical protection.

The NRC participated in a working group with representatives of DOT and the CNSC to develop draft NUREG-1886, "Joint Canada-United States Guide for Approval of Type B(U) and Fissile Material Transportation Packages," which was issued for comment in May 2008. This NUREG will provide the framework for U.S. and Canadian cooperation and acceptance of each country's Type B(U) and fissile materials transportation package design approvals for export and import. The NRC expects to publish a final regulation in FY 2009, after parallel review and comment in the United States and Canada.

Considerable effort has gone into bilateral inspection training activities, especially with regard to actions in Finland, Japan, South Korea, and Taiwan. In Finland, an NRC inspector spent two months observing at the Olkiluoto 3 construction site and participated in a technical exchange concerning quality assurance. The NRC participated in a dual vendor inspection of Dousan Heavy Industries while in South Korea in May 2008. Also in May, the vendor inspection team performed a vendor inspection at Mitsubishi Heavy Industries in Japan. Additionally, an NRC inspector observed the Lungmen Nuclear Power Plant construction project for 1 month in Taiwan. Future cooperation with these countries' regulatory bodies is expected as more vendors become active in the nuclear market.

STRATEGIC GOAL 2: SECURITY

Ensure Adequate Protection in the Secure Use and Management of Radioactive Materials

Strategic Outcome

The NRC has the following strategic outcome associated with the agency's goal to ensure the secure use and management of radioactive materials. Prevent any instances where licensed radioactive materials are used domestically in a manner hostile to the security of the United States.

RESULTS: In FY 2008, the NRC achieved its security goal strategic outcome.

PERFORMANCE MEASURES

The table on the following page lists the agency's annual performance measures and their outcomes for the past 6 years. The performance measures are used to determine the agency's success in achieving its security goal. The NRC met all of the FY 2008 security goal performance measure targets.

Analysis of FY 2008 Results

1. **Unrecovered losses or thefts:** This measure includes any loss or theft of radioactive nuclear sources that the NRC has determined to be risk significant. The measure tracks the NRC's performance in ensuring that those radioactive sources that the agency has determined to be risk significant for the public health and safety are accounted for at all times. The ability to account for these sources is vital to securing the Nation's critical infrastructure from "dirty bomb" attacks or other means of radioactive material dispersal. There was no loss or theft of radioactive nuclear material that the NRC determined to be risk significant during FY 2008.

2. **Thefts or diversion:** This measure includes the ability of NRC-licensed facilities to maintain adequate protective capabilities to prevent theft or diversion of nuclear material or sabotage that could result in harm to the public health and safety. There were no substantiated cases of theft or diversion of licensed, risk-significant radioactive sources or formula quantities of special nuclear material or attacks that resulted in radiological sabotage during FY 2008.

3. **Loss or inventory discrepancy:** This measure includes ensuring that special nuclear material is accounted for at all times and that no losses of this material occur that could lead to the creation of an improvised nuclear device or other type of nuclear device. Furthermore, the measure tracks whether the systems in place at NRC-licensed facilities maintain accurate inventories of special nuclear material that the facilities process, use, or store. There were no substantiated losses of formula quantities of special nuclear material or substantiated inventory discrepancies

FY 2008 Security Goal Performance Measures

Measure	2003	2004	2005	2006	2007	2008
1. Number of unrecovered losses or thefts of risk-significant radioactive sources is zero.	0	0	0	0	0	0
2. Number of substantiated cases of theft or diversion of licensed, risk-significant radioactive sources or formula quantities of special nuclear material, or attacks that result in radiological sabotage is zero.	0	0	0	0	0	0
3. Number of substantiated losses of formula quantities of special nuclear material or substantiated inventory discrepancies of formula quantities of special nuclear material that are judged to be caused by theft or diversion or by substantial breakdown of the accountability system is zero.	0	0	0	0	0	0
4. Number of substantial breakdowns of physical security or material control (i.e., access control containment or accountability systems) that significantly weaken the protection against theft, diversion, or sabotage is less than one.	0	0	0	0	0	0
5. Number of significant unauthorized disclosures of classified and/or safeguards information is zero.	0	0	0	0	0	0

of formula quantities of special nuclear material that were caused by theft or diversion or by substantial breakdown of the accountability system during FY 2008.

4. Substantial breakdowns of physical security: This measure includes any breakdowns in access control, containment, or accountability systems that significantly weakened the protection against theft, diversion, or sabotage for nuclear materials that the Commission has determined to be risk significant. There were no substantial breakdowns of physical security during FY 2008.

5. Significant unauthorized disclosures: This measure includes significant unauthorized disclosures of classified or safeguards information that cause damage to national security or public safety. This measure tracks whether information that can harm national security (classified information) or cause damage to the public health and safety (safeguards information) has been stored and used in such a way as to prevent its disclosure to the public,

terrorist organizations, other nations, or personnel without a need to know. There were no significant disclosures that caused damage to national security or public safety during FY 2008.

SECURITY ACTIVITIES

Security Inspections

The NRC continued to maintain vigilant oversight of security in the nuclear industry and to implement the agency's security procedures. There were no substantial breakdowns of physical security at any commercial nuclear power plant. This was determined by the NRC's implementation of its baseline security inspection program. This inspection effort resides within the "security cornerstone" of the agency's Reactor Oversight Process. The security cornerstone focuses on the following five key licensee performance attributes: access authorization, access control, physical protection systems, material control and accounting, and response to contingency events. Through the results obtained from all

oversight activities, including baseline security inspections and performance indicators, the NRC determines whether licensees comply with requirements and can provide high assurance of adequate protection against the design-basis threat for radiological sabotage.

The NRC regularly carries out force-on-force inspections at commercial operating nuclear power plants as part of its comprehensive security program. The agency uses these inspections to evaluate and improve the effectiveness of plant security programs to prevent radiological sabotage. The agency conducts force-on-force inspections at least once every 3 years at each commercial nuclear power plant and fuel facility.

Force-on-force inspections assess a nuclear power plant's ability to defend against the design-basis threat, which characterizes the adversary against which plant owners must design appropriate defenses, such as physical protection systems and response strategies. A full force-on-force inspection, spanning 2 weeks, includes both tabletop drills and simulated combat between a mock commando-type adversary force and the nuclear plant's security force. During the attack, the adversary force attempts to reach and damage key safety systems and components that protect the reactor's core (containing radioactive fuel) or the spent nuclear fuel pool, potentially causing a radioactive release to the environment. The nuclear power plant's security forces seeks to stop the adversaries from reaching the plant's equipment. In FY 2008, the agency completed 24 force-on-force inspections and submitted its third annual Report to Congress on the results of the security inspection program.

The agency also pursued recommended enhancements to its allegation and inspection programs based on a lessons-learned review that followed an agency investigation into reports of inattentive security officers at the Peach Bottom nuclear power plant in Pennsylvania.

Security Rulemaking

During FY 2008, the NRC continued security rulemaking activities to increase the stability of the security requirements that it has placed on its licensees. The proposed security rulemakings are intended to make security practices generically applicable and generically acceptable security practices. The rulemakings address the lessons learned from requirements imposed by Orders on licensees following the events of September 11, 2001, as well as addressing lessons learned from operating experience and force-on-force exercises. The NRC has nearly completed the rulemakings for 10 CFR Part 73, "Physical Protection of Plants and Materials," on security requirements and the requirements for new reactors to assess aircraft impact. The agency is developing draft regulatory guides to support these rulemakings.

This proposed rule was published in the *Federal Register* in October 2006 (71 FR 62664). The final rule will fulfill the Commission's intent to complete a thorough review of physical protection program requirements and orders issued after September 11, 2001, and make them generically applicable security requirements. The agency completed the fitness-for-duty rule, proposed revisions to the access authorization and physical protection rule, published a final rule revising the design-basis threats, and published a proposed rule for Nuclear Materials Management and Safeguards System database reporting. The agency also implemented interim fingerprinting requirements. Other significant additions to the security regulations include requirements for cyber security, mitigative strategies and response procedures for potential or actual aircraft attacks, and assessment and management of the interface between safety and security.

In addition, the agency made significant progress in the development of security infrastructure for new reactor licensing. The infrastructure includes the development of standard review plans for early site permits, design certification, and combined operating licenses as well as security assessment format and content guides. The NRC continued interactions with the U.S. Department of Homeland Security (DHS) on security infrastructure through periodic meetings. The NRC also completed its initial security review for the design certification of the General Electric ESBWR, provided technical support for a draft combined operating license regulatory guide, and completed its security review of the early site permit for the Vogtle plant.

The NRC continued to improve and formalize its working relationships with other Federal agencies. These activities included the development of a memorandum of agreement between the NRC and the U.S. Department of Energy on the harboring of transport vehicles at NRC-licensed sites. The NRC recognizes the importance of a coordinated approach to security among the agencies in the Federal Government charged with homeland security responsibilities.

Control of Radioactive Sources

In FY 2008, the NRC maintained its efforts to identify and mitigate the risk of terrorist threats through enhanced security and controls for the use, storage, and transportation of byproduct materials and spent nuclear fuel. In collaboration with the DHS, DOE, and other Federal, State, and local agencies, the NRC continued to assess the potential use of risk-significant sources in radiological dispersal devices and to coordinate efforts to enhance radioactive source protection and security.

The NRC worked with Agreement States to implement requirements imposed on licensees that enhance the security and control of risk-significant radioactive material, including development of an inspection program to verify the implementation of these measures. In FY 2008, the NRC and Agreement States issued orders or other regulatory requirements to these licensees to require fingerprinting for those persons with unescorted access to risk-significant radioactive material. The NRC also continued activities to implement the National Source Tracking rule, which requires licensees to report information that will be maintained in a database for tracking possession of risk-significant radioactive sources. The rule requires NRC and Agreement State licensees to report transactions involving the manufacture, transfer, receipt, and disposal of nationally tracked sources (i.e., Category 1 and 2 sources from the IAEA Code of Conduct for the Safety and Security of Radioactive Sources). In response to two U.S. Government Accountability Office (GAO) reports recommending the development of a tracking system for radioactive sources, the NRC developed and annually updates an interim database of nationally tracked sources. In response to a GAO investigation of the ease of obtaining a new license for radioactive sources, the NRC and Agreement States have implemented a process to

Gary Holahan, Deputy Director, Office of New Reactors, participating in an emergency preparedness exercise at the Waterford Nuclear Power Plant near New Orleans, LA.

screen new license applications or applicants to determine, with reasonable assurance, that the requested materials will be used as intended.

The NRC continued its significant participation in implementing portions of the International Atomic Energy Agency Code (IAEA) of Conduct on the Safety and Security of Radioactive Sources, as well as its participation in IAEA committees that are developing guidance documents for the security of radioactive sources during use, storage, and transport. The NRC's involvement in these committees enhances security and public safety and contributes to international and domestic regulatory consistency. Under 10 CFR Part 110, which was revised in December 2005, the NRC issued 50 licenses for the export of Category 1 and 2 materials as defined by the Code. The NRC is also developing plans to expand the National Source Tracking System to include Category 3 sources.

In FY 2008, the agency conducted an operational readiness review of the Enrichment Technology U.S., Inc., (ETUS) location at the Louisiana Energy Services (LES) site in Eunice, NM. The purpose of the readiness review was to determine if ETUS's program for the protection of classified matter was consistent with its NRC-approved Standard Practice Procedures Plan (SPPP) for the protection of

classified matter. Based on the results of the review, the NRC determined that the ETUS classified matter program was in compliance with its approved SPPP. Therefore, the NRC issued a facility security clearance for the use and storage of classified matter up to and including confidential-restricted data. The agency also conducted a protection of classified matter review of the LES International Standards Organization Container Storage (ISO) Pad in order to determine if the ISO Pad was sufficient for the temporary storage of classified matter and participated in an accreditation of the LES classified CROON Training network with the Department of Energy. The ISO Pad was built and added to the LES SPPP after NRC granted LES its initial facility security clearance. Therefore, the NRC performed an on site review of the LES ISO Pad to determine if it met the requirements for the protection of classified matter as described in the LES SPPP. Based on the ISO Pad review, the NRC notified LES that the Pad was approved for the temporary storage of classified matter. The agency also conducted an operational readiness review of General Electric-Hitachi's Separation of Isotopes by Laser Excitation (Silex) Test Loop Facility in Wilmington, NC, and Textron Defense Systems, a contractor to General Electric-Hitachi, who will be milling and refurbishing classified parts. In both cases, the agency granted facility security clearances for the use and storage of classified matter up to and including secret-restricted data.

In addition to operational readiness reviews that were conducted in support of classified storage programs for FY 2008, the agency also conducted safeguards information program reviews in support of the four advanced reactor vendors. The NRC conducted hands-on inspections at six different facilities operated by the four vendors in Virginia, Pennsylvania, North Carolina, and Japan and accredited the day-to-day safekeeping and storage practices for safeguards information. The safeguards information program reviews are intended to ensure compliance capabilities exist as directed by NRC information security standards. An engineering company in North Carolina was also visited by the NRC to evaluate its request for a safeguards information program.

SPENT FUEL

In FY 2008, the agency completed six security plan reviews for proposed independent spent fuel storage installations and issued security orders to five new independent spent fuel storage installation licensees. The NRC also reviewed and approved five spent fuel transportation routes.

ORGANIZATIONAL EXCELLENCE OBJECTIVES

Openness, Effectiveness, and Operational Excellence

The agency's Organizational Excellence objectives of Openness, Effectiveness, and Operational Excellence and their associated performance measures are shown below, as well as descriptions of agency actions that will be undertaken to address those measures that did not meet their targets. This will be the last year these objectives and performance measures will be reported in the Performance and Accountability Report since they are being discontinued after FY 2008.

Openness Objective measures not met and actions to resolve problem.

1b. & 1c. The requirements were not met. The agency continues to review internal procedures to improve agency timeliness in providing documents to the public. Internal processes are currently being reviewed, and improvements are being implemented to meet the timelines measure.

Effectiveness Objective measures not met and action to resolve problem.

1.a. There has been an increasing trend in the number of complex licensing action requests, reduced number of lower complexity actions such as orders, and reductions in efficiency caused by new staff and loss of experienced staff to attrition and movement within the agency. NRR did not see expected results of process enhancements because of the trend in more complex safety reviews.

Operational Excellence Objective measures not met and actions to resolve problems.

1.a. The agency has experienced a large growth in FTEs within the last year due to the New Reactor Program ramping up to receive applications from licensees to develop and construct new reactors. As a result, additional budget staff was hired to manage the program, which resulted in the agency exceeding the target for this measure. However, the Office of the Chief Financial Officer is currently developing a new budget process as directed by the Commission.

1.b. The NRC has initiated several actions to improve this measure. The Office of Human Resources has published "Staffing Process Enhancements" to speed up the hiring process. Additionally, a new element and standard covering the 45-day measure has been created for all Senior Executive Service positions.

Another significant issue in meeting the standard was the high volume of NRC hiring. For FY 2008, 521 new employees were hired.

ORGANIZATIONAL EXCELLENCE OBJECTIVES AND ASSOCIATED PERFORMANCE MEASURES

Measure	2003	2004	2005	2006	2007	2008
Objective 1: Openness						
1. Eighty-eight percent of selected openness output measures (below) achieve performance targets.	New measure in FY 2006			50%	66%	80%
a. Ninety percent of stakeholder formal requests for information receive an NRC response within 60 days of receipt.	New measure in FY 2006			100%	100%	100%
b. Ninety percent of nonsensitive, unclassified regulatory documents generated by the NRC and sent to the agency's Document Processing Center are released to the public by the 6th working day after the date of the document.	New measure in FY 2006			63%	75%	82%
c. Ninety percent of nonsensitive, unclassified regulatory documents received by the NRC are released to the public by the 6th working day after the document is added to the ADAMS main library.	New measure in FY 2006			77%	87%	66%
d. The NRC achieves a 71% user satisfaction score for the agency's public Web site greater than or equal to the Federal Agency Mean score based on results of the yearly American Customer Satisfaction Index for Federal Web sites.	New measure in FY 2006			70%	71%	71%
e. Complete 50% of Freedom of Information Act requests in 20 days (median).	New measure in FY 2006			61%	67%	71%
f. Issue ninety percent of Director's Decisions under 10 CFR 2.206, "Requests for Action under this Subpart," within 120 days.	New measure in FY 2006			100%	100%	100%
g. Make 90% of final significance determination process determinations within 90 days for all potentially greater-than-green findings.	New measure in FY 2006			92%	100%	100%
h. Ninety percent of stakeholders believe they were given sufficient opportunity to ask questions or express their views.	New measure in FY 2006			90%	96%	97%

Measure	2003	2004	2005	2006	2007	2008
i. At least 90% of Category 1, 2, and 3 meetings on regulatory issues for which public notices are issued at least 10 days in advance of the meeting.	New measure in FY 2006			92%	93%	90%
j. Complete all of the key stakeholder and public interactions for the reactor performance assessment cycle.	New measure in FY 2008					Met

Objective 2: Effectiveness

Measure	2003	2004	2005	2006	2007	2008
1. Seventy percent of selected processes deliver efficiency improvements.	New measure in FY 2006			25%	60%	80%
a. Reduce the average age at closure for licensing actions by 2.5%.	New measure in FY 2008					Not Met
b. At the rate of one per year, Category III license renewal applications will be considered for a 40-year license.	New measure in FY 2006			Not Met	Not Met	Met
c. Improve the timeliness of the review process for nuclear power reactor License Termination Plans by at least 30% over 3 years (FY 2006-FY 2008) as compared to the historical average.	New measure in FY 2006					38%
d. Implement process enhancements to permit improvement for the reactor rulemaking petition timeliness by 2.5%.	New measure in FY 2007				5%	Met
e. Reduce the staff cost for letters to DOE by 5%.	New measure in FY 2008					40%
2. No more than one instance per program where licensing or regulatory activities unnecessarily impede the safe and beneficial uses of radioactive materials.	New measure in FY 2006			0	0	0

Objective 3: Operational Excellence

Measure	2003	2004	2005	2006	2007	2008
1. Ninety percent of selected support processes deliver efficiency improvements.	New measure in FY 2006			50%	0%	0%
a. Five percent reduction of agency FTE used to develop and submit the FY 2008 and FY 2009 performance budgets.	New measure in FY 2006			0%	2%* increase	6% increase
b. Issue offer letter 80% of the time within 45 work days of the closing date of the announcement.	New measure in FY 2006			67%	31%	56%
2. Eighty percent of selected NRC management programs deliver intended outcomes.	New measure in FY 2005		60%	80%	100%	100%
a. Infrastructure management program: 80% of activities achieve their targets.	New measure in FY 2005		100%	100%	100%	100%
b. Financial Management & Budget and Performance Integration program: 70% of activities achieve their targets.	New measure in FY 2005		67%	67%	88%	100%
c. Expanded electronic government program: 75% of activities achieve their targets.	New measure in FY 2005		50%	75%	75%	75%
d. Management of Human Capital program: 80% of activities achieve their targets.	New measure in FY 2005		80%	100%	80%	100%

* FY 2007 PAR showed 12%. The data were error and recalculated to be 2%.

COSTING TO GOALS, PART REVIEWS, AND PROGRAM EVALUATIONS

COSTING TO GOALS

The NRC is working to improve its cost management capabilities to better align its costs with desired outcomes. This year's Performance and Accountability Report presents the full cost of achieving the safety and security goals for two of the agency's programs, Nuclear Reactor Safety and Nuclear Materials Safety. The cost of achieving the agency's safety goal was $904.2 million, and the cost of achieving the agency's security goal was $39.9 million (see Figure 20).

Figure 20
NRC SAFETY AND SECURITY COSTS
(In Millions)

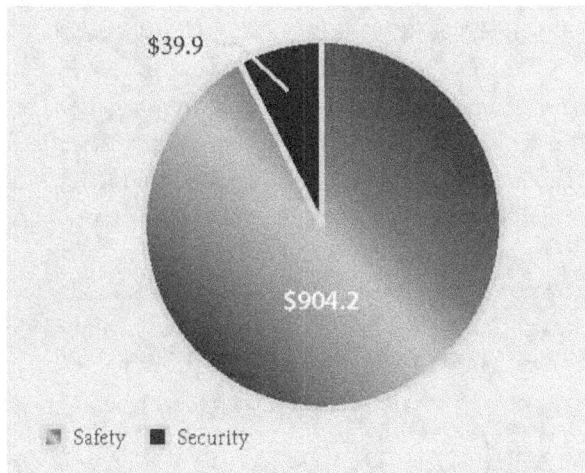

$39.9

$904.2

■ Safety ■ Security

PROGRAM ASSESSMENT RATING TOOL

The Office of Management and Budget (OMB) has conducted joint reviews with the NRC using the program assessment rating tool (PART) for all seven of the agency's major activities. The Office of Management and Budget has scored six of the programs as effective, the highest rating available, and one as moderately effective. There were no PART reviews in FYs 2006 and 2008. The following table shows the results of the NRC PART reviews:

NRC PART REVIEW RESULTS

Program	Year	Part Rating
Reactor Inspection and Performance Assessment	FY 2003	Effective
Fuel Facilities Licensing and Inspection	FY 2003	Effective
Nuclear Materials Users Licensing and Inspection	FY 2004	Effective
Reactor Licensing	FY 2005	Moderately Effective
Spent Fuel Storage and Transportation Licensing and Inspection	FY 2005	Effective
Decommissioning and Low-Level Waste	FY 2007	Effective
High-Level Waste Repository	FY 2007	Effective

PROGRAM EVALUATIONS

The NRC conducted a number of important self-assessments of its regulatory operations in FY 2008. The Office of Nuclear Reactor Regulation performed evaluations on operating licensing program, Reactor Oversight Process, and management work planning process.

Operator Licensing Program

A NRC review team evaluated the overall effectiveness of the Region II and Region III operator licensing programs and their adherence to the guidance contained in NUREG-1021, "Operator Licensing Examination Standards for Power Reactors," and other policy documents. The operator licensing programs are broken down into seven functional areas that are rated as "significant strength," "satisfactory," or "needs improvement." Overall, the operator licensing program in both Region II and Region III are being conducted in accordance with the examination standards. For both regions, six functional areas were assessed as satisfactory; one area—licensing assistant activities—was evaluated as a significant strength. The review team also commended the

regions' efforts to improve the quality of their Agencywide Documents Access and Management System examination packages.

Reactor Oversight Process

The NRC completed the 2007 Reactor Oversight Process (ROP) self-assessment in April 2008. The report, SECY-08-0046, "Reactor Oversight Process Self-Assessment for Calendar Year 2007," is available through the NRC public Web site.

The results of the CY 2007 self-assessment indicated that the ROP met its program goals and achieved its intended outcomes. The staff found the ROP objective, risk informed, understandable, and predictable, and the ROP met the agency goals of ensuring safety, openness, and effectiveness as listed in the NRC's Strategic Plan for Fiscal Years (FY) 2004–2009. The NRC staff maintained its focus on stakeholder involvement and continued to improve various aspects of the ROP. The staff implemented several ROP improvements in CY 2007 to address issues raised by the Commission, recommended by independent reviews, or obtained from internal and external stakeholder feedback.

The NRC inspection and assessment program independently verified that nuclear power plants were operated safely and securely. During the year, the staff made several improvements to the ROP, including the timeliness of significance determination process results, implementing enhancements to more fully address safety culture and oversight of licensees with performance problems, realigning inspection resources to improve effectiveness, and making changes to some performance indicators to better identify declining safety performance. However, the staff recognizes the need for further enhancements to the ROP and will continue to actively solicit input from the NRC's internal and external stakeholders. For example, the staff plans to explore ways in which substantive cross-cutting issues, traditional enforcement actions, and other insights could be used more effectively in the ROP.

Management Work Planning Process

In July 2007, the NRC engaged an independent management consulting firm to help assess its centralized work planning (CWP) efforts and make recommendations to improve the effectiveness of those efforts. The CWP is a significant initiative to implement CWP and project support within the Office of Nuclear Reactor Regulation (NRR). Its initial inception in 1999 changed the way many projects were initiated and managed in the NRR. The CWP effort was established with the following goals:

- Provide clear and consistent expectations and accountability for NRR work processes and products.
- Provide up-to-date, accessible workload information for planning, budgeting, and measuring work and organizational performance.
- Optimize the efficiency of NRR work processes by reducing process variances.
- Establish objective means of allocating and tracking the workload so that NRR resources are fully leveraged.

The consultants concluded that while the CWP effort has had a positive impact on project quality and execution, the agency can improve the quality of work and project planning, tracking, and management within NRR. The consultants recommended that the agency expand the organizational capacity of the CWP by adding additional project management support and business intelligence capabilities. In addition, the consultant recommended the agency migrate from its current information technology systems to an enterprise project management team.

DATA SOURCES AND QUALITY

The NRC's data collection and analysis methods are driven largely by the regulatory mandate that Congress entrusted to the agency. Specifically, the NRC's mission is to regulate the Nation's civilian use of byproduct, source, and special nuclear materials to ensure adequate protection of public health and safety, protect the environment, and promote the common defense and security. In undertaking this mission, the NRC oversees nuclear power plants, nonpower reactors, nuclear fuel facilities, interim spent fuel storage, radioactive material transportation, disposal of nuclear waste, and the industrial and medical uses of nuclear materials. Section 208 of the Energy Reorganization Act of 1974, as amended, requires the NRC to inform Congress of incidents or events that the Commission determines to be significant from the standpoint of public health and safety. To comply with the Energy Reorganization Act and to determine which events should be considered significant, the NRC developed the abnormal occurrence criteria. Based on those criteria, the NRC prepares the annual NUREG-0090, "Report to Congress on Abnormal Occurrences," which is available on the agency's public Web site at http://www.nrc.gov/reading-rm/doc-collections/nuregs/staff/sr0090.

One important characteristic of this report is that the data presented normally originate from external sources such as Agreement States and NRC licensees. The NRC finds these data credible because (1) agency regulations require Agreement States, licensees, and other external sources to report the necessary information; (2) the NRC maintains an aggressive inspection program that, among other activities, includes auditing licensee programs and evaluating Agreement State programs to ensure that they are reporting the necessary information as required by the agency's regulations; and (3) the agency has established procedures for inspecting and evaluating licensees. The NRC employs multiple database systems to support this process, including the Licensee Event Report Search System, the Accident Sequence Precursor Database, the Nuclear Materials Events Database, and the Radiation Exposure Information Report System. In addition, nonsensitive reports submitted by Agreement States and NRC licensees are available to the public through the NRC's Agencywide Documents Access and Management System accessible through the agency's public Web site http://www.nrc.gov.

As stated above, the NRC has established procedures for the systematic review and evaluation of events reported by both NRC and Agreement State licensees. The NRC's objective is to identify events that are significant from the standpoint of public health and safety, based on criteria that include specific

thresholds. The NRC verifies the reliability and technical accuracy of event information reported to the agency. The NRC periodically inspects licensees and reviews Agreement State programs. In addition, the NRC headquarters, regional offices, and Agreement States hold periodic conference calls to discuss event information. Events identified as meeting the abnormal occurrence criteria are validated and verified before being reported to Congress.

DATA SECURITY

Data security is ensured by the agency's automated information security program, which provides administrative, technical, and physical security measures to protect the agency's information, automated information systems, and information technology infrastructure. Specifically, these measures include the policies, processes, and technical mechanisms used to protect classified information, unclassified safeguards information, and sensitive unclassified information that is processed, stored, or produced on the agency's automated information systems. Data security for information maintained outside the NRC's infrastructure is provided by the hosting contractor or organization.

PERFORMANCE DATA COMPLETENESS AND RELIABILITY

To manage for results, it is essential for the agency to assess the completeness and reliability of the NRC performance data. Comparisons of actual performance with the projected levels are possible only if the data used to measure performance are complete and reliable. Consequently, the Reports Consolidation Act of 2000 requires the Chairman of the NRC to assess the completeness and reliability of the performance data used in this report. The process for ensuring the data is complete and reliable is that offices are required to complete a template for submission to the Chief Financial Officer for every performance measure, certifying the data submitted has been approved by the applicable Office Director.

DATA COMPLETENESS

The agency considers data to be complete if the agency reports actual performance data for every performance goal and indicator in the annual plan. Actual performance data include preliminary data if those are the only data available when the agency sends its report to the President and Congress. The NRC has reported actual or preliminary data for every strategic and performance goal measure; consequently, the data presented in this report meet these requirements for data completeness.

DATA RELIABILITY

The agency considers data to be reliable when agency managers and decisionmakers do not demonstrate either a refusal or a marked reluctance to use the data in carrying out their responsibilities. The data presented in this report meet this requirement for data reliability, since NRC managers and senior leaders regularly use the reported data in the course of their duties.

Waterford Nuclear Power Plant in St. Charles Parish, Killona, LA.

CHAPTER 3
FINANCIAL STATEMENTS AND AUDITORS' REPORT

U.S.NRC

United States Nuclear Regulatory Commission

Protecting People and the Environment

Photo Courtesy of the NRC Image Library.

NRC staff visiting the proposed high-level waste repository site at Yucca Mountain, NV.

A MESSAGE FROM THE
CHIEF FINANCIAL OFFICER

I am pleased to present the financial statements for the U.S. Nuclear Regulatory Commission (NRC) fiscal year (FY) 2008 Performance and Accountability Report. For the fifth consecutive year, an independent auditor has rendered an unqualified opinion on the NRC financial statements. This past year, the NRC successfully implemented the corrective actions necessary to improve its information system security controls and eliminated the last remaining internal control material weakness identified during prior audits.

Furthermore, the NRC continues to meet the requirements of Office of Management and Budget (OMB) Circular A-123, Appendix A, "Internal Controls Over Financial Reporting." During FY 2008, NRC assessed nine key processes and tested 56 controls in five of these key processes to meet the OMB circular requirements. For the third consecutive year, no material weaknesses were identified for NRC financial reporting.

During FY 2008, the agency continued implementing the President's Management Agenda and further improving its financial systems and processes. Some specific NRC accomplishments include the following:

- Outsourcing the NRC payment function to a shared service provider, reducing transaction costs, and improving payment accuracy and timeliness.
- Completing the Federal Information Security Management Act (FISMA) certification and accreditation for the NRC time and labor system.
- Establishing an educational grant program payment process with the U.S. Department of the Treasury's Automated Standard Application for Payment System that allows award recipients more timely access to grant funds.
- Implementing a streamlined process with a new information technology system for budget formulation that resulted in improved transparency and coordination during the FY 2010 budget development process.

In the future, the NRC plans to complete additional initiatives to achieve its financial management goals of improving controls while providing more timely and accurate information to stakeholders. The most significant initiative in this area involves the replacement of several legacy systems with an integrated Web-based financial management system hosted by a Government shared service provider. In FY 2008, NRC established an interagency agreement with a shared service provider and is currently defining system requirements working towards implementing this new core financial system by FY 2011. In conjunction with this effort, the NRC is also streamlining its business processes and modernizing its time and labor system to create more robust and user-friendly systems. These process changes and replacement systems will improve the NRC's efficiency and provide agency managers with substantially greater access to financial information for improved decisionmaking.

The NRC is proud of its financial management accomplishments in FY 2008 and looks forward to continued improvement in FY 2009 and beyond. The agency takes its responsibility for effective stewardship of taxpayer money very seriously. The NRC is committed to effective and efficient management of Government resources to achieve its strategic goals for ensuring the safety and security of the Nation's civilian use of nuclear materials.

J.E. Dyer
Chief Financial Officer
November 14, 2008

U.S.NRC
United States Nuclear Regulatory Commission
Protecting People and the Environment

PRINCIPAL STATEMENTS

BALANCE SHEET (IN THOUSANDS)

As of September 30,		2008		2007
Assets				
Intragovernmental				
Fund balance with Treasury (Note 2)	$	393,478	$	356,399
Accounts receivable (Note 3)		4,692		5,228
Other—advances and prepayments		4,121		3,244
Total intragovernmental		402,291		364,871
Accounts receivable, net (Note 3)		116,684		88,666
Property and equipment, net (Note 4)		35,475		31,832
Other		28		39
Total Assets	$	554,478	$	485,408
Liabilities				
Intragovernmental				
Accounts payable	$	12,360	$	9,038
Other (Note 5)		4,844		110,797
Total intragovernmental		17,204		119,835
Accounts payable		41,763		18,672
Federal employee benefits (Note 6)		7,059		6,833
Other (Note 5)		70,948		58,877
Total Liabilities		136,974		204,217
Net Position				
Unexpended appropriations		289,269		254,027
Cumulative results of operations (Note 8)		128,235		27,164
Total Net Position		417,504		281,191
Total Liabilities and Net Position	$	554,478	$	485,408

The accompanying notes to the principal statements are an integral part of this statement.

STATEMENT OF NET COST (IN THOUSANDS)

For the years ended September 30,	2008	2007
Nuclear Reactor Safety and Security		
Gross costs	$ 705,832	$ 582,212
Less: Earned revenue	(725,840)	(612,769)
Total Net Cost of Nuclear Reactor Safety and Security (Note 9)	(20,008)	(30,557)
Nuclear Materials and Waste Safety and Security		
Gross costs	238,219	204,495
Less: Earned revenue	(71,740)	(80,490)
Total Net Cost of Nuclear Materials and Waste Safety and Security (Note 9)	166,479	124,005
Net Cost of Operations	$ 146,471	$ 93,448

The accompanying notes to the principal statements are an integral part of this statement.

STATEMENT OF CHANGES IN NET POSITION (IN THOUSANDS)

For the years ended September 30,	2008	2007
Cumulative Results of Operations		
Beginning Balance	$ 27,164	$ 18,899
Budgetary Financing Sources		
Appropriations used	98,172	46,646
Non-exchange revenue (Note 11)	-	-
Transfers-in/out without reimbursement	29,025	45,826
Other Financing Sources		
Imputed financing from costs absorbed by others (Note 11)	26,911	27,627
Other—Revenue from excess collections	93,434	(18,386)
Total Financing Sources	247,542	101,713
Net Cost of Operations	(146,471)	(93,448)
Net Change	101,071	8,265
Cumulative Results of Operations	$ 128,235	$ 27,164
Unexpended Appropriations		
Beginning Balance	$ 254,027	$ 193,694
Adjustments:		
Change in accounting principle (Note 14)	-	(2,838)
Beginning Balance, as adjusted	254,027	190,856
Budgetary Financing Sources		
Appropriations received	133,414	109,817
Appropriations used	(98,172)	(46,646)
Total Budgetary Financing Sources	35,242	63,171
Total Unexpended Appropriations	289,269	254,027
Net Position	$ 417,504	$ 281,191

The accompanying notes to the principal statements are an integral part of this statement.

STATEMENT OF BUDGETARY RESOURCES (IN THOUSANDS)

For the years ended September 30,	2008	2007
Budgetary Resources		
Unobligated balance, brought forward, October 1	$ 72,160	$ 74,255
Recoveries of prior year unpaid obligations		
Actual	21,937	5,691
Budget authority		
Appropriation	926,074	824,893
Spending authority from offsetting collections		
Reimbursements earned—Collected	6,709	4,381
Reimbursements earned—Change in receivables	222	371
Change in unfilled customer orders—Advance received	1,645	1,433
Change in unfilled customer orders—Without advance	65	(93)
Subtotal—Spending authority from offsetting collections	8,641	6,092
Total Budgetary Resources	**$ 1,028,812**	**$ 910,931**
Status of Budgetary Resources		
Obligations incurred (Note 12)		
Direct	$ 941,942	$ 834,126
Reimbursable	7,880	4,645
Subtotal	949,822	838,771
Unobligated balance		
Apportioned	69,024	45,438
Exempt from apportionment	9,853	26,722
Subtotal	78,877	72,160
Unobligated balance, not available	113	-
Total Status of Budgetary Resources	**$ 1,028,812**	**$ 910,931**
Change in Obligated Balance		
Obligated balance, net		
Unpaid obligations brought forward, October 1	$ 270,894	$ 202,446
Obligations incurred, net	949,822	838,771
Gross outlays	(884,004)	(764,354)
Recoveries of prior year unpaid obligations, actual	(21,937)	(5,691)
Change in uncollected customer payments, from Federal sources	(287)	(278)
Obligated balance, net, end of period		
Unpaid obligations	318,626	274,745
Uncollected customer payments, from Federal sources	(4,138)	(3,851)
Total unpaid obligated balance, net, end of period	$ 314,488	$ 270,894
Net outlays		
Gross outlays	$ 884,004	$ 764,354
Offsetting collections	(8,354)	(5,814)
Distributed offsetting receipts	(763,640)	(669,245)
Net Outlays	**$ 112,010**	**$ 89,295**

The accompanying notes to the principal statements are an integral part of this statement.

NOTES TO PRINCIPAL STATEMENTS

NOTE 1. SUMMARY OF SIGNIFICANT ACCOUNTING POLICIES (ALL TABLES ARE PRESENTED IN THOUSANDS)

A. REPORTING ENTITY

The U.S. Nuclear Regulatory Commission (NRC) is an independent regulatory agency of the Federal Government that was created by the U.S. Congress to regulate the Nation's civilian use of byproduct, source, and special nuclear materials to ensure adequate protection of the public health and safety, to promote the common defense and security, and to protect the environment. Its purposes are defined by the Energy Reorganization Act of 1974, as amended, along with the Atomic Energy Act of 1954, as amended, which provide the foundation for regulating the Nation's civilian use of nuclear materials.

The NRC operates through the execution of its congressionally approved appropriations for Salaries and Expenses and for the Office of the Inspector General, including funds derived from the Nuclear Waste Fund. In addition, the U.S. Agency for International Development (USAID) provides transfer appropriations to develop nuclear safety, regulatory authorities, and independent oversight of nuclear reactors in Russia, Ukraine, Kazakhstan, and Armenia.

B. BASIS OF PRESENTATION

These principal statements were prepared to report the financial position and results of operations of the NRC as required by the Chief Financial Officers Act of 1990 and the Government Management Reform Act of 1994. These financial statements were prepared from the books and records of the NRC in conformance with generally accepted accounting principles (GAAP) of the United States, and the form and content for entity financial statements were specified by the Office of Management and Budget (OMB) in Circular No. A-136, "Financial Reporting Requirements." GAAP for Federal entities are the standards prescribed by the Federal Accounting Standards Advisory Board, which is the official body for setting the accounting standards of the U.S. Government. These statements are, therefore, different from the financial reports, also prepared by the NRC pursuant to OMB directives, which are used to monitor and control NRC's use of budgetary resources.

The NRC has not presented a Statement of Custodial Activity because the amounts involved are immaterial and incidental to its operations and mission.

C. BUDGETS AND BUDGETARY ACCOUNTING

Budgetary accounting measures the appropriation and consumption of budget spending authority or other budgetary resources and facilitates compliance with legal constraints and controls over the use of Federal funds. Under budgetary reporting principles, budgetary resources are consumed at the time of purchase. Assets and liabilities, which do not consume current budgetary resources, are not reported, and only those liabilities for which valid obligations have been established are considered to consume budgetary resources.

For the past 34 years, Congress has enacted no-year appropriations, which are available for obligation by the NRC until expended. For FY 2008, the Consolidated Appropriations Act of 2008 requires the NRC to recover approximately 90 percent of its new budget authority of $926.1 million by assessing fees. Under Public Law 110-161, the agency does not have to recover the $29 million for the Nuclear Waste Fund, $2 million for waste incidental to reprocessing, and $29.4 for generic homeland security. The $926.1 million does not include any amounts transferred from the U.S. Agency for International Development.

For FY 2007, the NRC recovered approximately 90 percent of its budget authority of $824.9 million less amounts derived from the Nuclear Waste Fund of $45.8 million, waste incidental to reprocessing of $2.5 million, and generic homeland security of $33.0 million.

D. Basis of Accounting

These financial statements reflect both accrual and budgetary accounting transactions. Under the accrual method, revenues are recognized when earned and expenses are recognized when a liability is incurred, without regard to receipt or payment of cash. Budgetary accounting is also used to record the obligation of funds prior to the accrual-based transaction. Interest on borrowings of the U.S. Department of the Treasury (Treasury) is not included as a cost to the NRC's programs and is not included in the accompanying financial statements.

E. Revenues and Other Financing Sources

The NRC is required to offset its appropriations by revenue received during the fiscal year from the assessment of fees. The NRC assesses two types of fees to recover its budget authority: (1) fees assessed under Title 10 of the *Code of Federal Regulations* (10 CFR), Part 170, "Fees for Facilities, Materials, Import and Export Licenses, and Other Regulatory Services under the Atomic Energy Act of 1954, as Amended," for licensing, inspection, and other services under the authority of the Independent Offices Appropriation Act of 1952 to recover the NRC's costs of providing individually identifiable services to specific applicants and licensees; and (2) annual fees assessed for nuclear facilities and materials licensees under 10 CFR Part 171, "Packaging and Transportation of Radioactive Material." All fees, with the exception of civil penalties, are exchange revenues in accordance with Statement of Federal Financial Accounting Standards No. 7, "Accounting for Revenue and Other Financing Sources and Concepts for Reconciling Budgetary and Financial Accounting."

For accounting purposes, appropriations are recognized as financing sources (appropriations used) at the time expenses are accrued. At the end of the fiscal year, appropriations recognized are reduced by the amount of assessed fees collected during the fiscal year to the extent of new budget authority for the year. Collections which exceed the new budget authority are held to offset subsequent years' appropriations. Appropriations expended for property and equipment are recognized as expenses when the asset is consumed in operations (depreciation and amortization).

As stated in Section C of this note, the NRC is required to recover approximately 90 percent of its budget authority through fee billing and to return the collections to the Treasury. In FY 2007 when fee revenue was recorded, the NRC also recorded a corresponding liability to the Treasury for the eventual collections. As the actual collections were returned to the Treasury, the liability was reduced. In FY 2008, a change was made to the accounting treatment for recording fee revenue and the corresponding transfer of fee revenue collections to Treasury. The NRC no longer records the liability to the Treasury when fee revenue is recorded and no longer reduces the liability as the collections are returned to Treasury. These changes were made to reflect appropriations law and to ensure U.S. Standard General Ledger (USSGL) compliance and consistency.

F. Fund Balance with Treasury

The NRC's cash receipts and disbursements are processed by the Treasury. The fund balances with the Treasury are primarily appropriated funds that are available to pay current liabilities and to finance authorized purchase commitments. Funds with Treasury represent NRC's right to draw on the Treasury for allowable expenditures. All amounts are available to NRC for current use.

G. Accounts Receivable

Accounts receivable consist of amounts owed to the NRC by other Federal agencies and the public. Amounts due from the public are presented net of an allowance for uncollectible accounts. The allowance is based on an analysis of the outstanding balances. Receivables from Federal agencies are expected to be collected; therefore, there is no allowance for uncollectible accounts.

H. NONENTITY ASSETS

Accounts receivable include nonentity assets of $28 thousand and $22 thousand at September 30, 2008, and 2007, respectively, and consist of miscellaneous penalties and interest due from the public, which, when collected, must be transferred to the Treasury.

I. PROPERTY AND EQUIPMENT

Property and equipment consist primarily of typical office furnishings, leasehold improvements, nuclear reactor simulators, and computer hardware and software. The costs of internal use software include the full cost of salaries and benefits from agency personnel involved in software development. The Agency has no real property. The land and buildings in which NRC operates are provided by the General Services Administration (GSA), which charges NRC rent that approximates the commercial rental rates for similar properties.

Property with a cost of $50 thousand or more per unit and a useful life of 2 years or more is capitalized at cost and depreciated using the straight-line method over the useful life. Other property items are expensed when purchased. Normal repairs and maintenance are charged to expense as incurred.

J. ACCOUNTS PAYABLE

The NRC uses an estimation methodology to calculate the accounts payable balance which represents costs for billed and unbilled goods and services received (prior to year end) that are unpaid. In FY 2007, the NRC used an algorithm that recognized accounts payable was a specific percentage of NRC's total expenses to date. Once this percentage was calculated, it was applied to an annualized expense figure. In FY 2008, the NRC implemented a revised methodology to calculate the accounts payable estimate. The new methodology involves analyzing the actual activity for the largest obligations to include in the estimate. For the remaining smaller obligations, the actual activity of a percentage of the obligations was analyzed, and an algorithm was developed to estimate the total amount to include in the accounts payable balance.

K. LIABILITIES NOT COVERED BY BUDGETARY RESOURCES

Liabilities represent the amount of monies or other resources that are likely to be paid by the NRC as the result of a transaction or event that has already occurred. No liability can be paid by the NRC absent an appropriation. Liabilities for which an appropriation has not been enacted are classified as "Liabilities Not Covered by Budgetary Resources." Also, the NRC liabilities arising from sources other than contracts can be abrogated by the Government acting in its sovereign capacity.

INTRAGOVERNMENTAL
The U.S. Department of Labor (DOL) paid Federal Employees Compensation Act (FECA) benefits on behalf of NRC which had not been billed or paid by the NRC as of September 30, 2008, and 2007, respectively.

FEDERAL EMPLOYEE BENEFITS
Federal employee benefits represent the actuarial liability for estimated future FECA disability benefits. The future workers' compensation estimate was generated by DOL from an application of actuarial procedures developed to estimate the liability for FECA, which includes the expected liability for death, disability, medical, and miscellaneous costs for approved compensation cases. The liability was calculated using historical benefit payment patterns related to a specific incurred period to predict the ultimate payments related to that period. These projected annual benefit payments were discounted to present value. The interest rate assumptions utilized for discounting benefits were 4.37 percent and 5.17 percent for FY 2008 and FY 2007, respectively.

OTHER
Accrued annual leave represents the amount of annual leave earned by NRC employees but not yet taken.

L. CONTINGENCIES

Contingent liabilities are those where the existence or amount of the liability cannot be determined with certainty pending the outcome of future events. The NRC is a party to various administrative proceedings, legal actions, environmental suits, and claims brought by or against it. Based on the advice of legal counsel concerning contingencies, it is the opinion of management that the ultimate resolution of these proceedings, actions, suits, and claims will not materially affect the agency's financial statements.

M. ANNUAL, SICK, AND OTHER LEAVE

Annual leave is accrued as it is earned, and the accrual is reduced as leave is taken. Each year, the balance in the accrued annual leave liability account is adjusted to reflect current pay rates. To the extent that current or prior year funding is not available to cover annual leave earned but not taken, funding will be obtained from future financing sources. Sick leave and other types of nonvested leave are expensed as taken.

N. RETIREMENT PLANS

The NRC employees belong to either the Federal Employees Retirement System (FERS) or the Civil Service Retirement System (CSRS). For FY 2008 and FY 2007, for employees belonging to FERS, the NRC withheld 0.8 percent of base pay earnings, in addition to Federal Insurance Contribution Act (FICA) withholdings, and matched the withholdings with an 11.2 percent contribution. The sum is transferred to the Federal Employees Retirement Fund. For employees covered by CSRS, NRC withholds 7 percent of base pay earnings. The NRC matched this withholding with a 7 percent contribution in FY 2008 and FY 2007.

The Thrift Savings Plan (TSP) is a retirement savings and investment plan for employees belonging to either FERS or CSRS. For employees belonging to FERS, NRC automatically contributes 1 percent of base pay to their account and matches contributions up to an additional 4 percent. The maximum percentage of base pay that an employee participating in FERS may contribute is unlimited in fiscal years 2008 and 2007. The Thrift Savings Plan (TSP) is a retirement savings and investment plan for employees belonging to either FERS or CSRS. The maximum percentage of base pay that an employee participating in FERS or CSRS may contribute is unlimited in fiscal years 2008 and 2007, subject to the maximum contribution of $15.5 thousand for both years. For employees participating in FERS, the NRC automatically contributes one percent of base pay to their account and matches contributions up to an additional four percent. For employees participating in CSRS, there is no NRC matching of the contribution. The sum of the employees' and NRC's contributions are transferred to the Federal Retirement Thrift Investment Board. The sum of the employees' and NRC's contributions are transferred to the Federal Retirement Thrift Investment Board.

The NRC does not report on its financial statements FERS and CSRS assets, accumulated plan benefits, or unfunded liabilities, if any, applicable to its employees. Reporting such amounts is the responsibility of the U.S. Office of Personnel Management. The portion of the current and estimated future outlays for CSRS not paid by NRC is, in accordance with Statement of Federal Financial Accounting Standards No. 5, "Accounting for Liabilities of the Federal Government," included in NRC's financial statements as an imputed financing source.

O. LEASES

The total capital lease liability is funded on an annual basis and included in NRC's annual budget. The NRC's capital leases are for personal property consisting of reproduction equipment which is installed at the NRC headquarters. For FY 2008 there are eight capital leases with terms of 5 years, consisting of two new capital leases added in FY 2008 with an interest rate of 3.99 percent, two capital leases that were added in FY 2007 with an interest rate of 4.58 percent, one capital lease in FY 2006 with an interest rate of 4.25 percent, and three capital leases for FY 2005 with an interest rate of 4.13 percent. The reproduction equipment is depreciated over 5 years using the straight-line method with no salvage value.

Operating leases consist of real property leases with GSA. The leases are for NRC's headquarters and regional offices. The GSA charges NRC lease rates which approximate commercial rates for comparable space.

P. U.S. Department of Energy Charges

Financial transactions between the U.S. Department of Energy (DOE) and the NRC are fully automated through the U.S. Treasury's Intragovernmental Payment and Collection (IPAC) System. The IPAC System allows DOE to collect amounts due from NRC directly from the NRC's account at the Treasury for goods or services rendered. Project manager verification of goods or services received is subsequently accomplished through a system-generated voucher approval process. The vouchers are returned to the Office of the Chief Financial Officer documenting that the charges have been accepted.

Q. Pricing Policy

The NRC provides goods and services to the public and other Government entities. In accordance with OMB Circular No. A-25, "User Charges," and the Independent Offices Appropriation Act of 1952, NRC assesses fees under 10 CFR Part 170 for licensing and inspection activities to recover the full cost of providing individually identifiable services.

The NRC's policy is to recover the full cost of goods and services provided to other Government entities where (1) the services performed are not part of its statutory mission and (2) the NRC has not received appropriations for those services. Fees for reimbursable work are assessed at the 10 CFR Part 170 rate with minor exceptions for programs that are nominal activities of the NRC.

R. Net Position

The NRC's net position consists of unexpended appropriations and cumulative results of operations. Unexpended appropriations represent appropriated spending authority that is unobligated and has not been withdrawn by the U.S. Treasury, and obligations that have not been paid. Cumulative results of operations represent the excess of financing sources over expenses since inception.

S. Use of Management Estimates

The preparation of the accompanying financial statements in accordance with generally accepted accounting principles requires management to make certain estimates and assumptions that affect the reported amounts of assets, liabilities, revenues, and expenses. Actual results could differ from those estimates.

T. Appropriation Transfers

The NRC is a party to allocation transfers with another Federal agency (parent) as a receiving (child) entity. Allocation transfers are legal delegations by one agency of its authority to obligate budget authority and outlay funds to another agency. A separate fund account (allocation account) is created in the U.S. Treasury as a subset of the parent fund account for tracking and reporting purposes. All allocation transfers of balances are credited to this account, and subsequent obligations and outlays incurred by the child entity are charged to this allocation account as they execute the delegated activity on behalf of the parent entity. All financial activity related to these allocation transfers (e.g., budget authority, obligations, and outlays) is reported in the financial statements of the parent entity from which the underlying legislative authority, appropriations, and budget apportionments are derived. The NRC receives allocation transfers, as the child, from U.S. Agency for International Development (USAID). These transfers are for the international development of nuclear safety and regulatory authorities in Russia, Ukraine, Kazakhstan, Georgia, and Armenia for the startup, operation, shutdown, and decommissioning of Soviet-designed nuclear power plants; the safe and secure use of radioactive materials; and the accounting for and protection of nuclear materials.

NOTE 2. FUND BALANCE WITH TREASURY

		2008		2007
Fund Balances				
Appropriated funds	$	371,714	$	301,751
Nuclear Waste Fund		21,764		41,300
Other fund types		-		13,348
Total	$	393,478	$	356,399
Status of Fund Balance with Treasury				
Unobligated balance				
Available				
Appropriated funds	$	78,877	$	72,160
Unavailable		113		-
Obligated balance not yet disbursed		314,488		270,894
Nonbudgetary funds with Treasury		-		13,345
Total	$	393,478	$	356,399

The Fund Balance with Treasury consists of unobligated and obligated balance budgetary accounts. It includes Nuclear Waste Fund activity. The Nuclear Waste Fund unobligated balance is $9.9 million and $26.7 million as of September 30, 2008, and 2007, respectively.

NOTE 3. ACCOUNTS RECEIVABLE

		2008		2007
Intragovernmental				
Receivables and reimbursements	$	4,692	$	5,228
Receivables with the Public				
Materials and facilities fees—billed	$	2,204	$	2,533
Materials and facilities fees—unbilled		116,162		90,718
Other		67		86
Total Accounts Receivable		118,433		93,337
Less: Allowance for uncollectible accounts		(1,749)		(4,671)
Accounts Receivable, Net	$	116,684	$	88,666

NOTE 4. PROPERTY AND EQUIPMENT, NET

Fixed Assets Class	Service Years	Acquisition Value	Accumulated Depreciation and Amortization	2008 Net Book Value	2007 Net Book Value
Equipment	5-8	$ 11,864	$ (10,578)	$ 1,286	$ 1,138
Leased equipment	5-8	1,712	(473)	1,239	841
IT software	5	50,907	(43,726)	7,181	4,686
IT software under development	-	12,110	-	12,110	12,988
Leasehold improvements	20	27,819	(17,738)	10,081	9,558
Leasehold improvements in progress	-	3,578	-	3,578	2,621
Total		$ 107,990	$ (72,515)	$ 35,475	$ 31,832

NOTE 5. OTHER LIABILITIES

	2008	2007
Intragovernmental		
Liability to offset net accounts receivable for fees assessed	$ -	$ 93,434
Liability from fees collected which will offset current year's appropriations	-	13,340
Liability to offset miscellaneous accounts receivable	28	22
Liability for advances from other agencies	74	88
Accrued workers' compensation	1,710	1,659
Accrued unemployment compensation	27	6
Employee benefit contributions	3,005	2,248
Total Intragovernmental Other Liabilities	$ 4,844	$ 110,797

The liability to offset the net accounts receivable for fees assessed represents amounts which, when collected, will be transferred to the Treasury to offset NRC's appropriations in the year collected. Beginning in 2008, this liability is no longer being recorded due to a change in methodology for fees recorded and transferred. See Note 1.

	2008	2007
Accrued annual leave	$ 43,675	$ 38,327
Accrued salaries	19,683	15,962
Contract holdbacks, advances, and other	6,929	4,588
Grants payable	661	-
Total Other Liabilities	$ 70,948	$ 58,877

Other liabilities, except accrued annual leave, contract holdbacks, and advances from others are current.

NOTE 6. LIABILITIES NOT COVERED BY BUDGETARY RESOURCES

	2008	2007
Intragovernmental		
FECA paid by DOL	$ 1,710	$ 1,659
Accrued unemployment compensation	27	6
Federal Employee Benefits		
Future FECA	7,059	6,833
Other		
Accrued annual leave	43,675	38,327
Total Liabilities not Covered by Budgetary Resources	$ 52,471	$ 46,825

NOTE 7. LEASES

	2008	2007
Assets under capital leases:		
Copiers and booklet maker	$ 1,712	$ 1,638
Accumulated depreciation	(473)	(797)
Net assets under capital leases	$ 1,239	$ 841

Future Lease Payments Due:

Fiscal Year	Capital	Operating	2008	2007
2008	$ -	$ -	$ -	$ 23,447
2009	362	32,322	32,684	20,778
2010	336	32,518	32,854	20,836
2011	284	32,353	32,637	20,537
2012	272	30,236	30,508	18,403
2013 and thereafter	14	48,603	48,617	23,412
Total Lease Liability	1,268	176,032	177,300	127,413
Add: Imputed Interest	107	-	107	86
Total Future Lease Payments	$ 1,375	$ 176,032	$ 177,407	$ 127,499

The capital lease liability of $1,268 thousand is included in Other Liabilities (Note 5).

NOTE 8. CUMULATIVE RESULTS OF OPERATIONS

	2008		2007	
Future funding requirements	$	(52,471)	$	(46,825)
Investment in property and equipment, net		35,475		31,832
Contributions from foreign cooperative research agreements		3,054		3,184
Change in Nuclear Waste Fund		21,439		38,933
Other		120,738		40
Cumulative Results of Operations	$	**128,235**	$	27,164

Future funding requirements represent the amount of future funding needed to pay the accrued unfunded expenses as of September 30, 2008, and 2007. These accruals are not funded from current or prior-year appropriations and assessments, but rather should be funded from future appropriations and assessments. Accordingly, future funding requirements have been recognized for the expenses that will be paid from future appropriations.

NOTE 9. STATEMENT OF NET COST

The programs as presented on the "Statement of Net Cost" are based on the annual performance budget and are described as follows:

Nuclear Reactor Safety and Security encompasses all NRC efforts to ensure that civilian nuclear power reactor facilities and research and test reactors are licensed and operated in a manner that adequately protects the public health and safety, the environment, and protects against radiological sabotage and theft or diversion of special nuclear materials. The Nuclear Reactor Safety and Security program contains the following activities: new reactors, nuclear reactor licensing and rulemaking, and nuclear reactor oversight, and incident response.

Nuclear Materials and Waste Safety and Security encompasses all NRC efforts to protect the public health and safety and the environment, and ensures the secure use and management of radioactive materials. The Nuclear Materials and Waste Safety and Security program contains five activities: fuel facilities licensing and inspection, nuclear materials users licensing and inspection, high-level waste repository, decommissioning and low-level waste, and spent fuel storage and transportation licensing and inspection.

For intragovernmental gross costs, the buyers and sellers are both Federal entities. For earned revenues from the public, the buyers of the goods or services are non-Federal entities.

NOTE 9. STATEMENT OF NET COST (CONTINUED)

For the years ended September 30,		2008		2007
Nuclear Reactor Safety				
Intragovernmental gross costs	$	205,183	$	157,582
Less: Intragovernmental earned revenue		(32,710)		(36,519)
Intragovernmental net costs		172,473		121,063
Gross costs with the public		500,649		424,630
Less: Earned revenues from the public		(693,130)		(576,250)
Net costs with the public		(192,481)		(151,620)
Total Net Cost of Nuclear Reactor Safety	$	(20,008)	$	(30,557)
Nuclear Materials and Waste Safety				
Intragovernmental gross costs	$	54,978	$	45,287
Less: Intragovernmental earned revenue		(6,011)		(7,154)
Intragovernmental net costs		48,967		38,133
Gross costs with the public		183,241		159,208
Less: Earned revenues from the public		(65,729)		(73,336)
Net costs with the public		117,512		85,872
Total Net Cost of Nuclear Materials and Waste Safety	$	166,479	$	124,005

NOTE 10. EXCHANGE REVENUES

		2008		2007
Fees for licensing, inspection, and other services	$	790,910	$	687,632
Revenue from reimbursable work		6,670		5,627
Total Exchange Revenues	$	797,580	$	693,259

NOTE 11. FINANCING SOURCES OTHER THAN EXCHANGE REVENUE

Appropriations Used

Collections were used to reduce the fiscal year's appropriations recognized:

	2008	2007
Funds consumed	$ 908,330	$ 757,892
Less: Collection from fees assessed	(763,640)	(669,246)
Less: Nuclear Waste Funding Used	(46,518)	(42,000)
Appropriations Used	$ 98,172	$ 46,646

Funds consumed include $72.2 million and $74.3 million through September 30, 2008, and 2007, respectively, of available funds from prior years.

Non-Exchange Revenue

	2008	2007
Civil penalties	$ 1,102	$ 450
Miscellaneous receipts	211	1,681
Contra-Revenue	(1,313)	(2,131)
Total Non-Exchange Revenue	$ -	$ -

Imputed Financing

	2008	2007
Civil Service Retirement System	$ 10,239	$ 10,593
Federal Employee Health Benefit	16,589	16,956
Federal Employee Group Life Insurance	79	71
Judgements Awards	4	7
Total Imputed Financing	$ 26,911	$ 27,627

NOTE 12. TOTAL OBLIGATIONS INCURRED

		2008		2007
Direct Obligations				
Category A	$	895,751	$	788,875
Exempt from Apportionment		46,191		45,251
Total Direct Obligations		941,942		834,126
Reimbursable Obligations		7,880		4,645
Total Obligations Incurred	$	949,822	$	838,771

Obligations exempt from apportionment are the result of funds derived from the Nuclear Waste Fund. Category A obligations consist of NRC appropriations only. Undelivered orders for the Nuclear Waste Fund are $ 11.6 million and $12.2 million, salaries and expenses are $ 228.4 million and $215.0 million, and the Office of the Inspector General are $ 1.5 million and $1.7 million through September 30, 2008, and 2007, respectively.

NOTE 13. NUCLEAR WASTE FUND

Included in the NRC's budget for FY 2008 and 2007 are $29.0 million and $45.8 million, respectively, provided from the Nuclear Waste Fund. Statement of Federal Financial Accounting Standards (SFFAS) No. 27, "Identifying and Reporting Earmarked Funds," lists three defining criteria for an earmarked fund. Generally, an earmarked fund is established by law to use specifically identified financing sources only for designated activities, and the statute provides explicit authority to retain current, unused revenues for future use. Also, the law includes a requirement to account for and report on the receipt and use of the financing sources as distinguished from general revenues.

In 1982, Congress passed the Nuclear Waste Policy Act of 1982 (Public Law 97-425) establishing the Nuclear Waste Fund (NWF) to be administered by the U.S. Department of Energy (DOE) (42 U.S.C. 10222). Given the terms of the statute, the NWF clearly meets the definition of an earmarked fund from DOE's perspective, and DOE does indeed report the NWF as an earmarked fund in its Performance and Accountability Report (PAR).

However, to the NRC, the NWF transfer is a source of financing; its receipt of NWF funds is a use of NWF resources. The NRC collects no revenue on behalf of the NWF and has no administrative control over it. Furthermore, the Treasury has no separate fund symbol for the NWF under the NRC's agency location code (ALC). The receipt and expenditure of NWF money is reported to Treasury under the NRC's primary Salaries and Expenses fund (X0200).

Based on these facts, the NWF is not an earmarked fund from NRC's perspective. However, in order to provide additional information to the users of these financial statements, enhanced disclosure of the fund is presented below.

The funding provided to the NRC in FY 2008 and 2007 was for the purpose of performing activities associated with DOE's application for a high-level waste repository at Yucca Mountain, NV. These activities included assistance to DOE with the application, review of the application, the conduct of thorough safety and security evaluations, preparation of the safety evaluation report, initiation of the inspection program, ensuring that the regulation process was made available to stakeholders and the general public, and to provide legal advice and representation for staff reviews and Commission actions.

The NWF amounts received, expended, obligated, and unobligated balances as of September 30, 2008, and 2007, are shown in the following:

	2008		2007	
Appropriations Received	$	29,025	$	45,826
Expended Appropriations	$	48,885	$	45,640
Obligations Incurred	$	46,191	$	45,247
Unobligated Balances	$	9,853	$	26,717

NOTE 14. CHANGE IN ACCOUNTING PRINCIPLE

As discussed in Note 1T, the NRC receives allocation transfers from USAID. In prior years, the NRC appropriately reported the proprietary activity related to the allocation transfers on its financial statements.

Effective in FY 2007, OMB Circular A-136, "Financial Reporting Requirements," mandated that a parent entity must report all budgetary and proprietary activity in its financial statements, whether material to a child entity or not. The effect of this reporting change on prior periods should be reported as a change in accounting principle consistent with SFFAS 21, "Reporting Corrections of Errors and Changes in Accounting Principles." The cumulative effect of the change on beginning unexpended appropriations is reported in the accompanying FY 2007 Statement of Changes in Net Position as follows:

Unexpended Appropriations:		
Beginning Balances, October 1, 2006	$	193,694
Less: USAID Allocation transfers		(2,838)
Restated beginning balance, October 1, 2006	$	190,856

NOTE 15. EXPLANATION OF DIFFERENCES BETWEEN THE STATEMENT OF BUDGETARY RESOURCES AND THE BUDGET OF THE U.S. GOVERNMENT

Statement of Federal Financial Standards (SFFAS) No. 7, "Accounting for Revenue and Other Financing Sources," requires the NRC to reconcile the budgetary resources reported on the Statement of Budgetary Resources to the prior fiscal year actual budgetary resources presented in the Budget of the U.S. Government and to explain any material differences. The NRC does not have any material differences between the Statement of Budgetary Resources and the Budget of the U.S. Government. The President's Budget with actual results for the NRC has not been published for FY 2008. It is expected to be published in February 2009.

NOTE 16. RECONCILIATION OF NET COST OF OPERATIONS TO BUDGETARY RESOURCES

For the years ended June 30,	2008	2007
Budgetary Resources Obligated		
Obligations incurred (Note 12)	$ 949,822	$ 838,771
Less: Spending authority from offsetting collections and recoveries	(30,578)	(11,783)
Less: Distributed offsetting receipts	(763,640)	(669,245)
Net Obligations	155,604	157,743
Other Resources		
Imputed financing from costs absorbed by others	26,911	27,627
Other—Revenue from excess collections	93,434	(18,386)
Non-Exchange Revenue	-	-
Net Other Resources Used to Finance Activities	120,345	9,241
Total Resources Used to Finance Activities	275,949	166,984
Resources Used to Finance Items not Part of the Net Cost of Operations	(19,841)	(79,278)
Total Resources Used to Finance the Net Cost of Operations	256,108	87,706
Components of the Net Cost of Operations that will not Require or Generate Resources in the Current Period	(109,637)	5,742
Net Cost of Operations	$ 146,471	$ 93,448

REQUIRED SUPPLEMENTARY INFORMATION
SCHEDULE OF BUDGETARY RESOURCES (IN THOUSANDS)

For the year ended September 30, 2008	Salaries & Expenses X0200	Office of Inspector General X0300	Nuclear Facility Fees X5280	Total
Budgetary Resources				
Unobligated balances, brought forward, October 1	$ 71,610	$ 546	$ 4	$ 72,160
Recoveries of prior year obligations				
Actual	21,624	313	-	21,937
Budget authority				
Appropriation	917,335	8,743	(4)	926,074
Spending authority from offsetting collections				
Reimbursements earned—Collected	6,709	-	-	6,709
Reimbursements earned—Change in receivables	222	-	-	222
Change in unfilled customer orders—Advance received	1,645	-	-	1,645
Change in unfilled customer orders—Without advance	65	-	-	65
Subtotal—Spending authority from offsetting collections	8,641	-	-	8,641
Total Budgetary Resources	$ 1,019,210	$9,602	$ -	$1,028,812
Status of Budgetary Resources				
Obligations incurred (Note 12)				
Direct	$ 933,139	$ 8,803	$ -	$ 941,942
Reimbursable	7,880	-	-	7,880
Subtotal	941,019	8,803	-	949,822
Unobligated balance				
Apportioned	68,338	686	-	69,024
Exempt from apportionment	9,853	-	-	9,853
Subtotal	78,191	686	-	78,877
Unobligated balance, not available	-	113	-	113
Total Status of Budgetary Resources	$ 1,019,210	$ 9,602	$ -	$1,028,812
Change in Obligated Balance				
Obligated balance, net				
Unpaid obligations, brought forward, October 1	$ 269,637	$ 1,257	$ -	$ 270,894
Obligations incurred, net	941,019	8,803	-	949,822
Gross outlays	(875,172)	(8,832)	-	(884,004)
Recoveries of prior year obligations, actual	(21,624)	(313)	-	(21,937)
Change in uncollected customer payments, from Federal sources	(287)	-	-	(287)
Obligated balance, net, end of period				
Unpaid obligations	317,711	915	-	318,626
Uncollected customer payments, from Federal sources	(4,138)	-	-	(4,138)
Total unpaid obligated balance, net, end of period	$ 313,573	$ 915	$ -	$ 314,488
Net outlays				
Gross outlays	$ 875,172	$ 8,832	$ -	$ 884,004
Offsetting collections	(8,354)	-	-	(8,354)
Distributed offsetting receipts	-	-	(763,640)	(763,640)
Net Outlays	$ 866,818	$ 8,832	$ (763,640)	$ 112,010

AUDITOR'S REPORT

UNITED STATES
NUCLEAR REGULATORY COMMISSION
WASHINGTON, DC 20555-0001

OFFICE OF THE
INSPECTOR GENERAL

November 10, 2008

MEMORANDUM TO: Chairman Klein

FROM: Hubert T. Bell
Inspector General

SUBJECT: RESULTS OF THE AUDIT OF THE UNITED STATES NUCLEAR REGULATORY
COMMISSION'S FINANCIAL STATEMENTS FOR FISCAL YEAR 2008
(OIG-09-A-01)

The Chief Financial Officers Act of 1990, as amended (CFO Act), requires the Inspector General (IG) or an independent external auditor, as determined by the IG, to annually audit the U.S. Nuclear Regulatory Commission's (NRC) financial statements in accordance with applicable standards. In compliance with this requirement, Urbach Kahn & Werlin, LLP (UKW) was retained by the Office of the Inspector General (OIG) to conduct this annual audit. Transmitted with this memorandum are the following UKW reports:

- Opinion on the Principal Statements.
- Opinion on Internal Control.
- Compliance with Laws and Regulations

NRC's Performance and Accountability Report includes comparative financial statements for FY 2008 and FY 2007. Therefore, it is important to note that R. Navarro & Associates, Inc. performed the audit of NRC's FY 2007 financial statements.

Objective of a Financial Statement Audit

The objective of a financial statement audit is to determine whether the audited entity's financial statements are free of material misstatement. An audit includes examining, on a test basis, evidence supporting the amounts and disclosures in the financial statements. An audit also includes assessing the accounting principles used and significant estimates made by management as well as evaluating the overall financial statement presentation.

UKW's audit and examination were made in accordance with auditing standards generally accepted in the United States of America; *Government Auditing Standards* issued by the Comptroller General of the United States; and Office of Management and Budget (OMB) Bulletin No. 07-04, *Audit Requirements for Federal Financial Statements*, as amended. The audit included obtaining an understanding of the internal controls over financial reporting and testing and evaluating the design and operating effectiveness of the internal controls. Because of inherent limitations in any internal control, there is a risk that errors or fraud may occur and not be detected. Also, projections of an evaluation of internal control over financial reporting to future periods are subject to the risk that the internal control may become inadequate because of changes in conditions, or that the degree of compliance with policies or procedures may deteriorate.

U.S.NRC
United States Nuclear Regulatory Commission
Protecting People and the Environment

FY 2008 AUDIT RESULTS

The results are as follows:

Financial Statements

* Unqualified opinion

Internal Controls

* Unqualified opinion
* Significant Deficiency
    - Estimation of accounts payable year-end balance

Compliance with Laws and Regulations

* Substantial noncompliance:
    - License Fee Billing System lack of certification and accreditation

OFFICE OF THE INSPECTOR GENERAL OVERSIGHT OF UKW PERFORMANCE

To fulfill our responsibilities under the CFO Act and related legislation for ensuring the quality of the audit work performed, we monitored UKW's audit of NRC's FY 2008 financial statements by:

* Reviewing UKW's audit approach and planning.
* Evaluating the qualifications and independence of UKW's auditors.
* Monitoring audit progress at key points.
* Examining the working papers related to planning and performing the audit and assessing NRC's internal controls.
* Reviewing UKW's audit reports to ensure compliance with *Government Auditing Standards* and OMB Bulletin No. 07-04, as amended.
* Coordinating the issuance of the audit reports.
* Performing other procedures deemed necessary.

UKW is responsible for the attached auditors' reports, dated November 7, 2008, and the conclusions expressed therein. OIG is responsible for technical and administrative oversight regarding the firm's performance under the terms of the contract. Our review, as differentiated from an audit in conformance with Government Auditing Standards, was not intended to enable us to express, and accordingly we do not express, an opinion on:

* NRC's financial statements.
* The effectiveness of NRC's internal control over financial reporting.
* NRC's compliance with laws and regulations.

However, our monitoring review, as described above, disclosed no instances where UKW did not comply, in all material respects, with applicable auditing standards.

It is noted that OIG performed similar oversight of R. Navarro & Associates, Inc.'s audit of NRC's FY 2007 financial statements.

Meeting with the Chief Financial Officer

At the exit conference on November 7, 2008, representatives of the Office of the Chief Financial Officer, OIG, and UKW discussed the issues in the report related to the results of the audit.

Comments of the Chief Financial Officer

In his response, the Chief Financial Officer (CFO) generally agreed with the auditors' recommendations. We will follow up on the CFO's implementation of planned corrective actions during FY 2009. The full text of the CFO's response follows this report.

We appreciate NRC staff's cooperation and continued interest in improving financial management within NRC.

INDEPENDENT AUDITORS' REPORT ON THE FINANCIAL STATEMENTS

Urbach Kahn & Werlin LLP
CERTIFIED PUBLIC ACCOUNTANTS

Inspector General
United States Nuclear Regulatory Commission

Chairman
United States Nuclear Regulatory Commission

We have audited the accompanying balance sheet of the United States Nuclear Regulatory Commission (NRC), as of September 30, 2008, and the related statements of net cost, changes in net position, and budgetary resources (Principal Statements) for the year then ended. The Principal Statements of NRC as of and for the year ended September 30, 2007 were audited by other auditors. We also examined the NRC's internal control over financial reporting as of September 30, 2008.

SUMMARY

We concluded that the NRC's 2008 Principal Statements are presented fairly, in all material respects, in conformity with accounting principles generally accepted in the United States of America. We also concluded that, although improvements are needed as noted below, the NRC had effective internal control over financial reporting (including the safeguarding of assets):

- The NRC should continue to enhance its procedures for determining accounts payable

We found one reportable instance of noncompliance with laws and regulations.

This report (including Appendices A through D) discusses: (1) these conclusions and our conclusions relating to other information presented in the Performance and Accountability Report, (2) management's responsibilities, (3) our objectives, scope and methodology, (4) management's response and our evaluation of their response, and (5) the current status of prior year findings and recommendations.

OPINION ON THE PRINCIPAL STATEMENTS

In our opinion, the Principal Statements referred to above present fairly, in all material respects, the financial position of the NRC as of September 30, 2008, and its net cost, changes in net position, and budgetary resources for the year then ended, in conformity with accounting principles generally accepted in the United States of America. The Principal Statements of NRC

as of and for the year ended September 30, 2007 were audited by other auditors, whose report, dated November 7, 2007, expressed an unqualified opinion on those statements.

As described in footnote 1 of the Principal Statements, the NRC revised its methodology for accounting for accounts payable as of September 30, 2008. We have not determined what impact, if any, this revised methodology may have had on the Principal Statements if applied in the prior year.

OPINION ON INTERNAL CONTROL

In our opinion, the NRC maintained, in all material respects, effective control over financial reporting (including safeguarding of assets) as of September 30, 2008 that provided reasonable assurance that misstatements, losses or noncompliance material in relation to the financial statements would be prevented on a timely basis. Our opinion is based on criteria established under 31 U.S.C. 3512 (c), (d), the Federal Managers' Financial Integrity Act, and the Office of Management and Budget (OMB) Circular A-123, *Management's Responsibility for Internal Control.*

However, we noted the matter summarized below and more fully described in Appendix A, involving the internal control and its operation that we consider to be a significant deficiency.

A control deficiency exists when the design or operation of a control does not allow management or employees, in the normal course of performing their assigned functions, to prevent or detect misstatements on a timely basis. A significant deficiency is a deficiency in internal control, or a combination of deficiencies, that adversely affects the NRC's ability to initiate, authorize, record, process, or report financial data reliably in accordance with generally accepted accounting principles such that there is more than a remote likelihood that a misstatement of the NRC's Principal Statements that is more than inconsequential will not be prevented or detected by the NRC's internal control.

The NRC should continue to enhance its procedures for determining accrued accounts payable

The NRC currently does not have a business process to record accounts payable and related accrued expenses in the general ledger at the transaction level. For the last several years, the NRC used an estimation methodology based on historical expenses to estimate these balances. Because of material variances in their prior estimates, and because the NRC transferred its bill paying function to the Department of Interior's National Business Center during fiscal year 2008, the NRC did not have adequate historical data to fully support its estimate recorded as of September 30, 2008. For September 30, 2008, the NRC requested its program managers to calculate, confirm or estimate the amounts of goods and services received but not yet paid for its 200 largest open obligations. An estimated amount for unbilled and/or unpaid goods and services was applied to the remaining balances based on the results of a sample of smaller obligations. We were able to perform adequate compensating procedures to determine the potential effect of this deficiency.

Specific details and the related recommendations for this finding are provided in Appendix A of this report.

A material weakness is a significant deficiency, or combination of significant deficiencies, that result in a more than remote likelihood that a material misstatement of the Principal Statements will not be prevented or detected by the NRC's internal control. We do not consider this matter to be a material weakness.

COMPLIANCE WITH LAWS AND REGULATIONS

The results of our tests of compliance with laws and regulations, exclusive of those referred to under the Federal Financial Management Improvement Act (FFMIA), disclosed no instances of noncompliance that are required to be reported under *Government Auditing Standards* and OMB Bulletin No. 07-04, *Audit Requirements for Federal Financial Statements*, as amended. Providing an opinion on compliance with laws and regulations was not an objective of our audit and, accordingly, we do not express such an opinion.

Under FFMIA, we are required to report whether the NRC's financial management systems substantially comply with the federal financial management systems requirements, applicable Federal accounting standards, and the United States Government Standard general ledger at the transaction level. To meet this requirement, we performed tests of compliance with the provisions of FFMIA section 803(a). The results of our tests disclosed one substantial noncompliance with federal financial management systems requirements.

The NRC did not complete its certification and accreditation (C&A) for the License Fee Billing System (FEES). The NRC is currently reevaluating its process for the modernization of its financial management systems as part of the core financial system replacement and has delayed the timeline for the replacement of FEES. Management intends to complete the C&A for the system by the end of the second quarter of FY 2009.

The current status of prior year findings and recommendations is included in Appendix B.

OTHER INFORMATION

The information in the Management's Discussion and Analysis section of the NRC's Performance and Accountability Report is not a required part of the Principal Statements, but is supplementary information required by accounting principles generally accepted in the United States of America. We have applied certain limited procedures, which consisted principally of inquiries of management regarding the methods of measurement and presentation of the supplementary information. However, we did not audit the information and express no opinion on it.

The Program Performance and Appendices listed in the table of contents are presented for additional analysis and are not a required part of the financial statements. Such information has not been subjected to the auditing procedures applied in the audit of the financial statements and, accordingly, we express no opinion on them.

MANAGEMENT RESPONSIBILITIES

Management is responsible for (1) preparing the Principal Statements in conformity with accounting principles generally accepted in the United States of America, (2) establishing, maintaining and assessing internal control to provide reasonable assurance that the broad control objectives of the Federal Managers Financial Integrity Act of 1982 are met; (3) ensuring that the NRC's financial management systems substantially comply with FFMIA; and (4) complying with applicable laws and regulations.

OBJECTIVES, SCOPE AND METHODOLOGY

We are responsible for planning and performing our audit to obtain reasonable assurance about whether the financial statements are free of material misstatement. An

UK&W

audit includes examining, on a test basis, evidence supporting the amounts and disclosures in the financial statements. An audit also includes assessing the accounting principles used and significant estimates made by management, as well as evaluating the overall financial statement presentation.

We are responsible for planning and performing our examination to obtain reasonable assurance about whether management maintained effective internal control over financial reporting (including safeguarding of assets) and compliance with applicable laws and regulations based on criteria established under 31 U.S.C. 3512 (c), (d), the Federal Managers' Financial Integrity Act, and OMB Circular A-123, *Management's Responsibility for Internal Control*. Our examination included obtaining an understanding of internal control related to financial reporting (including safeguarding assets) and compliance with laws and regulations (including execution of transactions in accordance with budget authority); testing relevant internal controls over financial reporting (including safeguarding assets) and compliance, evaluating the design and operating effectiveness of internal control; and performing such other procedures as we considered necessary in the circumstances. We did not test all internal controls relevant to operating objectives as broadly defined by the Federal Managers' Financial Integrity Act.

Because of inherent limitations in any internal control, misstatements due to error or fraud may occur and not be detected. Also, projections of any evaluation of the internal control to future periods are subject to the risk that the internal control may become inadequate because of changes in conditions, or that the degree of compliance with the policies or procedures may deteriorate.

We are also responsible for testing compliance with selected provisions of laws and regulations that have a direct and material effect on the financial statements. We did not test compliance with all laws and regulations applicable to the NRC. We limited our tests of compliance to those laws and

regulations required by OMB audit guidance that we deemed applicable to the financial statements for the fiscal year ended September 30, 2008. We caution that noncompliance may occur and not be detected by these tests and that such testing may not be sufficient for other purposes.

We conducted our audit and examinations in accordance with auditing standards generally accepted in the United States of America; *Government Auditing Standards*, issued by the Comptroller General of the United States; attestation standards established by the American Institute of Certified Public Accountants; and OMB Bulletin No. 07-04, *Audit Requirements for Federal Financial Statements*, as amended. We believe that our audit and examinations provide a reasonable basis for our opinions.

We also noted other less significant matters involving the NRC's internal control and its operation, which we have reported to the management of the NRC in a separate letter, dated November 7, 2008.

This report is intended solely for the information and use of the NRC OIG, the management of NRC, OMB, the Government Accountability Office and the Congress of the United States, and is not intended to be and should not be used by anyone other than these specified parties.

Urbach Kahn & Werlin L L P

Arlington, Virginia
November 7, 2008

APPENDIX A – SIGNIFICANT DEFICIENCY

In our report dated November 7, 2008, we described the results of our audit of the consolidated balance sheet of the Nuclear Regulatory Commission (NRC), as of September 30, 2008, and the related consolidated statements of net cost, changes in net position, and the combined statement of budgetary resources (Principal Statements) for the year then ended. The objective of our audit was to express an opinion on these financial statements. In connection with our audit, we also considered the NRC's internal control over financial reporting and tested the NRC's compliance with certain provisions of applicable laws and regulations that could have a direct and material effect on its financial statements. The following presents additional detail on the internal control deficiency discussed in that report.

1. **The NRC should continue to enhance its procedures for determining accrued accounts payable.**

The NRC currently does not have a business process to record accounts payable and related accrued expenses in the general ledger at the transaction level. For the last few years, the NRC has used an estimation methodology based on historical average percentage of actual accounts payable to expenses. The actual amount of accounts payable for a prior period was calculated through a review of subsequent disbursements. During fiscal year 2008, the NRC's management identified errors in its subsequent review procedures and found that their methodology was not reliable in estimating the September 30, 2007 non-federal accounts payable balance.

During fiscal year 2008, the NRC also transferred its bill paying function to the Department of Interior's National Business Center. Although management does not believe this transition has materially impacted its bill paying patterns for the fiscal year end, they did not have sufficient time to analyze this data to support their historical estimation methodology for the current fiscal year end.

For September 30, 2008, the NRC requested its program managers to calculate, confirm or estimate the amounts of goods and services received but not yet paid for its 200 largest open obligations. An estimated amount for unbilled and/or unpaid goods and services was applied to the remaining balances based on the results of a sample of smaller obligations.

While this new methodology should reduce the risk of misstatements in the recorded balance for non-federal accounts payable, the NRC has not fully documented its business processes and policies related to this methodology. In addition, the NRC has not established historical relationships between the accrued accounts payable balances and unliquidated obligations in order to corroborate the results of this process. We were able to perform adequate compensating procedures to determine the potential effect of this deficiency.

Without effective documented procedures and historical analysis, management cannot adequately ensure that the potential misstatement related to using this methodology rather than recording accounts payable and the related accrued expenses at the transaction level is appropriately immaterial.

We recommend that the NRC's Chief Financial Officer:

1. Ensure the NRC's long term plans for replacing the core financial management system evaluate the system requirements for recording accounts payable and related accrued expenses at the transaction level. (New)

2. Document the NRC's policies and procedures for calculating, estimating and recording accounts payable for the largest obligations quarterly. (New)

3. Consider the accounts payable process a high risk area in connection with the agency's management control program and conduct reviews and testing of the interim quarters for FY 2009 accordingly. (New)

4. Establish historical relationships between accrued expenses and unliquidated obligation levels that may support near term calculations of accounts payable and related accrued expenses. (New)

APPENDIX B – STATUS OF PRIOR YEAR FINDINGS AND RECOMMENDATIONS

Our assessment of the current status of reportable conditions and material weaknesses identified in prior year audits is presented below:

Prior Recommendation	Type	Fiscal Year 2008 Status
1. The NRC CFO should coordinate with the Office of Information Services and the Executive Director for Operations to ensure that any vulnerabilities of the general support systems and the financial management systems are addressed and resolved timely.	2007 Material Weakness/ Substantial Noncompliance with Laws and Regulations	Closed.
2. The NRC CFO should continue to define, design and implement compensating controls over the fee billing system.	2007 Significant Deficiency	Closed.

MANAGEMENT'S RESPONSE TO THE INDEPENDENT AUDITORS' REPORT ON THE FINANCIAL STATEMENTS

UNITED STATES
NUCLEAR REGULATORY COMMISSION
WASHINGTON, D.C. 20555-0001

OFFICE OF THE
CHIEF FINANCIAL OFFICER

November 7, 2008

MEMORANDUM TO: Stephen D. Dingbaum
                        Assistant Inspector General for Audits
                        Office of the Inspector General

FROM: J. E. Dyer
              Chief Financial Officer

SUBJECT: AUDIT OF THE FISCAL YEAR 2008 FINANCIAL STATEMENTS

We appreciate the collaborative relationship between the Office of the Inspector General, the auditors, and the Office of the Chief Financial Officer in supporting our continuing effort to improve financial reporting. We have reviewed the independent auditors' report of the agency's fiscal year 2008 financial statements and are in general agreement with the report and overall findings.

Our responses to the recommendations follow:

RECOMMENDATION 1

Ensure the NRC's long term plans for replacing the core financial management system evaluate the system requirements for recording accounts payable and related accrued expenses at the transaction level.

RESPONSE

Agree. The Office of the Chief Financial Officer (OCFO) will include system requirements for recording accounts payable and related accrued expenses at the transaction level in the functional requirements of the new core financial system.

RECOMMENDATION 2

Document the NRC's policies and procedures for calculating, estimating, and recording accounts payable for the largest obligations quarterly.

RESPONSE

Agree. The OCFO will document the policies and procedures for calculating, estimating and recording accounts payable for the largest obligations quarterly.

RECOMMENDATION 3

Consider the accounts payable process a high-risk area in connection with the agency's management control program and conduct reviews and testing of the interim quarters for FY 2009 accordingly.

RESPONSE

Agree. While we do not consider the accounts payable process to be a high-risk area in connection with our management control program, it merits the continued attention of management. NRC will conduct reviews and testing of the interim quarters for FY 2009 accordingly.

RECOMMENDATION 4

Establish historical relationships between accrued expenses and unliquidated obligation levels that may support near term calculations of accounts payable and related accrued expenses.

RESPONSE

Agree. The OCFO will begin to establish our understanding of the historical relationship between accrued expenses and unliquidated obligation levels through various means including trend analysis.

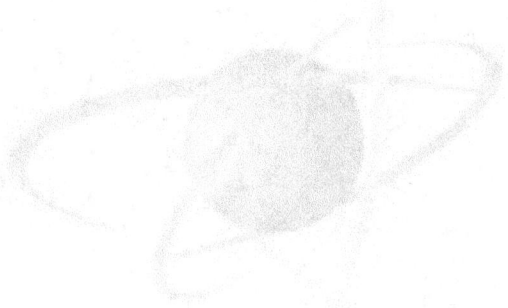

APPENDICES

Photo Courtesy of NRC Image Library.

NRC Region IV inspector Linda Gersey (right) surveys for gamma radiation at the Smith Ranch in situ leach uranium recovery facility, owned by Power Resources Inc., in eastern Wyoming. NRC staff conducted an unannounced inspection of the facility on September 23-25, 2008.

APPENDIX A
INSPECTOR GENERAL'S ASSESSMENT OF THE MOST SERIOUS MANAGEMENT AND PERFORMANCE CHALLENGES FACING THE NRC

UNITED STATES
NUCLEAR REGULATORY COMMISSION
WASHINGTON, D.C. 20555-0001

OFFICE OF THE
INSPECTOR GENERAL

September 30, 2008

MEMORANDUM TO: Chairman Klein

FROM: Hubert T. Bell
Inspector General

SUBJECT: INSPECTOR GENERAL'S ASSESSMENT OF THE MOST
SERIOUS MANAGEMENT AND PERFORMANCE
CHALLENGES FACING THE NUCLEAR REGULATORY
COMMISSION (OIG-08-A-20)

The *Reports Consolidation Act of 2000* requires the Inspector General of each Federal agency to summarize annually what he or she considers to be the most serious management and performance challenges facing the agency and to assess the agency's progress in addressing those challenges. In accordance with the act, I identified eight management and performance challenges that I consider to be the most serious. The list of eight challenges reflects (1) a new challenge concerning radiological waste; (2) the consolidation of prior challenges 2 and 7, which dealt with information handling and communication, into an overarching challenge about information management; and (3) rewording of three challenges to more precisely articulate the issues NRC is facing in 2008.

We appreciate the cooperation extended to us during this evaluation. The agency provided comments on this report, which have been incorporated as appropriate. If you have any questions or comments about this report, please feel free to contact Stephen D. Dingbaum, Assistant Inspector General for Audits, at 415-5915 or me at 415-5930.

Attachment: As stated

cc: Commissioner Jaczko
Commissioner Lyons
Commissioner Svinicki

APPENDIX A TABLE OF CONTENTS

EXECUTIVE SUMMARY

BACKGROUND

The Reports Consolidation Act of 2000 requires the Inspector General (IG) of each Federal agency to summarize annually what he or she considers to be the most serious management and performance challenges facing the agency and to assess the agency's progress in addressing those challenges.

PURPOSE

In accordance with the act's provisions, the Inspector General of the NRC updated what he considers to be the most serious management and performance challenges facing NRC. The IG evaluated the overall work of the Office of the Inspector General (OIG), the OIG staff's general knowledge of agency operations, and other relevant information to develop and update his list of management and performance challenges. As part of the evaluation, OIG staff sought input from NRC's Chairman, Commissioners, and management to obtain their views on what challenges the agency is facing and what efforts the agency has taken to address previously identified management and performance challenges.

RESULTS IN BRIEF

The IG identified eight challenges that he considers the most serious management and performance challenges facing NRC. The challenges he identified represent critical areas or difficult tasks that warrant high-level NRC management attention.

This year's list of challenges reflects several changes from last year's list.

Prior challenge 2, "Appropriate handling of information," was combined with prior challenge 7, "Communication with external stakeholders throughout NRC regulatory activities." The consolidation of these challenges resulted in the following description for new challenge 2, "Managing information to balance security with openness and accountability," which captures the need for both openness and protection of information.

Prior challenge 3, "Development and implementation of a risk-informed and performance-based regulatory approach," was revised to the current challenge 3, "Implementation of a risk-informed and performance-based regulatory approach." This change reflects the relative maturity of NRC's risk-informed and performance-based regulatory programs and their advancement beyond developmental efforts to implementation activities.

Prior challenge 4, "Ability to modify regulatory processes to meet a changing environment," specifically the potential for a nuclear renaissance, was reworded to more precisely focus on licensing issues. Current challenge 4 now states, "Ability to modify regulatory processes to meet a changing environment, to include the licensing of new nuclear facilities." Waste issues, formerly covered in challenge 4, are reflected in a new challenge 5, "Oversight of radiological waste."

Prior challenge 5, "Implementation of information technology," was reworded to current challenge 6, "Implementation of information technology and information security measures," to emphasize the need to ensure that information technology resources use technological solutions for information security when appropriate.

The chart that follows provides an overview of the eight most serious management and performance challenges as of September 30, 2008.

MOST SERIOUS MANAGEMENT AND
PERFORMANCE CHALLENGES FACING THE
NUCLEAR REGULATORY COMMISSION*
AS OF SEPTEMBER 30, 2008

(AS IDENTIFIED BY THE INSPECTOR GENERAL)

Challenge 1	Protection of nuclear material used for civilian purposes.
Challenge 2	Managing information to balance security with openness and accountability.
Challenge 3	Implementation of a risk-informed and performance-based regulatory approach.
Challenge 4	Ability to modify regulatory processes to meet a changing environment, to include the licensing of new nuclear facilities.
Challenge 5	Oversight of radiological waste.
Challenge 6	Implementation of information technology and information security measures.
Challenge 7	Administration of all aspects of financial management.
Challenge 8	Managing human capital.

*The most serious management and performance challenges are not ranked in any order of importance.

CONCLUSION

The eight challenges contained in this report are distinct, yet interdependent relative to the accomplishment of NRC's mission. For example, the challenge of managing human capital affects all other management and performance challenges.

The agency's continued progress in taking actions to address the challenges presented should facilitate successfully achieving the agency's mission and goals.

ABBREVIATIONS AND ACRONYMS

CFR	Code of Federal Regulations
COL	combined operating license
CUI	controlled unclassified information
DOE	U.S. Department of Energy
FY	fiscal year
IG	Inspector General
IT	information technology
MC&A	material control and accounting
NMSS	Office of Nuclear Material Safety and Safeguards
NMMSS	Nuclear Materials Management and Safeguards System
NRC	U.S. Nuclear Regulatory Commission
NSTS	National Source Tracking System
OIG	Office of the Inspector General
T&L	time and labor

I. BACKGROUND

On January 24, 2000, Congress enacted the Reports Consolidation Act of 2000, requiring Federal agencies to provide financial and performance management information in a more meaningful and useful format for Congress, the President, and the public. The act requires the Inspector General (IG) of each Federal agency to summarize annually what he or she considers to be the most serious management and performance challenges facing the agency and to assess the agency's progress in addressing those challenges.

II. PURPOSE

In accordance with the act's provisions, the NRC IG updated what he considers to be the most serious management and performance challenges facing the agency. The IG evaluated the overall work of the Office of the Inspector General (OIG), the OIG staff's general knowledge of agency operations, and other relevant information to develop and update his list of management and performance challenges.

In addition, OIG sought input from NRC's Chairman, Commissioners, and management to obtain their views on what challenges the agency is facing and what efforts the agency has taken or planned to address previously identified management and performance challenges.

III. EVALUATION RESULTS

The NRC's mission is to regulate the Nation's civilian use of byproduct, source, and special nuclear materials to ensure adequate protection of public health and safety, promote the common defense and security, and protect the environment. Like other Federal agencies, NRC faces management and performance challenges in carrying out its mission.

DETERMINATION OF MANAGEMENT AND PERFORMANCE CHALLENGES

Congress left the determination and threshold of what constitutes a most serious management and performance challenge to the discretion of the Inspectors General. As a result, the IG applied the following definition in identifying challenges:

Serious management and performance challenges are mission critical areas or programs that have the potential for a perennial weakness or vulnerability that, without substantial management attention, would seriously impact agency operations or strategic goals.

Based on this definition, the IG revised his list of the most serious management and performance challenges facing NRC. The challenges identified represent critical areas or difficult tasks that warrant high-level NRC management attention. The following chart provides an overview of the eight management challenges. The sections that follow provide more detailed descriptions of the challenges, descriptive examples related to the challenges, and examples of efforts that the agency has taken or are underway to address the challenges.

MOST SERIOUS MANAGEMENT AND
PERFORMANCE CHALLENGES FACING THE
NUCLEAR REGULATORY COMMISSION*
AS OF SEPTEMBER 30, 2008

(AS IDENTIFIED BY THE INSPECTOR GENERAL)

Challenge 1	Protection of nuclear material used for civilian purposes.
Challenge 2	Managing information to balance security with openness and accountability.
Challenge 3	Implementation of a risk-informed and performance-based regulatory approach.
Challenge 4	Ability to modify regulatory processes to meet a changing environment, to include the licensing of new nuclear facilities.
Challenge 5	Oversight of radiological waste.
Challenge 6	Implementation of information technology and information security measures.
Challenge 7	Administration of all aspects of financial management.
Challenge 8	Managing human capital.

*The most serious management and performance challenges are not ranked in any order of importance.

CHANGES TO MANAGEMENT CHALLENGES

This year's list of challenges reflects several changes from last year's list.

CONSOLIDATION OF TWO CHALLENGES

Prior challenges 2 and 7 were combined to form challenge 2, "Managing information to balance security with openness and accountability," which captures the need for both openness and protection of information.[1]

NEW WORDING FOR THREE CHALLENGES

Prior challenge 3 was revised to the current challenge 3 language, "Implementation of a risk-informed and performance-based regulatory approach."[2] This change reflects the relative maturity of NRC's risk-informed and performance-based regulatory programs and their advancement beyond developmental efforts to implementation activities.

Prior challenge 4 was reworded to more precisely focus on licensing issues.[3] New challenge 4 states, "Ability to modify regulatory processes to meet a changing environment, to include the licensing of new nuclear facilities."

Prior challenge 5 was reworded to current challenge 6, "Implementation of information technology and information security measures," to include emphasis on ensuring that information technology (IT) resources use technological solutions for information security when appropriate.[4]

---

1   2007 challenge 2, "Appropriate handling of information." 2007 challenge 7, "Communication with external stakeholders throughout NRC regulatory activities."

2   2007 challenge 3, "Development and implementation of a risk-informed and performance-based regulatory approach."

3   2007 challenge 4, "Ability to modify regulatory processes to meet a changing environment, specifically the potential for a nuclear renaissance."

4   2007 challenge 5, "Implementation of information technology."

NEW CHALLENGE

Waste issues, formerly covered in the writeup corresponding to challenge 4, are reflected in a new challenge 5, "Oversight of radiological waste." Managing current and future waste is a major issue for the nuclear industry and the Nation, and NRC must be prepared to support safe, sound, and long-lasting solutions for high- and low-level nuclear waste.

CHALLENGE 1

Protection of nuclear material used for civilian purposes.

NRC is authorized to grant licenses for the possession and use of radioactive materials and establishes regulations to govern the possession and use of those materials. NRC's regulations require that certain material licensees have extensive material control and accounting (MC&A) programs as a condition of their licenses. All other license applications (including those requesting authorization to possess small quantities of special nuclear materials) must develop and implement plans that demonstrate a commitment to accurately control and account for radioactive materials.

The issues facing NRC and the agency's actions to address each issue include the following:

Issue: Ensure that radioactive material is adequately protected to preclude its use for malicious purposes.

Action: NRC is enhancing its material licensing processes, including a new policy for onsite visits for issuing new material licenses, examinations of existing licenses to determine their legitimacy, and the formation of a working group to update and revise existing material licensing guidance.

Issue: Ensure adequate inspections to verify licensees' commitments to their material control and accounting programs.

Action: NRC is enhancing its inspection program. Currently, fuel cycle MC&A inspections are a shared responsibility between the Office of Nuclear Material Safety and Safeguards (NMSS) and Region II, with two MC&A inspectors in each location. Additionally, the Commission approved a staff proposed rulemaking effort to include enhancements to MC&A inspection frequency and on April 25, 2008, the staff provided its rulemaking plan to the Commission. The rulemaking is ongoing under the sponsorship of NMSS and the Office of Federal and State Materials and Environmental Management Programs.

Issue: Ensure reliable accounting of special nuclear materials in the NRC and U.S. Department of Energy's (DOE's) jointly managed Nuclear Materials Management and Safeguards System (NMMSS).

Action: NRC has been working since 2003 to resolve issues of material control and accounting in response to OIG-03-A-15, "Audit of NRC's Regulatory Oversight of Special Nuclear Materials." To improve the accuracy of material inventory information maintained in NMMSS, NRC approved the final rule on February 7, 2008, amending the Code of Federal Regulations (CFR) Title 10, Parts 40, 72, 74, and 150. This added requirements to track smaller quantities of special nuclear material. However, the Commission approved a DOE request to delay implementation by 1 year.

Issue: Implement the National Source Tracking System (NSTS) to ensure the accurate tracking of byproduct material, especially those materials with the greatest potential to impact public health and safety.

Action: NRC expects to have NSTS on line by December 31, 2008, initially populating the system with data submitted into an interim database by licensees during 2008. In addition, NRC has initiated several rulemakings to expand the materials tracked in NSTS.

Issue: Ensure that Agreement State programs are adequate to protect public health and safety and the environment, and are compatible with NRC's program.

Action: NRC continues to conduct about 10 to 12 reviews per year of Agreement State radioactive materials programs under NRC's integrated materials performance evaluation program.

CHALLENGE 2

Managing information to balance security with openness and accountability.

NRC employees create and work with a significant amount of sensitive information that needs to be protected. Such information includes sensitive unclassified information and classified national security information contained in written documents and various electronic databases.

In addressing continuing terrorist activity worldwide, NRC continually reexamines its information management policies and procedures. NRC faces the challenge of attempting to balance the need to protect sensitive information from inappropriate disclosure with the agency's goal of openness in its regulatory processes. Over the past year, NRC has made various efforts to improve public access to information while protecting sensitive information, including security-related information, from inappropriate disclosure.

The issues facing NRC and the agency's actions to address each issue include the following:

Issue: Manage information in accordance with new Federal Government policies for designating, marking, safeguarding, and disseminating controlled unclassified information (CUI).

Action: NRC will implement new CUI policies and procedures over a 5-year period once guidance has been issued by the National Archives and Records Administration. Safeguards information is exempt from the new regulations; therefore, NRC will continue to manage safeguards information according to current policies.

Issue: Ensure that sensitive information is handled in accordance with agency policies and procedures for public disclosure.

Action: NRC responded to congressional and public concern regarding an incident at a Nuclear Fuel Services, Inc., facility by reviewing and releasing a number of pertinent agency documents that had not been made publicly available. In addition, the NRC resumed public meetings on the facility's performance during the fall of 2007.

Action: NRC issued multiple announcements related to the appropriate handling of information. It also completed reviews of shared network drives and office files to ensure that personally identifiable information and Privacy Act information was adequately protected or removed if unnecessary.

Issue: Provide external stakeholders with clear and accurate information about regulatory programs and facilitate public participation in the regulatory process.

Action: The staff conducted monthly, public, working-level meetings with industry and public stakeholders to discuss ongoing changes to the Reactor Oversight Process. The staff also conducted public meetings near each operating reactor to discuss results of the NRC's annual assessment of the licensee's performance. Further, staff held an annual public meeting in November 2007, to present information on the overall security performance of the commercial reactor industry, and to respond to questions and solicit comments on nuclear security issues. Lastly, in November 2007, staff issued a revised communications plan for engaging Federal, Tribal, State, and local government stakeholders.

CHALLENGE 3

Implementation of a risk-informed and performance-based regulatory approach.

NRC's intent is to increase its safety focus on licensing and oversight activities through the application of a balanced combination of experience, deterministic models, and probabilistic analysis. This approach is known as risk-informed and performance-based regulation. Incorporating risk analysis into regulatory decisions is intended to improve the regulatory process by focusing both NRC and licensee attention and activities on the areas of highest risk.

The issues facing NRC and the agency's actions to address each issue include the following:

Issue: Ensure that the appropriate level of focus on risk-informed and performance-based regulation is maintained.

Action: NRC continues its work to improve the agency's risk-informed performance-based plan, including a recent expansion of the plan's objectives to more fully achieve a holistic, risk-informed, and performance-based regulatory structure.

Issue: Develop and implement risk-informed and performance-based regulation for fuel cycle facilities.

Action: The agency conducted risk analyses during an application review for a proposed gas centrifuge facility and continued implementation of an enhanced fuel cycle facility oversight process.

Issue: Ensure that the Reactor Oversight Process meets the agency's regulatory needs.

Action: NRC uses results of an annual self-assessment of the Reactor Oversight Process to better identify significant performance issues and to ensure that licensees take appropriate actions to maintain acceptable safety performance.

Issue: Ensure that research programs enhance the validity of current risk models, and also develop risk insights for new technologies, including program areas transitioning to risk-informed regulation.

Action: NRC continues to make progress in developing risk assessments. For example, NRC completed a review of the fire probabilistic risk assessment for two nuclear power plants. The agency also continues to develop tools that allow staff to make complex and probabilistic risk-assessment calculations on their desktop computers.

CHALLENGE 4

Ability to modify regulatory processes to meet a changing environment, to include the licensing of new nuclear facilities.

NRC faces the challenge of maintaining its core regulatory programs while adapting to changes in its regulatory environment. NRC must address a growing interest in licensing and constructing new nuclear power plants to meet the Nation's demand for energy production. By August 2008, NRC had received 12 combined operating license (COL) applications (Calvert Cliffs, South Texas Project, Bellefonte, North Anna, Lee, Shearon Harris, Grand Gulf, Vogtle, V.C. Summer, Comanche Peak, Levy County, and Victoria County). NRC expects to receive additional COL applications.

While responding to the emerging demands associated with licensing and regulating new reactors, NRC must maintain focus and effectively carry out its current regulatory responsibilities, such as inspections of the current fleet of operating nuclear reactors and fuel cycle facilities.

The challenges facing NRC and the agency's actions to address each challenge include the following:

NEW FACILITIES

Issue: Instituting a Construction Inspection Program.
- Developing strong control processes for project management to ensure the agency meets its new reactor review and licensing objectives.
- Developing technical review processes.
- Ensuring a comprehensive standard review plan and adequately documented safety evaluation reports.

Action: NRC is taking a design-centered review approach to optimize the COL application review process. The Office of New Reactors is in the process of developing a new construction inspection program in accordance with 10 CFR 52. The new program of "inspections, tests, analyses, and acceptance criteria" has been integrated into the 10 CFR Part 52 licensing process to create a design-specific, preapproved set of performance standards. Licensees must meet these standards and the Commission must find that the standards have been met before the licensee can load fuel and operate the plant.

Issue: Ensure that the process for reviewing applications for new facilities meets the public's demand for new energy sources while focusing on safety and effectiveness.

Action: NRC's preparations have been focused on issuing reactor design certifications, revising the regulation that governs early site permits, and engaging in ongoing interactions with nuclear plant designers and utilities regarding prospective new reactor applications and licensing activities.

EXISTING FLEET

Issue: Ensure the ability to review licensee applications for license renewals and power uprates submitted by industry in response to the Nation's demand for energy production.

Action: NRC continues to work with plant licensees to develop a schedule of anticipated license amendment requests for license renewals and power uprates. The agency has implemented a number of recommendations to improve the license renewal review process, to include closer management oversight of the renewal process, as well as to provide additional guidance to standardize the content of NRC's license renewal review reports.

Issue: Respond to a heightened public focus on license renewals resulting in contested hearings.

Action: NRC has open dialogs with the industry, licensees, and stakeholders, and appropriate comments have been incorporated into new inspection procedures. NRC staff explained details of the new procedures during breakout sessions at the agency's 2008 Regulatory Information Conference.

Issue: Ensure the ability to identify emerging operating and safety issues at all plants, including issues associated with extended and uprated licenses; consistently apply regulatory and review changes in response to these emerging issues across the existing fleet of reactors.

Action: Annually, agency staff communicate the status of the power uprate program to the Commission. The staff is currently revising Inspection Procedure 71004 to provide additional guidance on inspection planning, implementation, and documentation.

Issue: Establish and maintain effective, stable, and predictable regulatory programs or policies for all programs.

Action: NRC continues to interface with stakeholders, develop regulatory policy, update rules and technical guidance, provide technical lead and management for the Reactor Oversight Process, and support the development of programmatic changes when needed.

CHALLENGE 5

Oversight of radiological waste.

High-level radioactive waste is primarily in the form of spent nuclear fuel generated from commercial nuclear power reactors. NRC faces significant issues involving the potential licensing of the proposed Yucca Mountain, NV, repository for storing high-level radioactive waste. Additional challenges in the high-level waste area include the interim storage of spent nuclear fuel, certification of storage and transportation casks, and the oversight of decommissioned reactors and other nuclear sites.

Additionally, the amount of low-level waste continues to grow; however, no new disposal facilities have been built since the 1980s and unresolved issues will grow as the once-operational disposal facilities shut down.

The challenges facing NRC and the agency's actions to address each challenge include the following:

Issue: Address increasing quantities of radiological waste requiring interim or permanent disposal sites.

Action: NRC developed and implemented a risk-informed decisionmaking framework in connection with a wide range of nuclear waste storage issues. The NRC has conducted reviews using the framework for dry cask waste storage systems and concluded that such systems provide a safe means to store spent nuclear fuel with exceedingly low risk.

Issue: Address issues regarding the license application to construct a high-level radioactive waste repository at Yucca Mountain, NV.

Action: The NRC received the Yucca Mountain license application from DOE in June 2008. Consistent with direction in the Nuclear Waste Policy Act and the Energy Policy Act, the agency has been conducting high-level waste prelicensing activities to ensure appropriate standards and regulatory guidance are in place. Additionally, NRC is interacting with the applicant, the DOE, such that the licensing review for a potential Yucca Mountain high-level waste repository can be conducted in 3 to 4 years as directed by Congress. NRC is also preparing to publish a final revision to 10 CFR Part 63 to align agency regulations to new U.S. Environmental Protection Agency standards for radiation protection at a high-level waste repository.

Issue: Oversight of low-level waste disposal, including low-level radioactive waste disposal sites.

Action: NRC has informed fuel cycle and materials licensees about the potential need to store some low-level radioactive waste onsite for an extended period after the low-level waste disposal facility in Barnwell, SC, closed. NRC-updated guidance advises licensees to consider ways to minimize production of Class B and C low-level waste.

Issue: Oversight of nuclear waste issues associated with the decommissioning and cleanup of nuclear reactor sites and other facilities.

Action: NRC continues to hold public meetings with stakeholders and licensees to explore safe and secure storage options associated with decommissioning of plants, such as transitioning from spent pool storage to dry cask storage.

CHALLENGE 6

Implementation of information technology and information security measures.

NRC needs to continue upgrading and modernizing its IT capabilities both for employees and for public access to the regulatory process. Recognizing the need to modernize, the Office of Information Services established goals to improve the productivity, efficiency, and effectiveness of agency programs and operations, and enhance the use of information for all users inside and outside the agency. NRC also needs to ensure that system security controls are in place to protect the agency's information systems against misuse.

The issues related to this challenge and the agency's actions to address each issue include the following:

Issue: Upgrade and manage IT activities to improve the productivity, efficiency, and effectiveness of agency programs and operations.

Action: NRC recognizes that it continues to lag behind many other Federal agencies in terms of its IT infrastructure. For example, it recently upgraded software applications to include Microsoft Office Suite and Microsoft Outlook—both commonly used in the private and public sectors. In addition, the agency has begun to address longstanding telephone problems by upgrading the telephone system performance both with new enhanced features and service as well as bandwidth capabilities.

Issue: Implement a program to provide program office laptop computers with enhanced functionality, security, and support.

Action: The agency has set goals concerning laptops for the Office of Information Services to implement in the next several years. The agency has identified and is addressing its needs to (1) develop policies and standards for the use of laptop computers, (2) implement enterprise encryption and updating of operating systems to support the laptop program, and (3) provide secure wireless capability access. The use of laptop computers is expected to increase in the coming years.

Issue: Ensure that information systems are protected.

Action The NRC Computer Security Office was formed to provide an increased capability to oversee the integration of security controls into all IT projects and operations and to improve the security of automated information. The position of Chief Information Security Officer was established as the head of this office.

Action: NRC has made progress in correcting the two significant deficiencies identified in the 2007 evaluation of the Federal Information Security Management Act concerning its information systemwide security controls. As of August 2008, more than half of the agency's systems were certified and accredited; however, the agency needs to certify and accredit all of its systems. The agency is working towards this goal and expects to complete all certifications and accreditations by the end of FY 2009.

Action: NRC is awarding a contract in excess of $2 million to advance the organization's strengthening of security controls that protect NRC's information systems and information using a certification and accreditation process. By implementing this contract, NRC hopes to ensure that security controls for information systems are adequate, and that unauthorized access, use, disclosure, disruption, modification, or destruction of NRC's information systems or data can be detected and prevented.

CHALLENGE 7

Administration of all aspects of financial management.

NRC management is responsible for establishing and maintaining effective internal controls and financial management systems that meet the objectives of several statutes including the Federal Managers' Financial Integrity Act. This act mandates that NRC reasonably ensure that (1) obligations and costs comply with applicable law; (2) assets are safeguarded against waste, loss, unauthorized use, or misappropriation; and (3) revenues and expenditures are properly recorded and accounted for. This act encompasses programmatic and administrative areas, as well as accounting and financial management.

The issues related to this challenge and the agency's actions to address each issue include the following:

Issue: Replace or upgrade the agency's current financial systems, which are obsolete, overly complex, and inefficient.

Action: In June 2008, the Chairman approved the Financial Accounting and Integrated Management Information System Implementation project. The new system, which will replace five aging financial systems[5] with a single integrated core financial system, is expected to be operational in October 2010.

Action: NRC completed the eTravel pilot. eTravel is a Governmentwide initiative to improve internal efficiency. The paperless system will automate travel documentation and approval routing of most travel arrangements. The lessons learned from the pilot are currently under review and may result in a delay of full implementation from the planned date of December 2008.

Action: NRC plans to implement the upgrade to the Time and Labor (T&L) System during the second half

of FY 2009. The upgrade will provide a modern, Web-enabled version of the existing PeopleSoft T&L software. The system will include electronic approval of time, as well as other forms associated with leave, overtime, and compensatory time.

Action: In response to a business process improvement study that focused on time and labor and fee billing processes, the agency developed guidance for managing reporting codes. Initially, the number of reporting codes was reduced to fewer than 10,000; however, since January 2008, the number of codes has grown to approximately 20,000. The agency has issued further guidance and instituted a periodic review process to ensure that the new policy is consistently observed.

Issue: Ensure that the agency continues its efforts to monitor the effectiveness of existing controls over the fee billing process and implement additional controls to address weaknesses identified.

Action: NRC improved its internal control over fee billing by implementing additional detection controls. As a result, the agency's independent auditors downgraded the material weakness related to NRC's legacy Fee Billing System to a significant deficiency. The agency continues to conduct reviews to ensure that detection controls are working as intended and to seek ways to improve the fee billing certification process. These reviews have identified areas needing improvement.

In addition to the issues noted above, the agency has taken several steps to meet the challenge of administering all aspects of financial management. Those steps include implementing cross-servicing agreements for travel and contract support payment with an outside provider, evaluating the expansion of the cross-servicing effort to other NRC financial activities, and engaging in a thorough review of unliquidated funds, which resulted in funds being made available to fund high priority activities.

---

5   The five financial systems are Federal Financial System, Fee Billing System, Allotment/Allowance Financial Plan System, Cost Accounting System, and the Capitalized Property System.

CHALLENGE 8

Managing human capital.

NRC's human capital needs are changing due to the receipt of (1) applications to construct and operate the next generation of nuclear reactors, (2) DOE's license application to construct a nuclear waste repository, and (3) industry applications to increase the number of fuel cycle facilities. To effectively manage human capital as these changes progress, while continuing to accomplish the agency's mission, NRC must rigorously implement the following initiatives:

- Timely personnel security adjudication
- Space planning
- Recruitment and knowledge management

The issues related to this challenge and the agency's actions to address each issue include the following:

Issue: Achieve timely personnel security adjudication. Work start dates for NRC employees, contractors, and licensees are frequently delayed due to the time-consuming personnel security adjudication process currently in place for granting access authorization.

Action: The agency is reviewing its hiring process for external applicants, which includes the entire hiring and security process that occurs from identification of an active vacancy through the entrance-on-duty date, and will develop recommendations to expedite the process.

Action: In accordance with Executive Order 13467 dated June 30, 2008, "Reforming Processes Related to Suitability for Government Employment, Fitness for Contractor Employees, and Eligibility for Access to Classified National Security Information," NRC must develop reciprocity processes and procedures to accept applicable investigations and adjudications conducted by other Federal agencies.

Action: In November 2007, the Office of Administration

hired two additional personnel security specialists for the adjudication of personnel security cases. Three additional personnel security specialists were brought on board during the summer of 2008.

Action: The Human Resources Recruitment Activity Tracking System was modified to include security processing and adjudication status information. Reports from this system are shared with the program offices to keep managers informed of the status of their new hires.

Issue: NRC must continue to accomplish the agency's mission during workspace related changes agencywide. In headquarters, changes involve the use of multiple headquarters office buildings at various sites in Montgomery County, MD.

Action: NRC is implementing a Headquarters Strategic Housing Plan designed to meet space needs through FY 2009. This plan addresses workspace needs, workflow, and business processing structures. Beginning in 2013, the agency expects to begin occupying a new permanent building in an effort to reconsolidate headquarters staff. Once the moves to the new permanent building are complete, the agency will have headquarters staff consolidated in three buildings within the White Flint Complex in Rockville, MD. Furthermore, most NRC regional offices are seeking new office space for additional staff in order to meet increased workload demands.

Issue: NRC must continue to address anticipated increased workload demands and retirements with recruitment and knowledge management strategies.

Action: Since FY 2005 there have been 1,561 new employees added to the workforce.[6] In FY 2007, the agency exceeded its hiring goal of a 200 net gain of staff by bringing on board 417 new employees. During FY 2008, NRC is projected to bring on board 495 new employees with an estimated net gain of more than 200.

---

6   As of August 30, 2008, there were approximately 3,791 NRC staff.

Action: NRC maintains a recruitment program that includes participation in approximately 80 recruitment events each year at colleges, universities, and professional conferences. Other initiatives include developing new recruitment displays and videos to show at recruitment events, hiring additional human resource staff to perform critical human resources work, and upgrading the agency's Web-based job application tool.

Action: NRC is implementing knowledge management strategies[7] that include mentoring, early replacement hiring, and rehiring annuitants with or without use of a pension offset as applicable.[8] The agency also developed a knowledge management Web site, expressly for the purpose of retaining knowledge before key employees are promoted or retire.

IV. CONCLUSION

The eight challenges contained in this report are distinct, yet interdependent relative to the accomplishment of NRC's mission. For example, the challenge of managing human capital affects all other management and performance challenges.

The agency's continued progress in taking actions to address the challenges presented should facilitate successfully achieving the agency's mission and goals.

SCOPE AND METHODOLOGY

This evaluation focused on the IG's annual assessment of the most serious management and performance challenges facing the NRC. The challenges represent critical areas or difficult tasks that warrant high-level management attention. To accomplish this work, OIG focused on determining (1) current challenges, (2) the agency's efforts to address the challenges during FY 2008, and (3) future agency efforts to address the challenges.

OIG reviewed and analyzed pertinent laws and authoritative guidance, agency documents, and OIG reports, and sought input from NRC officials concerning agency accomplishments relative to the challenge areas and suggestions they had for updating the challenges. Specifically, because challenges affect mission critical areas or programs that have the potential to impact agency operations or strategic goals, NRC Commission members, offices that report to the Commission, the Executive Director for Operations, and the Chief Financial Officer were afforded the opportunity to share any information and insights on this subject.

OIG conducted this evaluation from June through August 2008. The major contributors to this report were Deputy Assistant Inspector General for Audits Anthony Lipuma, Team Leader Steven Zane, Team Leader Beth Serepca, Team Leader Sherri Miotla, and Senior Analyst Judy Gordon.

---

7   Knowledge management involves capturing critical information and making the right information available to the right people at the right time to assure that knowledge and experience of the current staff is passed on to the next generation of NRC staff.

8   This flexibility allows NRC to rehire a retiree to fill a position at full pay if the agency has experienced difficulty in filling a position, or if a temporary emergency exists.

APPENDIX B

MANAGEMENT DECISIONS AND FINAL ACTIONS ON OIG AUDIT RECOMMENDATIONS

U.S.NRC

United States Nuclear Regulatory Commission

Protecting People and the Environment

The U.S. Nuclear Regulatory Commission (NRC) maintains an excellent record in resolving and implementing NRC Office of the Inspector General's (OIG) audit recommendations. Section 5(b) of the Inspector General Act of 1978, as amended, requires agencies to report on final actions taken on OIG audit recommendations. The following table gives the dollar value of disallowed costs determined through contract audits conducted by the Defense Contract Audit Agency and NRC's OIG. Because of the sensitivity of contractual negotiations, the agency will not provide details of these contract audits in this report. As of September 30, 2008, there were no outstanding audits recommending that funds be put to better use.

MANAGEMENT REPORT ON OFFICE OF THE INSPECTOR GENERAL AUDITS WITH DISALLOWED COSTS

For the period October 1, 2007–September 30, 2008

Category	Number of Audit Reports	Questioned Costs	Unsupported Costs
1. Audit reports with management decisions on which final action had not been taken at the beginning of this reporting period.	0	$0	$0
2. Audit reports on which management decisions were made during this period.	1	$193,585	$0
3. Audit reports on which final action was taken during this report period. (i) Disallowed costs that were recovered by management through collection, offset, property in lieu of cash, or otherwise. (ii) Disallowed costs that were written off by management.	0 0	$0 $0	$0 $0
4. Reports for which no final action had been taken by the end of the reporting period.	1	$193,585	$0

MANAGEMENT DECISIONS NOT IMPLEMENTED WITHIN 1 YEAR

For the OIG audit reports listed in the following tables, the NRC made management decisions before October 1, 2007. As of September 30, 2008, NRC had not taken final action, including OIG final review and closure, on some issues. Completion of the activities listed in the column "Actions Pending" will complete agency action on the listed OIG audit and evaluation recommendations.

GOVERNMENT PERFORMANCE AND RESULTS ACT: REVIEW OF THE FY 1999 PERFORMANCE REPORT (OIG-01-A-03)

February 23, 2001

The OIG conducted this audit at the request of the chairman of the Senate Committee on Governmental Affairs to determine if NRC's FY 1999 performance data were valid and reliable and if the FY 2000 performance data would be more valid and reliable. The audit found that while NRC was improving and strengthening its performance reporting process, as interim policy guidance, the agency needed to institute management control procedures to produce valid and reliable data. The agency should then institutionalize the procedures in an NRC management directive (MD).

Open Recommendations	Actions Pending
1. Develop an NRC management directive (MD) to provide the management controls needed to ensure that the NRC produces credible Government Performance and Results Act (GPRA) documents.	The NRC issued interim guidance for performance management and reporting performance information in July 2001, consistent with GPRA requirements. In July 2002, the NRC issued a new MD and Handbook 4.8, "Performance Measurements," for intraagency review and comment. Staff subsequently decided that the agency should address performance measurement in the broader context of budget and performance integration. Therefore, the NRC decided to incorporate MD 4.8 into a revision of MD and Handbook 4.7, which will be titled "Planning, Budgeting, and Performance Management." Revised MD 4.7 and Handbook will clarify the roles and responsibilities in setting the agency's strategic direction, determining planned activities and resources, measuring and monitoring performance, and assessing performance.
3. Include guidance on reporting unmet goals in both the management directive and the interim policy guidance on implementing GPRA initiatives.	In August 2007, the Commission directed the Chief Financial Officer, in coordination with staff, to provide options for improving the agency's budget formulation process. Staff developed and implemented a new top-down budget process in formulating the agency's FY 2010 budget.
	Since a major section of MD and Handbook 4.7 addresses roles and responsibilities in the agency's budget formulation process, staff pushed back the update of MD and Handbook 4.7 to factor in lessons learned from the FY 2010 budget process. In late FY 2008, staff is considering lessons learned as part of an NRC task force that is reviewing the agency's budget formulation process and budget structure.
	Based on the task force's current schedule for issuing guidance on the agency's budget formulation process, staff expects to publish the MD and Handbook 4.7 in June 2009.

REVIEW OF NRC'S HANDLING AND MARKING OF SENSITIVE UNCLASSIFIED INFORMATION (OIG-03-A-01)

October 16, 2002

This OIG conducted this audit to assess NRC's program for handling, marking, and protecting of official use only (OUO) information, a category of sensitive unclassified information. The audit found that NRC's program and guidance for the handling and marking of sensitive unclassified information may not adequately protect OUO information from inadvertent public disclosure. The audit also found and that the agency does provide training on a regular basis to all NRC employees and contractors on handling and protecting sensitive unclassified information.

Open Recommendations	Actions Pending
1. Update the guidance for OUO documents to require clear identification of sensitive unclassified information to prevent its inadvertent disclosure.	Agency corrective actions require issuance of a revised management directive (MD) covering sensitive unclassified, nonsafeguards information (SUNSI) and a new MD covering safeguards information (SGI). The NRC issued MD 12.7, "NRC Safeguards Information Security Program," on SGI on June 25, 2008. The revision of SUNSI is on hold pending the issuance of standard Federal guidance on Controlled Unclassified Information (CUI) by the National Archives and Records Administration, which is the executive agent for implementing the CUI policy. NRC will revise SUNSI policy to align it with the CUI guidance. Updated guidance is currently due on October 31, 2009.
2. Mandate consistent use of defined markings on documents containing OUO information and clarify the markings that should be used on sensitive unclassified information.	

AUDIT OF NRC'S REGULATORY OVERSIGHT OF SPECIAL NUCLEAR MATERIALS (OIG-03-A-15)

May 23, 2003

The OIG conducted this audit to determine whether NRC adequately ensures that its licensees control and account for special nuclear material (SNM). The audit found that NRC's current levels of oversight of licensees' material control and accounting (MC&A) activities do not provide adequate assurance that all licensees properly control and account for SNM. The audit reported that NRC performs only limited inspections of licensees' MC&A activities and thus cannot assure the reliability of data in the Nuclear Materials Management and Safeguards System. The U.S. Department of Energy manages this computer database and shares it with the NRC as the national system for tracking certain private- and Government-owned nuclear materials.

Open Recommendations	Actions Pending
1. Conduct periodic inspections to verify that material licensees comply with MC&A requirements, including but not limited to visual inspections of licensees' SNM inventories and validation of report information.	NRC expects to issue a proposed rule in late 2009, with issuance of the final rule by December 2010. The final rule will enhance MC&A regulations, inspections, and the licensing process. The work on the rulemaking will include documentation of the technical basis for risk-informing the MC&A program and how the rulemaking will be applied to the program. By July 2011, NRC expects to have completed the application of risk-informing the MC&A program. The agency will determine inspection resources and frequencies for all types of materials licensees' MC&A inspections for SNM.
3. Document the basis of the approach used to risk-inform NRC's oversight of MC&A activities for all types of materials licensees.	

AUDIT OF NRC'S INCIDENT RESPONSE PROGRAM (OIG-04-A-20)
September 16, 2004

The OIG conducted this audit to determine whether the NRC performs its incident response program in a timely and effective manner, provides adequate support to licensees, and maintains readiness and qualifications of staff. The audit found that while NRC has improved its program since the Three Mile Island 2 accident on March 29, 1979, the agency needs to do more to ensure that the program is performed consistently, is more fully understood by licensees, and maintains a well-defined process for demonstrating staff are qualified and ready to respond.

Open Recommendations	Actions Pending
4. Periodically review regional incident response programs to ensure NRC's incident response program is carried out consistently across the agency.	To implement the Incident Response Self-Assessment Program, the agency began by developing a self-assessment plan that was tested in NRC Region II. In April 2008, the agency performed a self-assessment in Region I. Another self-assessment was completed for Region IV in October 2008. By July 2009, the NRC plans to institute self-assessments in all of the NRC regions.

INDEPENDENT EVALUATION OF NRC'S IMPLEMENTATION OF THE FEDERAL INFORMATION SECURITY MANAGEMENT ACT FOR FY 2004 (OIG-04-A-22)
September 30, 2004

This was an independent evaluation of NRC's implementation of the Federal Information Security Management Act for FY 2004. The review found that while NRC had made improvements to its automated information security program, the agency still needs to make additional improvements.

Open Recommendations	Actions Pending
Two of the original 16 recommendations remain open.	Due to the sensitive nature of the OIG's review and recommendations in this area, the agency will not include specific details in this report. As of September 30, 2008, completion of agency actions on this OIG audit report requires recertification and reaccreditation of some systems and updating of a business continuity plan. The NRC is completing these actions in accordance with a prioritization of information technology security activities, based on a mission perspective and security risk. Consequently, most of these activities were completed in the first half of FY 2008, but completion of the recertification and reaccreditation of the telecommunication system will be delayed until early FY 2009. Staff will track these agency plans to completion through NRC's FY 2008 Plan of Action and Milestones required by the Federal Information Security Management Act.

SYSTEM EVALUATION OF THE GENERAL LICENSE TRACKING SYSTEM (OIG-04-A-24)
September 30, 2004

The OIG conducted this evaluation as part of the OIG's review of NRC's implementation of the Federal Information Security Management Act for FY 2004. The objective was to review and evaluate the managerial, operational, and technical controls for the General License Tracking System (GLTS). The GLTS facilitates the tracking and accountability of NRC general licensees and generally licensed devices. The review found that the GLTS's security documentation did not always follow required guidelines, that security protection requirements were not consistent within the security documentation, and that NRC was not tracking all action items resulting from testing the system's security controls.

Open Recommendations	Actions Pending
1. Update the GLTS Security Plan to describe all controls currently in place. In-place controls are those marked at least at Level 3 in the self-assessment and that were documented as "passed" in the last Security Test and Evaluation Report, or in any test and evaluation on controls added since publication of that report.	As of September 30, 2008, the agency has completed all documents required for the GLTS certification and accreditation (C&A) effort. The newly revised GLTS system security plan describes all controls, currently in place, inherited from the General Support System on which it resides and planned controls. GLTS has been through the security test and evaluation (ST&E). The ST&E report has been received and reviewed. Staff will compile the C&A documentation, place it into ADAMS, and formally submit it to the designated approval authority for approval through the Computer Security Office for authority-to-operate.
3. Update the GLTS Business Continuity Plan.	The agency updated the GLTS contingency (business continuity) plan in May 2008. The agency tested the GLTS contingency plan and reported results to the Computer Security Office on June 10, 2008.
4. Update the GLTS Security Plan and GLTS self-assessment to consistently define the protection requirements (confidentiality, integrity, and availability).	During development of the updated GLTS System Security Plan (SSP), the NRC advised the contractor of the need to ensure consistency in defining the protection requirements and controls. With completion of the revised SSP and security test and evaluation, the annual security self-assessment was not required for FY 2008. However, during the next 3-year cycle before the agency reevaluates the SSP, the annual security self-assessments will be required and FSME will ensure that controls and protection requirements continue to be consistently defined. The security categorization prepared for the current C&A effort determined that GLTS is a major application, with a moderate security categorization for each protection objective (confidentiality, integrity, and availability).

System Evaluation of the Integrated Personnel Security System (OIG-05-A-08)
January 14, 2005

The OIG conducted this evaluation as part of its review of NRC's implementation of the Federal Information Security Management Act for FY 2004. The objective was to review and evaluate the management, operational, and technical controls for the Integrated Personnel Security System (IPSS), which replaced NRC employee security information contained in paper files and in a less-capable automated data system. The review found that the IPSS's security test and evaluation were not comprehensive and independent, security documentation was not always consistent with National Institute of Standards and Technology (NIST) guidelines, and security protection requirements were not consistent within the security documentation.

Open Recommendations	Actions Pending
1. Recertify and reaccredit IPSS based on an independent, comprehensive, and fully documented assessment of all management, operational, and technical controls.	The agency has established completion dates in order to integrate the certification and accreditation of IPSS with the implementation of Homeland Security Presidential Directive 12 and to allow time for resolution of operational issues. Therefore, staff expects certification and accreditation of IPSS to be completed by March 31, 2009.
2. Update the IPSS Risk Assessment Report to include listed changes.	NRC staff expects to update the IPSS Risk Assessment Report to include the specified items by December 31, 2008.
3. Update the IPSS System Security Plan to include listed changes.	NRC staff expects to update the IPSS Security Plan to include the specified items by December 31, 2008.
4. Update the IPSS System Security Plan to include a section on planning for security in the life cycle and a section on incident response capability.	NRC staff expects to update the IPSS Security Plan by December 31, 2008. It will include sections on planning for security in the life cycle and incident response capability.
5. Update the IPSS System Security Plan to describe all controls currently in place. In-place controls are those marked at least at Level 3 in the self-assessment and that were documented as passed in the last Security Test and Evaluation Report (or in any test and evaluation on controls added since publication of that report.)	The agency expects to update the IPSS Security Plan by December 31, 2008, and will describe all controls currently in place.
8. Update the IPSS System Security Plan and IPSS self-assessment to consistently define the protection requirements (confidentiality, integrity, and availability).	The agency expects to update the security plan and IPSS self-assessment by December 31, 2008, to consistently define protection requirements.

AUDIT OF NRC's BUDGET FORMULATION PROCESS (OIG-05-A-09)
January 31, 2005

The OIG conducted the audit to determine whether the budget formulation portion of the NRC's Planning, Budgeting, and Performance Management process is effectively used to develop and collect data to align resources with strategic goals and is efficiently and effectively coordinated with program and support offices. The audit found that NRC effectively develops and collects data to align resources with strategic goals, prepares the budget in alignment with the Strategic Plan, and successfully conducts Office of Management and Budget-required program assessment rating tool evaluations. The audit also found the agency needed additional internal coordination and communication efforts.

Open Recommendations	Actions Pending
1. Clarify the roles and responsibilities of the Chief Financial Officer and the Executive Director for Operations in the budget formulation process.	A revision of MD and Handbook 4.7, "Planning, Budgeting, and Performance Management," will clarify roles and responsibilities and document the budget formulation process, including decisionmaking, and will provide for a logical, comprehensive sequencing of events for obtaining early Commission direction and approval.
2. Document the decisionmaking process and the roles and responsibilities of the program review committee.	In August 2007, the Commission directed the Chief Financial Officer, in coordination with staff, to provide options for improving the agency's budget formulation process. Staff developed and implemented a new top-down budget process in formulating the agency's FY 2010 budget.
3. Document the budget formulation process to ensure a logical, comprehensive sequencing of events that provides for obtaining early Commission direction and approval.	Since a major section of MD and Handbook 4.7 addresses roles and responsibilities in the agency's budget formulation process, the agency decided that the update of the MD and Handbook 4.7 should be pushed back to factor in lessons learned from the FY 2010 budget process. In late FY 2008, NRC staff were considering lessons learned as part of an NRC task force that is reviewing the agency's budget formulation process and budget structure.
	Based on the task force's current schedule for issuing guidance on the agency's budget formulation process, the agency expects to publish the MD and Handbook 4.7 in June 2009. (MD and Handbook 4.7 will also address the decisionmaking roles and responsibilities of the program review committee.)

AUDIT OF NRC's TELECOMMUNICATIONS PROGRAM (OIG-05-A-13)
June 7, 2005

The OIG conducted this audit to evaluate controls over the use of NRC telecommunications services and the physical security of NRC telecommunications systems. The OIG found that the agency needs to strengthen controls over the use of telecommunications services and the physical security of NRC telecommunications systems.

Open Recommendation	Action Pending
3. Revise Management Directive and MD Handbook 2.3 "Telecommunications" to include effective management controls over NRC headquarters staff use of agency telecommunications services.	The revised management directive and handbook is in final concurrence for publication by February 27, 2009.

AUDIT OF NRC's DECOMMISSIONING PROGRAM (OIG-05-A-17)
September 21, 2005

The OIG conducted this audit to determine whether NRC's decommissioning program achieves desired performance results as stated in the Strategic Plan and reported in the Performance and Accountability Report. The audit found that while NRC's decommissioning program has processes in place to monitor, evaluate, and report on performance, some performance results could not be verified. In addition, although staff implemented most of the recommendations from an FY 2003 self-evaluation of the program, the agency had not made progress on a few recommendations.

Open Recommendation	Action Pending
1. Clarify and disseminate expectations for generating and maintaining supporting documentation for performance data to staff responsible for preparing and collecting performance data.	Revised Management Directive 4.7, "Planning, Budgeting, and Performance Management," will include clarifications of expectations for generating and maintaining supporting documentation for performance data.
	In August 2007, the Commission directed the Chief Financial Officer, in coordination with staff, to provide options for improving the agency's budget formulation process. The agency developed and implemented a new top-down budget process in formulating the FY 2010 budget.
	Since a major section of MD and Handbook 4.7 addresses roles and responsibilities in the agency's budget formulation process, staff decided to postpone update of MD and Handbook 4.7 to include a lessons learned from the FY 2010 budget process. In late FY 2008, lessons learned were being considered by an NRC task force that is reviewing the agency's budget formulation process and budget structure.
	Based on the task force's current schedule for issuing guidance on the agency's budget formulation process, staff expects to publish MD and Handbook 4.7 in June 2009.

SYSTEM EVALUATION OF SECURITY CONTROLS FOR STANDALONE PERSONAL COMPUTERS AND LAPTOPS (OIG-05-A-18)

September 22, 2005

The OIG conducted this evaluation as part of their review of NRC's implementation of the Federal Information Security Management Act for FY 2005, with the objectives of evaluating the effectiveness of NRC security policies, procedures, practices, and controls for standalone personal computers (PCs) and laptop computers. The review found that security controls for standalone PCs and laptops were not adequate, that the devices were not monitored for compliance with Federal regulations, and agency information technology coordinators' understanding of disposal practices for these devices were not consistent.

Open Recommendations	Actions Pending
2. Develop and require users to sign a rules-of-behavior agreement accepting responsibility for implementing security controls on standalone PCs and laptops.	The agency has developed standard rules of behavior that the Office of Human Resources and the National Treasury Employees Union (NTEU) have been reviewing since the beginning of May 2008. Upon completion of the review, the NRC will implement new rules. The agency will require all NRC system users to sign the rules annually. Staff will make rules available by the first quarter of fiscal year 2009.
3. Develop and implement procedures for verifying all required security controls are implemented on standalone PCs and laptops.	The Computer Security Office (CSO) is finalizing procedures for verifying security controls for standalone PCs and laptops and expects to have them completed in the first quarter of fiscal year 2009.
4. Provide users with guidance on compliance with Executive Order (EO) 13103, "Computer Software Piracy," for standalone PCs and laptops.	The agency will develop and disseminate clear guidance on compliance with EO 13103 for standalone PCs and laptops as part of the standard rules of behavior as discussed above under Recommendation 2. The agency will develop the rules of behavior, including review by the National Treasury Employees Union, by the end of FY 2009.
5. Develop and require users to sign a rules-of-behavior agreement acknowledging their compliance with EO 13103, "Computer Software Piracy," for standalone PCs and laptops.	As part of the development of the standard rules of behavior as discussed above under Recommendation 2 and Recommendation 4, a standard rules-of-behavior agreement for users to acknowledge their compliance with EO 13103 for standalone PCs and laptops will be developed, and offices will be notified of the requirement for all users of such devices to sign the agreement as a condition of using the devices. The agency will develop the rules of behavior, including review by the National Treasury Employees Union, by the end of FY 2009.
6. Develop and implement procedures for monitoring compliance with EO 13103, "Computer Software Piracy," for standalone PCs and laptops.	Procedures for monitoring compliance with EO 13103 for standalone PCs and laptops will be developed and issued as part of the standard rules of behavior as discussed above under Recommendation 2. The agency will develop the rules of behavior, including review by the National Treasury Employees Union, by the end of FY 2009.

NRC's GENERIC COMMUNICATIONS PROGRAM (OIG-05-A-19)
September 30, 2005

The OIG conducted this audit to assess the effectiveness of the Generic Communications Program, specifically whether NRC generic communications are issued in accordance with the Generic Communications Program and other regulatory requirements, and how NRC tracks licensee actions on generic communications. The audit found that NRC has an established framework for developing and issuing certain generic communications, but that weaknesses exist in NRC's internal controls over generic communications in controls for oversight of licensee actions.

Open Recommendations	Actions Pending
1. Include safeguards advisories, as well as any other agency communication tool that meets the definition of a generic communication, in the formal Generic Communications Program to ensure compliance with regulatory requirements.	Proposed new Management Directive (MD) 8.18, "NRC Generic Communications Program," defines the scope of NRC's generic communications, defines organizational roles and responsibilities for each generic communications product, and establishes security advisories and information assessment team advisories as additional agency generic communications products. The MD is in final concurrence. The agency expects to issue it in FY 2009.
3. Implement controls to ensure a systematic, consistent tracking methodology from initiation to closure for each agency-issued generic communication.	In June 2006, NRC established an interoffice working group to evaluate the current process for initiating, developing, tracking, and distributing generic communications, and to recommend process changes. The working group decided to incorporate the tracking system into the project tracking NRO requests for additional information (licensee responses and inquiries). The agency has completed final acceptance testing of the generic communication tracking system. The agency expects to implement the system in FY 2009.
4. Direct the development of a methodology that will allow the staff to gauge the effectiveness of agency-issued generic communications.	Proposed new MD 8.18, "NRC Generic Communications Program," defines the scope of NRC's generic communications and defines organizational roles and responsibilities for each generic communications product, including the conduct of effectiveness reviews. In addition, it clearly identifies those generic communications that require effectiveness reviews. The MD is in final concurrence. The agency expects to issue it in FY 2009.

AUDIT OF NRC'S OFFICE OF NUCLEAR SECURITY AND INCIDENT RESPONSE (OIG-06-A-09)
February 16, 2006

This audit was an independent evaluation of the operations of the Office of Nuclear Security and Incident Response (NSIR), formed in April 2002, specifically focusing on NSIR's management of emergent work, communications with stakeholders, and implementation of the recommendations from the organizational assessment performed in 2003. The audit found that while NSIR accomplished a great deal since its inception, it needed to focus on refining and formalizing its day-to-day operations to improve its ability to meet its mission.

Open Recommendations	Actions Pending
2. Review the Emergent Work Process to ensure emergent work is accurately documented to assist with workforce and budget decisions.	NSIR is integrating this system into its work planning management system. The Electronic Document and Action Tracking System (EDATS) will track emergent and unbudgeted work. This recommendation will be completed when the NRC fully implements EDATS throughout the agency.

AUDIT OF THE BYPRODUCT MATERIALS LICENSE APPLICATION & REVIEW PROCESS (OIG-06-A-11)
March 10, 2006

As part of a larger effort to determine whether NRC's oversight of byproduct material provides reasonable assurance that licensees account for and control the materials, the OIG directed this audit towards determining if NRC ensures, through its license application and review process, that only legitimate entities receive NRC byproduct material licenses. It concluded that because NRC has not conducted vulnerability assessments of all aspects of the materials program, there may be vulnerabilities in the license application and review process that could be exploited by individuals with malevolent intent.

Open Recommendations	Actions Pending
1. Conduct a complete vulnerability assessment of the materials program, including the license application and review process, and the methods used by licensees to purchase byproduct material from sellers.	In September 2007, the Commission approved a comprehensive plan to address needed changes in NRC's process for issuing licenses for radioactive sources. The plan called for an independent, external review panel to identify potential weaknesses or security gaps in the NRC's materials licensing program. The plan also called for the establishment of a materials program working group to provide recommendations to address any identified security gaps or weaknesses. The independent panel issued its report and recommendations on the NRC's materials licensing program in March 2008. Staff has incorporated the panel's recommendations into the overall corrective action plan for the materials licensing program. The materials program working group expects to issue its report in October 2008.

continued

AUDIT OF THE BYPRODUCT MATERIALS LICENSE APPLICATION & REVIEW PROCESS (OIG-06-A-11)

continued

Open Recommendations	Actions Pending
2. Modify the license application and review process to mitigate the risks identified in the vulnerability assessment.	Staff issued revised prelicensing guidance in September 2008, to directly address the vulnerability demonstrated by the U.S. Government Accountability Office's covert investigation of the NRC's materials licensing process. As noted in action pending above, two additional groups, an independent external review panel and a materials working group, have made recommendations to enhance the NRC's materials licensing program. The agency has incorporated some of these recommendations into an overall corrective action plan for the materials licensing program. The agency is still evaluating other solutions.

NRC'S BASELINE SECURITY AND SAFEGUARDS INSPECTION PROGRAM (OIG-06-A-21)

September 8, 2006

The audit of NRC's drug testing program found that the NRC's Drug-Free Workplace Plan was not in compliance with Federal guidance that requires the plan to receive U.S. Department of Health and Human Services's (HHS's) approval and that it was missing a required clause.

Open Recommendations	Actions Pending
1. Provide the required initial and refresher security training courses for regional security inspectors at the frequency needed to support qualification requirements.	Phase 1 of NRC's corrective actions is to develop foundation security courses such as "Security Fundamentals" and "Reactor Technology for Security." The Security Fundamentals course is under review with expected delivery in FY 2008. Both courses have been reviewed and delivered.
	A pilot for the "Reactor Technology for Security" course was completed in June 2007 and is under review based on comments received from course participants and lessons learned. The expected delivery was in FY 2008. The course has been reviewed and delivered. Complete.
	A 3-day annual security refresher course for security inspectors from all four NRC regions was conducted in November 2006, and was scheduled for November 13–15, 2007. Complete.
	This course is now listed in the NRC course catalog. Phase 2 of NRC's corrective action is to develop four modules of advanced security field courses. These are being reviewed, and NRC is pursuing contracts with outside Federal agencies to provide portions of this specialized training. The agency expects Phase 2 courses to be available by FY 2009. All Phase 2 courses have been developed and are scheduled in FY 2009.
	continued

NRC's Baseline Security and Safeguards Inspection Program (OIG-06-A-21) *continued*

Open Recommendations	Actions Pending
4. Update the security inspector training program to ensure course material is current and relevant.	Staff are developing revisions of the training requirements in NRC Manual Chapter (MC) 1245, Appendix C4, "Safeguards Inspector Technical Proficiency Training and Qualification Journal," and Office of Nuclear Security and Incident Response Office Procedure ADM-109, "Training Development and Qualification Programs." The agency expects to issue these materials in FY 2009. As the agency finalizes and publishes the courses in response to Recommendation 1 in the NRC Training Catalog, staff will also update MC 1245 and ADM-109. The agency continues to develop revisions. Staff anticipates completing action in FY 2009.
6. Include guidance in the baseline security and safeguards inspection procedures to ensure inspectors review an adequate number of sample items to assess the effectiveness of the licensee's security program.	As a result of the inspection program assessment process, and on the basis of recommendations received from the IG Audit conducted in 2006, the agency has revised security baseline inspection procedures. The revision effort, which included standardizing the inspection procedure sample sizes, was completed on October 6, 2008. The NRR inspection manual chapter coordinator possesses these procedures, and they are in the change management and declaration process with a projected publication date of mid-November 2008. The program implementation schedule is for January, 1 2009 (to coincide with the beginning of the calendar year inspection cycle).
7. Implement training on how to select an adequate number of sample items.	Along with the effort to revise the security baseline inspection procedures, NSIR provided training and familiarization on the standardization and determination of sample sizes through presentation and open discussion during the annual counterpart conference in November 2007. The agency provided further familiarization by allowing the inspectors to continue to review the revised procedures prior to finalization and implementation.

Audit of the NRC's Process for Releasing Commission Decision Documents (OIG-06-A-22)
September 8, 2006

This audit assessed the NRC's process for evaluating SECY papers and staff requirements memoranda for public release pursuant to relevant legal and regulatory requirements. The audit concluded that while the NRC has a process for handling Freedom of Information Act (FOIA) requests, there are weaknesses in the internal controls needed to ensure full compliance with the FOIA.

Open Recommendations	Actions Pending
1. Develop a program to ensure NRC compliance with the FOIA's automatic disclosure requirements.	The Commission has modified procedures; however, closure of this recommendation requires the revision of Management Directive (MD) 3.4, "Release of Information to the Public," to address document screening for compliance with Title 5 of the United States Code, 5 U.S.C. 552 (a)(1) and (a)(2). The Commission expects to issue revised MD 3.4 by December 31, 2008.

EVALUATION OF THE NRC'S USE OF PROBABILISTIC RISK ASSESSMENT IN REGULATING THE COMMERCIAL NUCLEAR POWER INDUSTRY (OIG-06-A-24)
September 29, 2006

This evaluation determined if the NRC follows prevailing good practices in probabilistic risk assessment (PRA) methods and data in its use of PRA, uses prevailing good practices in PRA methods and uses data appropriately in its regulation of nuclear power plant licensees, and achieves the objectives of the PRA policy statement. The evaluation concluded that although the NRC employs prevailing good practices in the regulation of nuclear power plants, the NRC lacks formal, documented processes and associated configuration control for PRA computer models and software.

Open Recommendations	Actions Pending
3. Conduct a full verification and validation (V&V) of the Systems Analysis Program for Hands-On Integrated Reliability Evaluations (SAPHIRE) Version 7.2 and the Graphical Evaluation Module (GEM). (SAPHIRE and GEM are software programs used to perform evaluations of SPAR models and to provide risk results based on the events or initiators evaluated.)	Because development of SAPHIRE Version 8 is in progress, a full V&V of SAPHIRE Version 7.2 would not be an effective use of resources. Therefore, the release of SAPHIRE, Version 8, for general use by April 2010 will close this recommendation, allowing sufficient time to complete independent V&V activities.

AUDIT OF THE NRC'S TECHNICAL TRAINING CENTER (OIG-O7-A-05)
January 9, 2007

This audit identified opportunities to improve the economy, efficiency, and effectiveness of the Technical Training Center's operations.

Open Recommendations	Actions Pending
1. Revise MD 13.1 to require that property inventories should include independent verification of the property by someone other than the property holder.	All property custodians received interim guidance requiring property inventories to include independent verification by someone other than the property holder, in preparation for the FY 2008 biennial inventory, which is currently ongoing. The FY 2008 biennial inventory plan was developed and executed to comply with this requirement. Staff assigned to revise Management Directive (MD) 13.1 have also been conducting the biennial inventory and have been unable to dedicate sufficient time to complete the MD revision. Additional required changes to MD 13.1 were identified since the last update provided to the Office of the Inspector General on February 29, 2008, (e.g., definition of sensitive items). An update to MD 13.1 incorporating all the required changes is currently under staff review. Staff will complete the review and incorporation of comments by August 31, 2008, at which time they will transmit the MD revision to offices and regions for review and comment. The final approval process concludes February 27, 2009.

continued |

AUDIT OF THE NRC's TECHNICAL TRAINING CENTER (OIG-O7-A-05) *continued*

Open Recommendations	Actions Pending
3. Update and finalize training policies and procedures.	Staff completed procedures by the dates reported in the NRC's response to the OIG, with the following exceptions: • OP-401, "Course Scheduling." The original scheduled completion date was September 28, 2008. Procedure development is now tied to the resolution of Recommendations 6 and 7 of IG Evaluation (Audit) OIG 08-A-13, action on which should conclude on June 30, 2009. • OP-402, "Course Registration." The implementation of iLearn (the NRC's Learning Management System) has automated the process previously performed by staff and, as a result, rendered the subject procedure unnecessary. • OP-403, "Course Administration." An update to the procedure reflecting the implementation of LMS is due on December 20, 2008.
9. Periodically rotate cognizant instructor responsibilities.	OP-404, "Training Materials Control" addresses this recommendation in part. By memorandum dated August 25, 2008, the OIG stated that this recommendation will close upon development and implementation of additional policy requiring periodic rotation of cognizant instructor responsibilities.
10. Establish a more formal method to track and trend Technical Training Center course evaluations and periodically analyze trends for appropriate action.	Staff will modify OP-403 (or develop a new procedure) to address this recommendation by December 20, 2008.
11. Include questions specific to instructor performance on all course evaluations.	Staff will modify OP-403 (or develop a new procedure) to address this recommendation by December 20, 2008.

U.S.NRC
United States Nuclear Regulatory Commission
Protecting People and the Environment

AUDIT OF THE NRC'S REGULATION OF NUCLEAR FUEL CYCLE FACILITIES (OIG-07-A-06)
January 10, 2007

This audit determined whether the NRC has an effective and efficient approach to fuel cycle facility oversight. The audit found that the NRC could enhance the current Fuel Cycle Facility Oversight Program by developing and implementing a framework modeled after a structured process, such as the Reactor Oversight Process (ROP).

Open Recommendations	Actions Pending
1. Fully develop and implement a framework for the Fuel Cycle Facility Oversight Program (FCFOP) that is consistent with a structured process, such as the Reactor Oversight Process (ROP).	Agency corrective actions consist of initiatives related to improving fuel cycle oversight, including performing a structured evaluation of integrated safety analysis (ISA) annual updates, providing fuel cycle input to a revision of NRC enforcement policy, and completing a safety culture pilot plan. The staff has completed the review of the 2007 ISA annual updates and has developed changes to the review process. The ISA update review will conclude following the review of the next annual updates at the end of 2008. The staff has drafted proposed changes to the NRC enforcement policy to align the policy with revisions to Title 10 of the Code of Federal Regulations, Part 70, "Domestic Licensing of Special Nuclear Material," (10 CFR Part 70). The staff is conducting public meetings with fuel cycle industry representatives to develop final comments. Enforcement policy revision will conclude when staff issues the new policy at the end of 2008. The most lengthy corrective action is the two-phase NMSS Safety Culture Project Plan. Phase I consists of information gathering, which is complete. Phase II consists of developing a strategic plan to implement the pilot, followed by implementation. The safety culture pilot will conclude when Phase II ends in August of 2009.

AUDIT OF THE NRC's BADGE ACCESS SYSTEM (OIG-07-A-10)

January 23, 2007

This audit determined whether the current badge access system meets its required operational capabilities and provides for the security, availability, and integrity of the system data.

Open Recommendations	Actions Pending
8. Write and implement badge access system operating procedures that provide system user guidance and address Recommendations 5 through 7.	The badge access system operating procedures were updated to enhance system user guidance as part of the updated manual for both the personnel security branch and the facilities security branch in November 2007. An update to Recommendation 8 is currently scheduled for December 29, 2008.
10. Replace the current visitor badges with expiring paper badges.	The NRC was unsuccessful in utilizing paper badges in the past (sticker-type badges damaged clothing or simply fell off). As part of the consulting services contract for Homeland Security Presidential Directive 12 (HSPD-12), the contractor recommended that temporary date-stamped, clip-on visitor badges could be a feasible alternative to the current permanent visitor badges. The clip-on temporary visitor badges would be date-stamped and valid only for 1 day at a time. The NRC will make the decision whether to convert to the clip-on visitor badge by June 30, 2009.
13. In accordance with NRC requirements for listed systems, develop an access system security plan, and appoint an information system security officer.	ADM received several security categorization documents for updating to newer templates, causing a delay in the process. Since ACCESS is a listed system on a fully enclosed network, the Office of Information Systems (OIS) contractor did not give this task a high priority, causing additional delay. Once approved, the staff will forward the security categorization documentation, which officially lists the Information System Security Officer for ACCESS, with the remainder of the certification and accreditation (C&A) documentation. Since ACCESS is not on the agency priority list for C&A this fiscal year, the staff should provide the C&A package for approval by March 31, 2009.
15. Complete the actions necessary to address the access weaknesses contained in the penetration test reports.	ACCESS is on a fully enclosed network environment and does not connect to any other system or the Internet. Due to other high priorities, ADM has determined that it is not cost-effective or imperative to correct the findings from the penetration tests with the current, closed network, since the implementation of HSPD-12 will result in system upgrade or replacement. Many of the findings were related to weaknesses present only if the system is connected to other systems or to the Internet. ADM will work with the CSO to ensure that CSO corrects any issues during system upgrade or replacement. The Division of Facilities and Security (DFS) will then determine a schedule to correct those actions impacting any weaknesses still in the upgraded system. An update to Recommendation 15 is currently scheduled for December 29, 2008.

AUDIT OF THE NRC'S NUCLEAR MATERIALS EVENTS DATABASE (OIG-07-A-11)

March 23, 2007

Open Recommendations	Actions Pending
1. Develop and implement written procedures for the operation of the Fuel Cycle Nuclear Material Event Database (FCNMED) to ensure that the mechanism is available for staff to share and access data on Category I fuel cycle facilities.	In January–April 2008, the staff reviewed event reports in FCNMED to identify and redact SUNSI and other sensitive information. The staff placed redacted event reports in public ADAMS on May 13, 2008. The Nuclear Materials Events Database (NMED) contractor placed them in NMED very soon after. The staff has created an automated system whereby each event report from a Category I fuel cycle facility is withheld from public disclosure until after the project staff has reviewed the report and released it in its entirety or in a redacted form. The new Idaho National Laboratory (INL) contract, which started October 1, 2008, includes the retirement of FCNMED by February 2009.
3. Conduct a quality assurance review of the FCNMED data to ensure that the database includes all pertinent data.	The staff will complete by January 12, 2009, a quality assurance review of NMED data to assure that all redacted FCNMED reports and pertinent data are available in NMED.

SUMMARY REPORT AND PERSPECTIVES ON BYPRODUCT MATERIAL SECURITY AND CONTROL (OIG-07-A-12)

March 30, 2007

While the NRC has implemented or planned a variety of measures to regulate and provide for the security of byproduct material in the post-September 11 era, the agency in its approach to byproduct material security, has not adequately identified and evaluated byproduct material security risks. Specifically, the NRC has not conducted an impartial and comprehensive look inwards at its own business and regulatory processes. Consequently, the agency is not aware of potential weaknesses and vulnerabilities in its byproduct material security program. Furthermore, the NRC's approach has resulted in agency policy and practices that do not consider the full range of potential consequences of a radiological dispersal device (RDD, or "dirty bomb").

Open Recommendations	Actions Pending
1. Convene an independent panel of experts external to the agency to identify agency vulnerabilities concerning the NRC's materials licensing and tracking programs, and to validate the agency's ongoing byproduct-material security efforts.	In September 2007, the Commission approved a comprehensive plan to address needed changes in the NRC's process for issuing licenses for radioactive sources. The plan called for an independent, external review panel to identify potential weaknesses or security gaps in the NRC's materials licensing program. The independent panel issued its report and recommendations on the NRC's materials licensing program in March 2008. The staff has incorporated the panel's recommendations into the overall corrective action plan for the materials licensing program.

AUDIT OF THE NRC'S NONCAPITALIZED PROPERTY (OIG-07-A-14)
July 12, 2007

This audit determined whether the NRC has established and implemented an effective system of management controls for maintaining accountability and control of noncapitalized property.

Open Recommendations	Actions Pending
2. Incorporate property management duties and responsibilities into all property custodian and alternate property custodian performance evaluations.	The NRC offices received the third memorandum on this subject on October 30, 2007. All offices have responded, and all but two have completed the requested action. The remaining offices are targeted to incorporate property management duties and responsibilities into all property custodian and alternate property custodian (if applicable) performance plans by October 31, 2008.
7. Modify MD 13.1, "Property Management," to reference, where applicable, MD 12.5, "NRC Automated Information Security Program," to include procedures for coordinating with OIS regarding missing property that contains or may contain personally identifiable information (PII).	Staff assigned to revise MD 13.1 have also been conducting the biennial inventory and so have been unable to dedicate sufficient time to complete the MD revision. Additional required changes to MD 13.1 were identified since the last update provided to the Office of the Inspector General on February 29, 2008 (e.g., definition of sensitive items). The staff is currently reviewing an update to MD 13.1 incorporating all the required changes. The review and incorporation of comments should conclude by August 31, 2008, at which time the offices and regions will review and comment on the MD 13.1 revision. The final approval process should conclude by February 27, 2009. The modified NRC Form 395 "Report of Property for Survey" now includes a requirement to report any missing property containing PII to the CSO. An update to Recommendation 7 is scheduled for February 27, 2009.
11. Work with the OIG to modify MD 13.1 to develop a process for notifying the OIG Assistant Inspector General for Investigations of all reports (Form 395 "Report of Property for Survey") of missing sensitive property and missing nonsensitive property with a current value of at least $1,000.	Staff has worked in collaboration with the OIG Assistant Inspector General for Investigations and has agreed to forward all completed NRC Form 395s reporting missing property with a depreciated value of $1,000 or more to his organization. The revision of MD 13.1 will include this notification process. As stated in Recommendation 7, the anticipated date for final issuance of MD 13.1 is February 27, 2009.

THE NRC'S STATUS OF RECOMMENDATIONS: AUDIT OF THE NRC'S LICENSE RENEWAL PROGRAM (OIG-07-A-15)

September 5, 2007

The Office of the Inspector General conducted an audit of the license renewal review program, and while acknowledging the existence of a comprehensive license renewal review process, the OIG identified several areas where improvements would enhance program operations and made eight recommendations. The Office of Executive Director issued a status report on September 11, 2008, which indicated Recommendations 1, 2, 5, 6, and 8 are closed, and Recommendations 3, 4, and 7 are resolved. An update of the status of the recommendations is due by February 27, 2008.

Open Recommendations	Actions Pending
3. Clarify guidance and adjust procedures for auditor's and inspector's removal of licensee-provided documents from license-renewal sites.	The license renewal staff, in a joint effort with the inspection program staff, the regions, and the Office of General Counsel developed consistent guidance for removal of applicant or licensee documents from applicant or licensee sites.
4. Establish requirements and management controls to standardize the conduct and depth of license renewal operating experience reviews.	The staff provided additional guidance and management controls to standardize the conduct and depth of license renewal operating experience reviews. The Project Manager Handbook includes enhanced guidance in "Operating Experience Review Responsibilities." All regional offices participated in a conference call to ensure consistent implementation of these expectations. The OIG will close this recommendation once additional guidance is provided to reflect management's expectations that license renewal audit teams will independently verify that the operating experience information is provided by the licensee in its application.
7. Establish a review process to determine whether or not Interim Staff Guidance (ISG) meets the provisions of 10 CFR 54.37 (b), "Additional Records and Recordkeeping Requirements," and document accordingly.	The staff continues to enhance the current guidance, "Process for Interim Guidance Development and Implementation," to determine and document whether the ISG meets the provisions of 10 CFR 54.37(b). The staff plans to issue the approved ISG by March 31, 2009.

REVIEW OF THE NRC'S PROCESS FOR PLACING DOCUMENTS IN THE ADAMS PUBLIC AND
NONPUBLIC LIBRARIES (OIG-07-A-16)
September 6, 2007

This audit determined the effectiveness and consistency with which staff profiles and processes documents for entry into the public or nonpublic ADAMS libraries.

Open Recommendations	Actions Pending
1. Update MD 3.4 so that it reflects the underlying principles of how to determine whether an official agency record should be public or nonpublic, and describes the relationship with other agency reviews for information sensitivity (e.g., personally identifiable information, SUNSI).	The staff has updated Management Directive (MD) 3.4, "Release of Information to the Public." MD 3.4 now reflects the underlying principles of how to determine if an official agency record (OAR) should be made public or remain nonpublic. It further explains the relationship with other agency reviews for information sensitivity. On May 1, 2008, the staff sent MD 3.4 to the Office of the Commission (OCM) for review and concurrence. On August 4, 2008, OIS received 10 questions on the MD. OIS provided the Office of Executive Director of Operations (EDO) with responses to the questions for review. Publication of the updated MD 3.4 is targeted for the second quarter of FY 2009.
2. Create a supplemental guidance document that is updated routinely to include, to the extent practicable, categories of information routinely not made public.	The staff has completed a supplemental guidance document titled "Guidance for Determining the Public Availability of NRC Documents," which identifies the categories of documents that are routinely not made public. Additionally, the guidance document includes the categories of information that are routinely made public. The OIS maintains the final version of this new guidance document, referenced in the revised MD 3.4 and on the NRC internal Web site at http://www.internal.nrc.gov/2008_MD-Companion-Doc.pdf. The updated MD 3.4 will require all offices to routinely monitor the guidance document and notify OIS when it requires modification. Offices will review and update the supplemental guidance document on an annual basis. Interim changes will also be accommodated.
3. After MD 3.4 and supporting guidance are updated and consolidated, conduct a training-needs analysis and develop appropriate training for staff with responsibility for determining whether ADAMS records should be publicly or non-publicly available.	OIS staff is working with the Office of Human Resources to develop appropriate training for staff with responsibility for determining whether ADAMS records should be publicly or nonpublicly available. Once the training is developed, it will become a part of the existing ADAMS training program available to staff at the Professional Development Center. Once implemented, the staff will make informed decisions when determining whether documents should be publicly or nonpublicly available. We currently estimate that the revised training courses will be available in the second quarter of FY 2009.

continued

Open Recommendations	Actions Pending
4. Develop a mechanism to indicate the rationale for designating a document as public or nonpublic. This rationale should be sufficiently detailed to allow for an assessment of whether the staff applies agency criteria correctly.	During the MD 3.4 concurrence phase, the Office of General Counsel (OGC) recommended that staff must document the rationale only for nonpublic designated documents. The OIS discussed this with Office of the Inspector General (OIG) staff and OIG agreed with the OGC recommendation. To document the rationale for nonpublic designations in the ADAMS document profile, staff must reference the appropriate item number in the "Guidance for Determining the Public Availability of NRC Documents." The rationale tag will be a permanent part of each OAR's metadata and will permit an assessment of whether agency criteria are being applied correctly. On May 1, 2008, OIS sent MD 3.4 to the Office of the Commission (OCM) for review and concurrence. On August 4, 2008, OIS received 10 questions on the MD and provided responses to the questions to the Office of the Executive Director for Operations (EDO) for review. Publication is targeted for the second quarter of FY 2009.
5. Require offices to use the mechanism developed in response to Recommendation 4 to provide the rationale for public or nonpublic designation of official agency records.	The revised MD 3.4 requires all staff to use the mechanism described in our response to Recommendation 4. Publication of the MD will communicate this to agency staff. On May 1, 2008, MD 3.4 went to the OCM for review and concurrence. On August 4, 2008, the OIS received 10 questions on the MD. The OIS provided responses to the questions to the EDO for their review. Publication is targeted for the second quarter of FY 2009.
6. Conduct periodic assessments of the accuracy with which NRC staff apply the agency's criteria for designating records as public or nonpublic by assessing a random sample of records against the agency's criteria for making these determinations.	The NRC will conduct annual assessments of the accuracy with which the staff applies the agency criteria for designating records as public or nonpublic by assessing a random sample of records against the agency criteria for making these determinations after the issuance of MD 3.4. On May 1, 2008, MD 3.4 went to the OCM for review and concurrence. On August 4, 2008, the OIS received 10 questions on the MD. The OIS provided responses to the questions to the Office of the Executive Director for Operations (EDO) for review. Publication is targeted for the second quarter of FY 2009.
8. Add a nonpublic pending review category to the electronic regulatory information distribution system (ERIDS) notifications and clarify the language in the notifications to convey the need to finalize the document availability as either public or nonpublic.	The updated ADAMS software now includes a change that clearly identifies documents with "Non-Public Pending Review" status in the ERIDS notifications sent to staff. This update, ADAMS Release 4.7, was deployed to staff in August and September 2008.

Audit of Assessment of Security at NRC Buildings in Rockville and Bethesda, MD and Las Vegas, NV (OIG-07-A-18)

September 25, 2007

These security assessments determined the adequacy of physical security and emergency planning measures of the identified NRC buildings.

Open Recommendations	Actions Pending
10. Apply Mylar film to any remaining exterior doors and windows where it has not yet been installed.	Staff prepared a statement of work and reimbursable work order on September 12, 2008, for the operation and maintenance contractor to place the additional Mylar film on any remaining exterior doors and windows. The contractor has installed Mylar film on all remaining exterior doors and windows as of October 2, 2008. The staff has completed actions related to this recommendation, pending closure by OIG.
11. Post signs near vehicle entrance directing pedestrians further west along Marinelli Avenue, and paint "Crosswalk" to direct pedestrians along a safe path to two controlled entry points.	Implementation of HSPD-12 included an overall assessment of physical access controls at the headquarters complex. An NRC consultant completed an assessment of Recommendation 11 on February 29, 2008. Based on that assessment, staff is preparing a proposed plan and cost analysis to install a security fence to enclose the rear of the complex. The fence will control pedestrian traffic entering at the P1 levels to the One White Flint North and Two White Flint North buildings. Due to the complexity of the terrain and associated easements with the NRC property, the NRC awarded an architectural and engineering contract to Oudens & Knoop on September 26, 2008. Oudens & Knoop anticipate completing the design phase of this project in 45 days. The construction phase of this project will start in the spring of 2009. Recommendation 11 is scheduled for completion on June 30, 2009.
13. Refresh and increase width of painted pedestrian walkways in garage, and add additional lighting.	Repainting the walkways and crosswalks was completed on May 30, 2008. To enhance the garage lighting in walkways and crosswalks, Administration has ordered additional, more energy-efficient LED (light-emitting diode) lights. These lights are capable of providing more lumens and will enhance lighting for pedestrians. Recommendation 13 is scheduled for completion on November 17, 2008.
21. Develop post orders for guards that specifically address contingency plans for events that may occur.	NRC staff attended a meeting with the Federal Protective Service (FPS) and the onsite guard force on May 2, 2008, to complete and update the Las Vegas Hearing Facility Guard Post Orders. *continued*

AUDIT OF ASSESSMENT OF SECURITY AT NRC BUILDINGS IN ROCKVILLE AND BETHESDA, MD AND LAS VEGAS, NV (OIG-07-A-18) *continued*

Open Recommendations	Actions Pending
23. Develop and refine operational and security plans in preparation for future public hearings.	NRC staff supported the development of an NRC Information Guide for Atomic Safety and Licensing Board Proceedings at the Las Vegas Hearing Facility. This document is in pamphlet form and will serve as an informational handout for members of the public who wish to attend an adjudicatory proceeding. The pamphlet includes requirements for entrance and screening, prohibited items, etiquette, and parking. The pamphlet was published in December 2007. As stated in the response to Recommendation 21, on May 2, 2008, the NRC has coordinated Guard Post Orders and contingency plans with FPS and the security force.
26. Develop implementing procedures for specific topics too sensitive to include in the occupant emergency plan.	As stated in the responses to Recommendations 21 and 23, administration coordinated the revised operational, security, and contingency plans with the FPS and the onsite guard force to include sensitive topics not included in the occupant emergency plan.
27. Conduct tabletop, functional, or full-scale exercises to assess ability to respond to large demonstrations, evacuations, a large influx of personnel attending hearings, media control, etc.	On June 16, 2008, the staff conducted a 4-hour table-top exercise, testing security and crisis response capabilities with Las Vegas Hearing Facility personnel, local law enforcement, and the FPS regional commander.

INDEPENDENT EVALUATION OF THE NRC'S IMPLEMENTATION OF THE FEDERAL INFORMATION
SECURITY MANAGEMENT ACT FOR FY 2007 (OIG-07-A-19)
September 28, 2007

An independent evaluation of the NRC's implementation of the Federal Information Security Management Act for FY 2007 found that the NRC information security program needed improvements.

Open Recommendation	Action Pending
1. Review and correct as needed all security categorizations so that they consistently reflect the information types that reside on the systems.	The OIG's recommendation is now part of the agency's security categorization process by reviewing current line of business or service type, subfunction or service component, and any other related mission types.
2. Categorize all NRC major applications and general support systems in accordance with Federal Information Processing Standard (FIPS) 199, "Standards for Security Categorization of Federal Information and Information Systems."	The agency has completed categorization of all major applications and general support systems in accordance with FIPS 199.
3. Conduct annual self-assessments in accordance with current Office of Management and Budget and the National Institute for Standards and Technology guidance.	The agency has completed annual control testing on all NRC-owned major applications and general support systems.
10. Develop and implement a methodology for identifying which listed systems reside on the NRC network and which do not.	The agency continues to update the system inventory database reporting tool to reflect which listed systems reside on the NRC network and which do not. The OIS works with system owners on the procedure to ensure the system database reflects changes in a timely and efficient fashion. Currently, 95 percent of our systems in inventory reflect the correct system type. The NRC is also working on restructuring its database to make reporting and data entry more efficient. Database restructuring is now complete, pending closure by OIG.
11. Develop and implement quality assurance procedures for the Plan of Action and Milestones (POA&Ms).	In addition to documenting the procedures, CSO will also undertake other steps related to improving the quality of POA&M information. This will include: • documentation of procedures for conducting independent verification and validation of POA&M to assure their adequacy as part of the security assessment review process • acquiring additional contract support to assist in establishing a compliance review process in which CSO will review security documentation, conduct vulnerability scanning, and meet with each system owner on an annual basis to verify *continued*

INDEPENDENT EVALUATION OF THE NRC'S IMPLEMENTATION OF THE FEDERAL INFORMATION
SECURITY MANAGEMENT ACT FOR FY 2007 (OIG-07-A-19) *continued*

Open Recommendation	Action Pending
11. Develop and implement quality assurance procedures for the Plan of Action and Milestones (POA&Ms). *continued*	the status of remediation efforts; to assess the comprehensiveness of planned corrective action; and to validate the accuracy of tasks, responsibilities, and milestones for each outstanding weakness. These activities will take place quarterly targeting approximately 25 percent of the overall number of POA&M. The estimated completion date is fourth quarter FY 2009.
12. Follow NIST guidance and only issue Interim Approval to Operate (IATO) with documentation that includes accurate identification of risks, risk mitigation plans, and security plans.	The NRC has implemented the change in the C&A process and has posted relevant accreditation decision process information on the project management methodology (PMM) Web site. The agency's new designated approving authority (DAA) makes a decision based on the results of the security certification package, which provides the DAA with the essential information needed to make a credible, risk-based decision for authorization to operate, interim approval to operate (IATO), or denial of authorization to operate information systems. All systems with IATO will be revisited to ensure a new procedure is followed before the issuing of IATO.
13. Develop and implement quality assurance procedures to ensure that certification and accreditation documentation is consistent with NIST guidance.	The NRC has developed an evaluation criteria checklist for three additional documents. The agency will continue to develop the evaluation checklist and will distribute the checklist to all system owners and certifying agents. The NRC is currently soliciting feedback from certifying agents and system owners on the checklist as developed so far. The NRC also plans to use contract support for reviewing and providing feedback on documents and packages to system owners.
14. Develop and implement procedures for ensuring that employees and contractors with significant IT security responsibilities are identified, that they receive security awareness and training, and that the individual and associated training are readily correlated. This recommendation replaces Recommendation 10 from OIG-05-A-21, "Independent Evaluation of NRC's Implementation of FISMA for Fiscal Year 2005."	All NRC offices have provided their identification of individuals with significant IT security responsibilities to CSO. CSO will request updates on the identification on an annual basis. CSO provided system administrators with a Microsoft Windows server security course, and 14 staff members attended the course. CSO also provided system owner training to system owners in August and September 2008. Fifty-four percent of system owners attended the course. The iLearn system will list the course, enabling others to take it. CSO is developing a role-based training plan and expects to have the plan completed by the end of the first quarter of FY 2009.

APPENDIX C
SUMMARY OF FINANCIAL
STATEMENT AUDIT AND
MANAGEMENT ASSURANCES

U.S.NRC
United States Nuclear Regulatory Commission
Protecting People and the Environment

The Enrico Fermi Nuclear Generating Station, a nuclear power plant on the shore of Lake Erie, in Frenchtown Charter Township, Monroe County, MI.

SUMMARY OF FINANCIAL STATEMENT AUDIT AND MANAGEMENT ASSURANCES

SUMMARY OF FINANCIAL STATEMENT AUDIT

Audit Opinion—Unqualified

Restatement—No

Material Weaknesses	Beginning Balance	New	Resolved	Consolidated	Ending Balance
Information Systemwide Security Controls	1	-	(1)	-	-
Total Material Weaknesses	1	-	(1)	-	-

SUMMARY OF MANAGEMENT ASSURANCES

Effectiveness of Internal Control over Financial Reporting (FMFIA § 2)

Statement of Assurance—Unqualified

There are no Material Weaknesses for Internal Control Over Financial Reporting.

Effectiveness of Internal Control over Operations (FMFIA § 2)

Statement of Assurance—Unqualified

Material Weaknesses	Beginning Balance	New	Resolved	Consolidated	Reassessed	Ending Balance
Information Systemwide Security Controls	1	-	(1)	-	-	-
Total Material Weaknesses	1	-	(1)	-	-	-

Conformance with Financial Management System Requirements (FMFIA § 4)

Statement of Assurance—Systems Conform to Financial Management System Requirements

There are no nonconformances with Financial Management System Requirements.

Compliance with Federal Financial Management Improvement Act (FFMIA)

	Agency	Auditor
Overall Substantial Compliance	No	No
1. Systems Requirements	No	No
2. Accounting Standards	Yes	Yes
3. United States Standard General Ledger at Transaction Level	Yes	Yes

Michael Johnson, front row right, Director of the Office of New Reactors, and members of his staff receive the Victoria County application from Ken Ainger, center, of Exelon.

APPENDIX D

VERIFICATION AND VALIDATION OF NRC'S MEASURES AND METRICS

U.S.NRC

United States Nuclear Regulatory Commission

Protecting People and the Environment

Arkansas Nuclear One is the only nuclear power plant in Arkansas. It is a two-unit, pressurized-water reactor located in Russellville, AR.

THE NRC'S DATA COLLECTION PROCEDURES

In the Performance and Accountability Report, the U.S. Nuclear Regulatory Commission (NRC) measures the agency's performance against its strategic goals related to safety and security. The agency obtained or derived most of the data used in this measurement from the NRC's abnormal occurrence (AO) data and from reports submitted by licensees. The agency has amended the AO criteria to ensure that the criteria are consistent with both the NRC Strategic Plan for fiscal years (FY) 2008–2013 and the NRC rulemaking on Title 10 of the *Code of Federal Regulations* (10 CFR) Part 35, "Medical Use of Byproduct Materials."

The NRC developed its AO criteria to comply with Section 208 of the Energy Reorganization Act of 1974, as amended. The Act requires the NRC to inform Congress of unscheduled incidents or events that the Commission determines to be significant to public health and safety. The agency includes events that meet the AO criteria in the yearly publication of NUREG-0090, "Report to Congress on Abnormal Occurrences." In 1997, the Commission determined NUREG-0090 should also include events that meet AO criteria that occur at Agreement State-licensed facilities. Therefore, all events, whether they occur at an Agreement State-licensed facility or an NRC-licensed or regulated facility, fall under the agency's AO criteria and reporting requirements.

Data for AOs originate from external sources, such as Agreement States and NRC licensees. The NRC has established procedures for the systematic review and evaluation of events reported by NRC licensees and Agreement State licensees. The NRC believes these data are credible for the following reasons:

(1) Regulations require that external sources, such as Agreement States and licensees, report the needed information to the NRC.

(2) The NRC maintains an aggressive inspection program that audits licensees and evaluates Agreement State programs to determine whether they are reporting information as required by regulations.

(3) The NRC has procedures for reviewing and evaluating licensees.

The NRC database systems that support this process include the Licensee Event Report Search System (LERSearch), the Accident Sequence Precursor (ASP) Database, the Nuclear Materials Event Database (NMED), and the Radiation Exposure Information Report System.

The objective of this systematic review and evaluation of licensee and Agreement State data is to identify events that are significant from the standpoint of public health and safety, based on criteria that include specific thresholds. The NRC uses a number of sources to determine the reliability and the technical accuracy of event information reported by licensees and Agreement States. Such sources include (1) NRC licensee reports, (2) NRC inspection reports, (3) Agreement State reports, (4) periodic review of Agreement State regulatory programs, (5) NRC consultant and contractor reports, and (6) U.S. Department of Energy operating experience weekly summaries. In addition, there are daily interactions and exchanges of event information between headquarters and the regional offices, as well as periodic conference calls between headquarters, the regions, and Agreement States to discuss event information. The NRC headquarters program offices, regional offices, and agency management validate and verify events that meet the AO criteria before submission of the information to Congress.

The agency action review meeting provides another opportunity for the NRC's senior management to discuss significant events, licensee performance issues, trends, and the actions the NRC needs to take to mitigate recurrences.

The NRC's computer security program maintains strict data protection. It also provides administrative, technical, and physical security measures to protect the agency's information, automated information systems, and information technology infrastructure. These measures include special safeguards to protect classified information, unclassified safeguards information, and sensitive unclassified information that are processed, stored, or produced on designated automated information systems.

STRATEGIC GOAL 1 – SAFETY

Ensure Adequate Protection of Public Health and Safety and the Environment

NUCLEAR REACTOR SAFETY

Strategic Outcomes:

- Prevent the occurrence of any nuclear reactor accidents.
- Prevent the occurrence of any inadvertent criticality events.
- Prevent the occurrence of any acute radiation exposures resulting in fatalities.
- Prevent the occurrence of any releases of radioactive materials that result in significant radiation exposures.
- Prevent the occurrence of any releases of radioactive materials that cause significant adverse environmental impacts.

VERIFICATION:

Licensees report any nuclear reactor events at their facilities in licensee event reports (LERs). Through review of LERs, the NRC staff would identify any nuclear reactor accidents, deaths from acute radiation exposures, events that result in significant radiation exposure or releases of radioactive materials that cause significant adverse environmental impacts that meet the criterion for an abnormal event. During periodic meetings, NRC's AO coordinators discuss each potential AO to determine whether it meets the AO reporting criteria. In addition, the NRC specialists periodically conduct inspections to assess licensee compliance with reporting criteria as well as radiological and environmental release criteria. If a licensee reports an event involving core damage, NRC inspectors carefully investigate the event to ensure the validity of the information in the report. Providing an additional layer of verification, an NRC-employed resident inspector monitors each reactor facility on a real-time basis. The resident inspector verifies the safe operation of the facility and is aware of any instances in which core damage has occurred or radiation has been released from the reactor in excess of reporting limits.

The NRC staff evaluates potential AO events using specific criteria. The NRC's Office of Nuclear Regulatory Research makes the final determination of which events should be recommended to the Commission as abnormal occurrences. NRC Management Directive 8.1, "Abnormal Occurrence Reporting Procedure," describes the abnormal occurrence reporting process.

VALIDATION:

Prevent the occurrence of any nuclear reactor accidents. The NRC Severe Accident Policy Statement defines nuclear reactor accidents as those events that result in substantial damage to the reactor fuel, whether or not serious offsite consequences occur.

Prevent the occurrence of any inadvertent criticality events. Events collected under this strategic outcome are actual occurrences of accidental criticality. Such events could compromise public health and safety, the environment, and the common defense and security. Events of this magnitude are rare. If such an event occurred, the NRC would conduct a prompt and thorough investigation to determine root causes and consequences of the event. The agency would also take necessary actions to mitigate the situation and prevent recurrence.

Prevent the occurrence of any acute radiation exposures resulting in fatalities. Determining whether or not any deaths result from acute radiation exposure is essential to protecting public health and safety. Events of this magnitude are rare. If such an unlikely event occurred, the NRC would conduct a prompt and thorough investigation to determine root causes and consequences of the event. The agency would also take any necessary actions to mitigate the situation and prevent recurrence. This strategic outcome measure is a direct measurement of the occurrence of radiation-related deaths at nuclear reactors.

Prevent the occurrence of any releases of radioactive materials that result in significant radiation exposures. Nuclear power generation produces radiation, a form of energy that can be harmful if not properly controlled. Measuring the number of events resulting in significant radiation exposures, as well as any deaths from radiation exposure, indicates whether radiation-related deaths and illness are being prevented. The NRC defines significant radiation exposures as those that result in unintended permanent functional damage to an organ or a physiological system. This should be determined by a physician, in accordance with Abnormal Occurrence Criterion I.A.3.

Prevent the occurrence of any releases of radioactive materials that cause significant adverse environmental impacts. The radiation produced in the process of generating power from nuclear materials can also harm the environment if it is not properly controlled. A radiation release that has the potential to adversely affect the environment is currently undefined. As a surrogate for this performance measure, the NRC collects data on the frequency with which radioactive material is released into the environment in excess of specified limits. NUREG-0090, Appendix A, Criterion I.B.1, defines such releases as those involving, "the release of radioactive material to an unrestricted area in concentrations which, if averaged over a period of 24 hours, exceed 5,000 times the values specified in Table 2 of Appendix B [Annual Limits on Intake (ALIs) and Derived Air Concentrations (DACs) of Radionuclides for Occupational Exposure; Effluent Concentrations; Concentrations for Release to Sewerage.] to 10 CFR Part 20, unless the licensee has demonstrated compliance with 20.1301 [10 CFR 20.1301, "Dose Limits for Individual Members of the Public,"] using 20.1302(b)(1) or 20.1302 (b)(2)(ii)." The essence of the criterion is that events that result in unintended permanent functional damage to an organ or a physiological system, as determined by a physician, are used as the measure for events that result in releases of radioactive material causing an adverse impact on the environment. Licensees report such events in LERs, which are sent to the NRC as reportable occurrences. This strategic outcome measure is a direct measurement of instances in which harmful impacts on the environment occur from nuclear reactors.

Performance Measures:

■ Number of new conditions evaluated as red (high safety significance) by the NRC's Reactor Oversight Process (ROP). *Reactor Safety Target: Less than or equal to 3*

VERIFICATION:

The NRC collects data for this performance measure in two ways as part of the agency's Reactor Oversight Process (ROP). The NRC inspectors collect inspection findings at least once every 3 months. Inspectors use formal, detailed inspection procedures to review plant operations and maintenance. As part of the ROP significance determination process, NRC managers review inspection findings. Licensees collect the data for performance indicators and submit them to the NRC at least once every 3 months. The significance of the data is determined by thresholds for each indicator. The NRC conducts inspections of licensees' processes for collecting and submitting the data to ensure completeness, accuracy, consistency, timeliness, and validity.

The NRC enhances the quality of its inspections through inspector feedback, periodic reviews of results, and a rigorous inspector qualification program. The quality of performance indicators is improved through continuous feedback from licensees and inspectors that is incorporated into guidance documents. The NRC publishes the inspection findings and performance indicators on the agency's Web site and incorporates feedback received from all stakeholders, as appropriate.

VALIDATION:

The inspection findings and performance indicators used by the ROP cover a broad range of plant operations and maintenance. The NRC managers review significant issues that are identified and inspectors conduct supplemental inspections of selected aspects of plant operations, as appropriate. Plants that are identified as having performance issues, as well as a self-assessment of the ROP, are reviewed by senior agency managers on an annual basis, and the results are reported to the Commission.

This measure is the number of new red inspection findings during the fiscal year plus the number of new red performance indicators during the fiscal year. Programmatic issues at multiunit sites that result in red findings for each individual unit are considered separate conditions for purposes of reporting for this measure. A red performance

indicator and a red inspection finding that are due to an issue with the same underlying causes are also considered separate conditions for purposes of reporting for this measure. Red inspection findings are included in the fiscal year in which the final significance determination was made. Red performance indicators are included in the fiscal year in which the ROP external Web page was updated to show the red indicator.

- Number of significant accident sequence precursors (ASPs) of a nuclear accident.
  Reactor Safety Target: Zero

VERIFICATION:

The Commission has an ASP program to systematically evaluate United States nuclear power plant operating experience to identify, document, and rank those operating events that were most significant in terms of the potential for inadequate core cooling and core damage (i.e., precursors). The ASP program evaluation process has five steps. First, the NRC screens operating experience data to identify events or conditions that may be potential precursors to a nuclear accident. The data the NRC evaluates include LERs from a Licensee Event Report Search System (LERSearch) database; incident investigation team or augmented inspection team reviews; the NRC's daily screening of operational events; and other events the NRC staff identifies as candidates. Second, the NRC conducts an engineering review, using specific criteria, to identify those events requiring detailed analyses as candidate precursors. Third, the NRC staff calculates a conditional core damage probability by mapping failures observed during the event to accident sequences in risk models. Fourth, the preliminary potential precursor analyses are provided to the NRC staff and the licensee for independent peer review. However, for ASP analyses of noncontroversial, low-risk precursors in which the ASP results reasonably agree with the significant determination process (SDP) results, formal peer reviews by licensees may not be performed. The NRC staff will continue to perform an in-house review process for all analyses. Lastly, the NRC provides findings from the analyses to the licensee and the public.

It must also be noted that there is a time lag in obtaining ASP analysis results since they are often based on LERs

(submitted up to 60 days after an event) and most analyses take approximately 6 months to finalize. Final data will be reported in the year in which the event occurred.

VALIDATION:

The ASP program identifies significant precursors as those events that have a 1,000 (10^{-3}) or greater probability of leading to a nuclear reactor accident. Significant accident sequence precursor events have a conditional core damage probability (CCDP) or ΔCDP of $> 1 \times 10^{-3}$.

- Number of operating reactors whose integrated performance entered the Manual Chapter 0350 process, the multiple/repetitive degraded cornerstone column, or the unacceptable performance column of the Reactor Oversight Process (ROP) Action Matrix.
  Reactor Safety Target: Less than or equal to 3

VERIFICATION:

The NRC uses the ROP to collect data for this performance measure on a continuous basis and publishes it every 3 months. NRC inspectors use detailed formal procedures to conduct inspections of licensee performance; the NRC managers review the results to ensure the completeness, accuracy, consistency, timeliness, and validity of the data.

The NRC enhances the quality of its inspections through inspector feedback, periodic reviews of results, and a rigorous inspector qualification program. The agency also improves inspection quality through continuous feedback from licensees and inspectors that is incorporated into guidance documents. The NRC publishes the data on the agency's Web site and incorporates feedback received from all stakeholders, as appropriate.

VALIDATION:

The information collected by the ROP covers a broad range of plant operations and maintenance. The NRC managers review significant issues and inspectors conduct supplemental inspections of selected aspects of plant operations, as appropriate. Plants that are identified as having performance issues are reviewed by senior agency managers on an annual basis, and the results are reported to the Commission. The same is true of the agency's self-assessment of the ROP.

This measure is the number of plants that have entered the Manual Chapter 0350 process, the multiple/repetitive degraded cornerstone column, or the unacceptable performance column during the fiscal year (i.e., were not in these columns or process the previous fiscal year). Data for this measure are obtained from the NRC external Web action matrix summary page that provides a matrix of the five columns with the plants listed within their applicable column and notes the plants in the Manual Chapter 0350 process. For reporting purposes, plants that are the subject of an approved deviation from the action matrix are included in the column or process in which they appear on the Web page.

■ Number of significant adverse trends in industry safety performance.
  Reactor Safety Target: Less than or equal to 1

VERIFICATION:

The NRC derives data for this performance measure from data supplied by all power plant licensees in LERs, from monthly operating reports, as well as from performance indicator data submitted for the ROP. These data are required by by 10 CFR 50.73, Section 50.73, "Licensee Event Report System," plant-specific technical specifications, or the ROP. Detailed NRC guidelines and procedures are in place to control each of these reporting processes. The NRC reviews these procedures for appropriateness both periodically and in response to licensee feedback. The NRC also conducts periodic inspections of licensees' processes for collecting and submitting the data to ensure completeness, accuracy, consistency, timeliness, and validity.

All licensees report the data at least once every 3 months. The NRC staff reviews all of the data and conducts inspections to verify safety significant information. The NRC also employs a contractor to review the licensee data, input them into a database, and compile them into various indicators. The agency has established quality assurance processes for

this work and included these in the statement of work for the contract. The agency controls the experience and training of key personnel through the administration of the contract. The contractor identifies discrepancies to both licensees and the NRC for resolution. The NRC reviews the indicators and publishes them on the agency's Web site on a quarterly basis. When appropriate, the agency also incorporates feedback from licensees and the public.

The NRC sets the target value based on the expected addition of several indicators and a change in the long-term trending methodology.

VALIDATION:

The data and indicators that support reporting against this performance measure provide a broad range of information on nuclear power plant performance. The NRC staff tracks indicators and applies statistical techniques to provide an indication of whether industry performance is improving, remaining steady, or degrading over time. If the staff identifies any adverse trends, the NRC addresses the problem through its processes for addressing generic safety issues and issuing generic communications to licensees. The NRC is developing additional, risk-informed indicators to enhance the current set of indicators. In doing so, the staff considers the costs and benefits of collecting the data through ongoing, extensive interactions with industry regarding the indicators. The Industry Trends Program is reviewed by senior agency managers on an annual basis, and the staff reports the results to the Commission.

■ Number of events with radiation exposures to the public and occupational workers from nuclear reactors that exceed Abnormal Occurrence Criteria I.A.
  Reactor Safety Target: Zero

VERIFICATION:

Licensees report overexposures through the Sequence Coding and Search System (SCSS) LER database. The Oak Ridge National Laboratory maintains the database by receiving all LERs and coding them into the searchable database. The SCSS LER database is used to identify those

LERs that report overexposures. The NRC resident inspectors stationed at each nuclear power plant provide a high degree of assurance that plants do, in fact, report all events that meet reporting criteria. In addition, the NRC conducts inspections if there is any indication that an exposure exceeded, or could have exceeded, a regulatory limit. Finally, areas of the facility that may be subject to radiation contamination have monitors that record radiation levels. These monitors would immediately reveal any instances of high levels of radiation exposure.

VALIDATION:

Overexposure to radiation is a potential danger from the operation of nuclear power plants. Such exposure to radiation in excess of the applicable regulatory limits may potentially occur through either a nuclear accident or other malfunctions at the plant. Consequently, tracking the number of overexposures that occur at nuclear reactors is an important indicator of the degree to which safety is being maintained.

■ Number of radiological releases to the environment from nuclear reactors that exceed applicable regulatory limits.

Reactor Safety Target: 0

VERIFICATION:

As with worker overexposures, licensees report environmental releases of radioactive materials that are in excess of regulations or license conditions through the SCSS LER database maintained at the Oak Ridge National Laboratory. The NRC uses the SCSS database to identify those LERs reporting releases and applies the number of reported releases to this measure. The NRC also conducts periodic inspections of licensees to ensure that they properly monitor and control releases to the environment through effluent pathways. In addition, onsite monitors record any instances in which the plant releases radiation into the environment. If the inspections or the monitors reveal any indication of an accident or an inadvertent release, the NRC conducts followup inspections.

VALIDATION:

The generation of nuclear power creates radioactive materials. Nuclear power plants release these radioactive materials into the environment in a strictly controlled manner. The NRC has established regulatory controls that limit the amount of radioactive material released and the resultant dose to members of the public. Because releases in excess of regulatory limits have the potential to endanger public safety and harm the environment, the NRC tracks all releases of radioactive materials. The NRC inspects every nuclear power plant for compliance with regulatory requirements and specific license conditions related to radioactive releases. If the licensee violates regulations or license conditions, the inspection program includes escalating enforcement actions based on the severity of the event.

This performance measure includes dose values that are classified as being as low as reasonably achievable (ALARA), contained in 10 CFR Part 50, Appendix I, "Numerical Guides for Design Objectives and Limiting Conditions for Operation to Meet the Criterion 'As Low as is Reasonably Achievable' for Radioactive Material in Light-Water-Cooled Nuclear Power Reactor Effluents," as well as the public dose limits contained in 10 CFR Part 20, "Standards for Protection Against Radiation." Because the performance measure includes ALARA values, which are not safety limits, and because Appendix I to 10 CFR Part 50 allows licensees to temporarily exceed, for good reason, the ALARA dose values, the performance measure is set to 2.

STRATEGIC GOAL 1–SAFETY

Ensure Adequate Protection of Public Health and Safety and the Environment

NUCLEAR MATERIALS AND WASTE SAFETY

Strategic Outcomes:

■ Prevent the occurrence of any inadvertent criticality events.

■ Prevent the occurrence of any acute radiation exposures resulting in fatalities.

- Prevent the occurrence of any releases of radioactive materials that result in significant radiation exposures.

- Prevent the occurrence of any releases of radioactive materials that cause significant adverse environmental impacts.

VERIFICATION:

Prevent the occurrence of any inadvertent criticality events. Inadvertent criticality events must be reported, regardless of whether they result in exposures or injuries to workers or the public, and regardless of whether they result in adverse impacts to the environment. Licensees immediately report criticality events to the NRC Headquarters Operations Center by telephone through the cognizant licensee safety officer. The licensee must submit followup written reports to the NRC within 30 days of the initial report. The written report must contain specific information concerning the event, as specified by 10 CFR 70.50(c)(2) and 10 CFR 76.120(d)(2). The NRC then dispatches an inspection team to confirm the reliability of the data. The agency also tracks the event through the Nuclear Materials Event Database (NMED). The NRC would immediately investigate an event of this nature. Should an event meeting this threshold occur, it would be reported to the NRC through a number of sources but primarily through required licensee notifications. These events are summarized in event notifications and preliminary notifications, which are used to widely disseminate the information to internal and external stakeholders.

The fuel facilities, materials, high-level waste repository, decommissioning, and spent fuel storage and transportation inspection programs are key elements in verifying the completeness and accuracy of licensee reports. The integrated materials performance evaluation program (IMPEP) also provides a mechanism to verify that NRC regions are consistently and properly collecting and reporting events received from the licensees, and entering them into NMED.

The NRC has taken a number of steps to improve the timeliness and completeness of materials event data. These steps include assessment of the NMED data during monthly staff reviews, emphasis and analysis during the IMPEP reviews, NMED training in headquarters, the regions, and Agreement States, and discussions at all meetings of Agreement States and of the conference of radiation control program directors (CRCPD).

VALIDATION:

Events collected under this strategic outcome are actual occurrences of accidental criticality. Such events could compromise public health and safety, the environment, and the common defense and security. Events of this magnitude are rare. If such an event occurred, it would result in prompt and thorough investigation to determine root causes, consequences, and actions that would mitigate the situation and prevent recurrence. Therefore, the strategic outcome of "no inadvertent criticalities" represents a valid measure of whether the NRC has ensured the adequate protection of public health and safety.

In assessing the validity of the data being collected as appropriate for the strategic outcome, the staff has determined that there is a logical relationship between the data collected and the strategic outcome. Given the magnitude and rarity of a criticality event, the NRC believes the probability that it would not be aware of an inadvertent criticality is very small.

VERIFICATION:

Prevent the occurrence of any acute radiation exposures resulting in fatalities. Determining whether or not a death resulted from acute radiation exposure is essential to the protection of public health and safety. Should an event meeting this threshold occur, it would be reported to the NRC, the Agreement State, or both through a number of sources but primarily through required licensee notifications. These events are summarized in event notifications and preliminary notifications, which are used to widely disseminate the information to internal and external stakeholders.

The fuel facilities, materials, high-level waste repository, decommissioning, and spent fuel storage and transportation inspection programs are key elements in verifying the completeness and accuracy of licensee reports. The IMPEP also provides a mechanism to verify that Agreement States and NRC regions are consistently collecting and reporting events received from the licensees, and entering them into NMED.

The NRC has taken a number of steps to improve the timeliness and completeness of materials event data. These steps include assessment of the NMED data during monthly staff reviews, emphasis and analysis during the IMPEP reviews, NMED training in headquarters, the regions, and Agreement States, and discussions at all Agreement States and conference of radiation control program directors (CRCPD) meetings.

VALIDATION:

The NRC had designed its regulatory process (including licensing, inspection, guidance, regulations, and enforcement activities) to ensure that there are no fatalities caused by acute radiation exposure. In the unlikely event that a death should occur, NRC or Agreement State technical specialists, with input from expert consultants, will decide whether the cause of a death is acute radiation exposure or exposure to other radioactive hazardous materials (for fuel cycle activities, this extends to other hazardous materials used with, or produced from, licensed material, consistent with 10 CFR Part 70, "Domestic Licensing of Special Nuclear Material").

NRC believes the data collected to meet this strategic outcome are free from bias. NRC does not use statistical sampling of data to determine results. Rather, the agency reviews all events data to determine if it has met the strategic outcome. Two important data limitations in determining this strategic outcome are (1) delay time for receiving information and (2) failure of NRC to become aware of an event that results in a fatality. To address the first limitation, NRC regulations and procedures associated with event reporting include specific requirements for timely notifications; however, there is a lag time separating the occurrence of an event and the known consequences of an event.

On the second limitation, the NRC believes the probability that it would not be aware of a fatality caused by acute radiation exposure is very small. Periodic licensee inspections and regulatory reporting requirements are sufficient to ensure that the agency would be aware of an event of this magnitude.

If such an event occurred, it would result in a prompt and thorough investigation of the event to determine its root causes and consequences as well as actions that would mitigate the situation and prevent recurrence. In addition to these immediate actions, the NRC holds periodic meetings where staff and management review events that appear to meet this strategic outcome.

VERIFICATION:

Prevent the occurrence of any releases of radioactive materials that result in significant radiation exposures. The NRC defines this strategic outcome as any discharge or dispersal of radioactive materials from the intended place of confinement, or discharge or dispersal of radioactive wastes during storage, transport, or disposal, which causes significant radiation exposures to a member of the public or an occupational worker. A significant radiation exposure is one that directly results in unintended permanent functional damage to an organ or physiological system, as determined by a physician, in accordance with AO Criterion I.A.3. (This metric does not include exposures from sealed sources. Exposure from sealed sources would be counted under the performance measure, "Number of events with radiation exposures to the public and occupational workers from radioactive material that exceed AO Criterion I.A.")

Should an event meeting this threshold occur, it would be reported to the NRC, the Agreement State, or both through a number of sources but primarily through required licensee notifications. These events are summarized in event notifications and preliminary notifications, which are used to widely disseminate the information to internal and external stakeholders. The NMED is an essential system for the NRC Office .... (NMSS) and Office... (FSME) to collect information on such events.

The fuel facilities, materials, high-level waste repository, decommissioning, and spent fuel storage and transportation inspection programs are key elements in verifying the completeness and accuracy of licensee reports. The IMPEP also provides a mechanism to verify that Agreement States and NRC regions are consistently collecting and reporting events received from the licensees, and entering them into NMED.

The NRC has taken a number of steps to improve the timeliness and completeness of materials event data. These steps include assessment of the NMED data during monthly staff reviews, emphasis and analysis during the IMPEP reviews, NMED training in headquarters, the regions and Agreement States, and discussions at all Agreement State and CRCPD meetings.

VALIDATION:

Significant radiation exposures are exposures that result in unintended permanent functional damage to an organ or a physiological system, as determined by a physician, in accordance with AO Criterion I.A.3. Events of this magnitude are rare. In the unlikely event that a significant exposure should occur, NRC or Agreement State technical specialists, with input from expert consultants, decide if the permanent functional damage is caused by conditions related to acute radiation exposures or exposure to other radioactive hazardous materials (for fuel cycle activities, this extends to other hazardous materials used with, or produced from, licensed material, consistent with consistent with 10 CFR Part 70, "Domestic Licensing of Special Nuclear Material").

NRC does not use statistical sampling of data to determine results. Rather, the agency reviews all event data to determine if the strategic outcome has been met. Two important data limitations in determining this strategic outcome are (1) delay time for receiving information and (2) failure of NRC to become aware of an event that results in a fatality. To address the first limitation, the NRC regulations and procedures associated with event reporting include specific requirements for timely notifications; however, there is a lag time separating the occurrence of an event and the known consequences of an event. On the second limitation, NRC believes the probability that it would not be aware of a fatality due to acute radiation exposure is very small. Periodic licensee inspections and regulatory reporting requirements are sufficient to ensure that the agency would be aware of an event of this magnitude.

If such an event occurred, it would result in a prompt and thorough investigation to determine root causes, consequences, and actions that would mitigate the situation and prevent recurrence. In addition to these immediate actions, the NRC holds periodic meetings, where staff and management review events that appear to meet this strategic outcome.

VERIFICATION:

Prevent the occurrence of any releases of radioactive materials that cause significant adverse environmental impacts. Releases that have the potential to cause adverse environmental impact are currently undefined. As a surrogate, we will use any discharge or dispersal of radioactive materials from the intended place of confinement or discharge or dispersal of radioactive wastes during storage, transport, or disposal that exceeds the limits for reporting abnormal occurrences as given in Abnormal Occurrence Criterion 1.B.1.

Should an event meeting this threshold occur, it would be reported to the NRC, the Agreement State, or both through a number of sources but primarily through required licensee notifications. These events are summarized in event notifications and preliminary notifications, which are used to widely disseminate the information to internal and external stakeholders.

The fuel facilities, materials, high-level waste repository, decommissioning, and spent fuel storage and transportation inspection programs are key elements in verifying the completeness and accuracy of licensee reports. The IMPEP also provides a mechanism to verify that Agreement States and NRC regions are consistently collecting and report events received from the licensees and entering them into NMED.

The NRC has taken a number of steps to improve the timeliness and completeness of materials event data. These steps include assessment of the NMED data during monthly staff reviews, emphasis and analysis during the IMPEP reviews, NMED training in headquarters, the regions, and Agreement States, and discussions at all Agreement State and CRCPD meetings.

U.S.NRC
United States Nuclear Regulatory Commission
Protecting People and the Environment

VALIDATION:

Releases that have the potential to cause an adverse environmental impact are those that exceed the limits for reporting abnormal occurrences as given by AO Criterion 1.B.1. The NRC has designed its regulatory process (including licensing, inspection, guidance, regulations, and enforcement activities) to ensure that there are no releases of radioactive materials that cause significant adverse environmental impacts.

Events of this magnitude are rare. In the unlikely event of a release of radioactive materials (for fuel cycle activities, this extends to other hazardous materials used with, or produced from, licensed material, consistent with 10 CFR Part 70), NRC and Agreement State technical experts, with possible input from expert consultants, decide whether the release caused a significant adverse environmental impact.

The NRC does not look at statistical sampling of data to determine results. Rather, the agency reviews all event data to determine if the strategic outcome has been met. Two important data limitations in determining this strategic outcome are (1) delay time for receiving information and (2) failure of NRC to become aware of an event that results in a fatality. To address the first limitation, NRC regulations and procedures associated with event reporting include specific requirements for timely notifications; however, there is a lag time separating the occurrence of an event and the known consequences of an event. On the second limitation, the NRC believes the probability that it would not be aware of a fatality caused by acute radiation exposure is very small. Periodic licensee inspections and regulatory reporting requirements are sufficient to ensure that the agency would be aware of an event of this magnitude.

If such an event occurred, the NRC would promptly investigate the event to determine its root causes, consequences, and actions that would mitigate the situation and prevent recurrence. In addition to these immediate actions, the NRC holds periodic meetings, where staff and management review events that appear to meet this strategic outcome.

Performance Measures:

- Number of events with radiation exposures to the public or occupational workers from radioactive material that exceed AO Criteria 1.A.
  Materials Safety Target: Less than or equal to 2
  Waste Safety Target: Zero

VERIFICATION:

This performance measure includes any event involving licensed radioactive materials that results in significant radiation exposures to members of the public or occupational workers that exceed the dose limits of the AO reporting criteria. The NRC defines significant radiation exposure as exposure that results in unintended permanent functional damage to an organ or a physiological system, as determined by a physician, according to AO Criterion 1.A. However, this excepts some medical applications of radioactive materials that involve the intentional application of extremely high doses of radioactive materials.

Should an event meeting this threshold occur, it would be reported to the NRC, the Agreement State, or both through a number of sources, but primarily through required licensee notifications. These events are summarized in event notifications and preliminary notifications, which are used to widely disseminate the information to internal and external stakeholders.

The fuel facilities, materials, high-level waste repository, decommissioning, and spent fuel storage and transportation, inspection programs are key elements in verifying the completeness and accuracy of licensee reports. The IMPEP also provides a mechanism to verify that Agreement States and NRC regions consistently collect and report such events and enter them into NMED.

The NRC has taken a number of steps to improve the timeliness and completeness of materials event data. These steps include assessment of the NMED data during monthly staff reviews; emphasis and analysis during the IMPEP reviews; NMED training in headquarters, the regions, and Agreement States; and discussions at all Agreement State and CRCPD meetings.

VALIDATION:

There is a logical basis for using events involving radiation exposures that exceed AO Criteria I.A. as a performance measure for ensuring the protection of public health and safety. The NRC considers an event an abnormal occurrence if it significantly impacts public health or safety. The NRC has designed its regulatory process (including licensing, inspection, guidance, regulations, and enforcement activities) to mitigate the likelihood of an event that would exceed AO Criteria I.A.

Events of this magnitude are rare. In the unlikely event that an abnormal occurrence should occur, NRC or Agreement State technical specialists will confirm whether the criteria were met, with input provided by expert consultants, as necessary.

The NRC does not use statistical sampling of data to determine results. Rather, the agency reviews all event data to determine if the performance measure has been met. Two important data limitations in determining this strategic outcome are (1) delay time for receiving information and (2) failure of NRC to become aware of an event that results in a fatality. To address the first limitation, NMSS and FSME procedures and NRC regulations associated with event reporting include specific requirements for timely notifications; however, there is a lag time separating the occurrence of an event and the known consequences of an event.

On the second limitation, the probability of the NRC being unaware of a fatality caused by acute radiation exposure is very small. Periodic licensee inspections and regulatory reporting requirements are sufficient to ensure that the agency would be aware of an event of this magnitude. If such an event occurred, the NRC would promptly and thoroughly investigate the event to determine its root causes, consequences, and actions to mitigate the situation and prevent recurrence. In addition to these immediate actions, the NRC holds periodic meetings where staff and management validate the occurrence of these events.

■ Number of radiological releases to the environment that exceed applicable regulatory limits.
Materials Safety Target: Less than or equal to 2
Waste Safety Target: Zero

VERIFICATION:

This performance measure is defined as a radiological release to the environment from any of the following activities: fuel facilities process and fabrication, nuclear materials licensing, high-level waste repository licensing, decommissioning, spent fuel storage and transportation, as well as other activities that exceed applicable regulations as defined in 10 CFR 20.2203(a)(3). A 30-day written report is required on such releases. The nuclear materials safety performance measure target is to have no more than five releases a year that meet these reporting criteria. The nuclear waste safety target is to have no releases that meet the reporting criteria.

Should an event meeting this threshold occur, it would be reported to the NRC, the Agreement State, or both through a number of sources but primarily through required licensee notifications. These events are summarized in event notifications and preliminary notifications, which are used to widely disseminate the information to internal and external stakeholders.

The fuel facilities, materials, high-level waste repository, decommissioning, and spent fuel storage and transportation inspection programs are key elements in verifying the completeness and accuracy of licensee reports. The IMPEP also provides a mechanism to verify that Agreement States and NRC regions are consistently collecting and reporting events received from the licensees and entering them into NMED.

The NRC has taken a number of steps to improve the timeliness and completeness of materials event data. These steps include assessment of the NMED data during monthly staff reviews; emphasis and analysis during the IMPEP reviews; NMED training in headquarters, the regions, and Agreement States; and discussions at all Agreement State and CRCPD meetings.

VALIDATION:

The regulations in 10 CFR Part 20 provide standards for protection against radiation. There is a logical basis for tracking releases subject to the 30-day reporting requirement under 10 CFR 20.2203(a)(3)(ii) as a performance measure for ensuring the protection of the environment. The NRC designed its regulatory process (including licensing, inspection, guidance, regulations, and enforcement activities) to ensure that releases of radioactive materials that exceed regulatory limits are infrequent.

In the unlikely event that a release to the environment exceeds regulatory limits, NRC or Agreement State technical specialists, with input from expert consultants, will confirm whether the criteria were met.

The NRC does not look at statistical sampling of data to determine results. Rather, the agency reviews all event data to determine if the strategic outcome has been met. Two important data limitations in determining this strategic outcome are (1) delay time for receiving information and (2) failure of NRC to become aware of an event that results in a fatality. To address the first limitation, NMSS and FSME procedures and NRC regulations associated with event reporting include specific requirements for timely notifications; however, there is a lag time separating the occurrence of an event and the known consequences of an event.

On the second limitation, it is unlikely that the NRC would be unaware of a fatality caused by acute radiation exposure. Periodic licensee inspections and regulatory reporting requirements are sufficient to ensure that the agency would be aware of an event of this magnitude.

If such an event occurred, the NRC would promptly investigate the event to determine its root causes, consequences, and actions that would mitigate the situation and prevent recurrence. In addition to these immediate actions, the NRC holds periodic meetings where staff and management review events that appear to meet this strategic outcome.

STRATEGIC GOAL 2 – SECURITY

Ensure the secure use and management of radioactive materials

Strategic Outcome:

- Prevent instances where licensed radioactive materials are used domestically in a manner hostile to the security of the United States.

Performance Measures:

- Unrecovered losses or thefts of risk-significant radioactive sources are 0.

Under AO Criterion I.C.1, the agency counts any unrecovered lost, stolen, or abandoned sources that exceed the values listed in 10 CFR Part 110, Appendix P, "Category 1 and 2 Radioactive Material." Excluded from reporting under this criterion are events involving sources that are lost, stolen, or abandoned under the following conditions:

(1) Sources abandoned in accordance with the requirements of 10 CFR 39.77(c).

(2) Sealed sources contained in labeled, rugged source housing.

(3) Recovered sources with sufficient indication that doses in excess of the reporting thresholds specified in AO Criteria I.A.1 and I.A.2 did not occur during the time the source was missing.

(4) Unrecoverable sources lost under such conditions that doses in excess of the reporting thresholds specified in AO Criteria I.A.1 and I.A.2 were not known to have occurred.

(5) Other sources that are lost or abandoned and declared unrecoverable; for which the agency has determined that the risk-significance of the source is low based on the location (e.g., water depth) or physical characteristics (e.g., half-life, housing) of the source and its surroundings; where all reasonable efforts have been made to recover the source; and where it has been determined that the source is not recoverable and would not be considered a realistic safety or security risk under this measure.

VERIFICATION:

Losses or thefts of radioactive materials that are greater than or equal to 1,000 times the quantity specified in 10 CFR Part 20, Appendix C, "Quantities of Licensed Material Requiring Labeling," must be reported (following the guidelines of 10 CFR 20.2201(a)) by telephone to the NRC Headquarters Operations Center or Agreement State immediately (within 4 hours) if the licensee believes that an exposure could result to persons in unrestricted areas. If an event meeting the thresholds described above occurs, it would be reported through a number of sources but primarily through this required licensee notification. Events that are publicly available are then entered and tracked in NMED, which is an essential system used to collect and store information on such events. Separate methods are used to track events that are not publicly available. Additionally, licensees must meet the reporting and accounting requirements in 10 CFR Part 73, "Physical Protection of Plants and Materials," and 10 CFR Part 74, "Material Control and Accounting of Special Nuclear Material."

The NRC's inspection programs are key elements in verifying the completeness and accuracy of licensee reports. The IMPEP also provides a mechanism to verify that Agreement States and NRC regions are consistently collecting and reporting events received from the licensees and are entering these events in NMED. In some cases, upon receiving a report, the NRC or Agreement State initiates an independent investigation that verifies the reliability of the reported information.

The regulation in 10 CFR 20.2201(b) requires a a written report within 30 days for lost or stolen sources that are greater than or equal to 10 times the quantity specified in Appendix C to 10 CFR Part 20 if the source is still missing at that time. In addition, 10 CFR 20.2201(d) requires a second written report within 30 days of a licensee learning any additional substantive information. The NRC interprets this requirement as including reporting the recovery of sources.

The NRC issued guidance in the form of a regulatory issue summary (RIS 2005-21, "Clarification of the Report Requirements in 10 CFR 20.2201") to clarify the current 10 CFR 20.2201(d) requirement for reporting the recovery of a risk-significant source. FSME will ask the Agreement States to send copies of the RIS (or equivalent document) to their licensees. The NRC issued the National Source Tracking System final rule in November 2006. Implementation of this system will create and maintain an inventory of risk-significant sources. This rulemaking codifies and clarifies reporting requirements for risk-significant sources (including reporting timeframes) by adding specific requirements to 10 CFR 20.2201, "Reports of Theft or Loss of Licensed Material," for risk-significant sources, including a requirement for licensees to report the recovery of a risk-significant source within 30 days of recovery. In conjunction with this rulemaking, FSME will modify its Procedure SA-300 to specifically require Agreement States to report the recovery of a risk-significant source to the NRC Headquarters Operations Center immediately after being notified by a licensee.

VALIDATION:

Events collected under this performance measure are actual losses, thefts, or diversions of materials described above. Such events could compromise public health and safety, the environment, and the common defense and security. Events of this magnitude are expected to be rare. The information reported under 10 CFR Part 73 and 10 CFR Part 74 is required so that the NRC is aware of events that could endanger public health and safety or national security. Any failures at the level of the strategic plan would result in immediate investigation.

If an event subject to the reporting requirements described above occurs, the NRC would promptly and thoroughly investigate of the event to determine root causes, consequences, and actions to mitigate the situation and prevent recurrence.

■ Number of substantiated cases of actual theft or diversion of licensed risk-significant radioactive sources or a formula quantity of special nuclear material or number of acts that result in radiological sabotage is 0.

VERIFICATION:

In AO Criterion I.C.2, a "substantiated" case means a situation that requires additional action by the agency or other proper authorities because of an indication of loss, theft, or unlawful diversion that cannot be refuted following an investigation. Such a situation might include an allegation of diversion, a report of lost or stolen material, a statistical processing difference, or other indication of loss of material control or accountability. Section 70.4, "Definitions," of 10 CFR defines a "formula quantity of special nuclear material." Radiological sabotage is defined in 10 CFR 73.2, "Definitions." Within 1 hour of an occurrence, licensees subject to the requirements of 10 CFR Part 73 must call the NRC to report any breaches of security or other event that may potentially lead to theft or diversion of material or to sabotage at a nuclear facility. The NRC's safeguards requirements are described in 10 CFR 73.71, "Reporting of Safeguards Events"; 10 CFR Part 73, Appendix G, "Reportable Safeguards Events"; and 10 CFR 74.11, "Reports of Loss or Theft or Attempted Theft or Unauthorized Production of Special Nuclear Material." An information assessment team composed of NRC headquarters and regional staff members would immediately assess any significant events to determine further actions such as coordination with the intelligence community and law enforcement. In accordance with 10 CFR 73.71(d), the licensee must also file a written report within 60 days of the incident, describing the event and the steps that the licensee took to protect the nuclear facility. This information will enable the NRC to adequately assess whether radiological sabotage has occurred.

VALIDATION:

Events subject to reporting requirements are those that endanger the public health and safety and the environment through deliberate acts of theft or diversion of material or through sabotage directed against the nuclear facilities that the agency licenses. Events of this type are extremely rare. If such an event occurs, it would result in a prompt and thorough investigation of the event to determine root causes, consequences, and actions to mitigate the situation

and prevent recurrence. The investigation both ensures the validity of the information and assesses the significance of the event.

■ Number of substantiated losses of a formula quantity of special nuclear material or substantiated inventory discrepancies of a formula quantity of special nuclear material that are judged to be significant relative to normally expected performance or regulatory limits and that are judged to be caused by theft or diversion or substantial breakdown of the accountability system is 0.

VERIFICATION:

Licensees must record events associated with AO Criterion I.C.3 within 24 hours of the identified event in a safeguards log maintained by the licensee. The licensee must retain the log as a record for 3 years after the last entry is made or until termination of the license. The NRC relies on its safeguards inspection program to ensure the reliability of recorded data. The NRC makes a determination of whether a substantiated breakdown has resulted in a vulnerability to radiological sabotage, theft, diversion, or unauthorized enrichment of special nuclear material. When making substantiated breakdown determinations, the NRC evaluates the materials event data to ensure that licensees are reporting and collecting the proper event data.

VALIDATION:

"Substantiated" means a situation that requires additional action by the agency or other proper authorities because of an indication of loss, theft, or unlawful diversion that cannot be refuted following an investigation. Such a situation may include an allegation of diversion, a report of lost or stolen material, a statistical processing difference, a system breakdown closely related to the material control and accounting program (such as an item control system associated with the licensee's facility information technology system), or other indication of loss of material control or accountability. Section 70.4 of 10 CFR defines a formula quantity of special nuclear material. Events collected under this performance measure may indicate a vulnerability to radiological sabotage, theft, diversion, or loss of special nuclear materials. Such events could compromise public health and safety, the environment, and the common defense and security. The NRC relies on its safeguards inspection program to help validate the reliability of recorded data and determine whether a breakdown of a physical protection or material control and accounting system has actually resulted in vulnerability.

■ Number of substantial breakdowns of physical security or material control (i.e., access control containment or accountability systems) that significantly weaken the protection against theft, diversion, or sabotage is 0.

VERIFICATION:

AO Criterion I.C.4 defines "substantial breakdown" as a red finding in the security oversight program or significant performance problems and operational events resulting in a determination of overall unacceptable performance or in a shutdown condition (inimical to the effective functioning of the Nation's critical infrastructure). Radiological sabotage is defined in 10 CFR 73.2. Immediately after a known occurrence, the NRC requires licensees to report any known breakdowns of physical security, based on the requirements in 10 CFR 73.71 and Appendix G to 10 CFR Part 73. If a licensee reports such an event, the headquarters operations officer prepares an official record of the initial event report. Upon notification of such an event, the NRC immediately begins responding with the activation of its information assessment team. A licensee must follow its initial telephone notification with a written report submitted to the NRC within 30 days.

The licensee maintains a safeguards log in which it records breakdowns of physical protection resulting in a vulnerability to radiological sabotage, theft, diversion, or loss of special nuclear materials or radioactive waste within 24 hours in a safeguards log maintained by the licensee. The licensee must retain the log as a record for 3 years after the last entry is made or until termination of the license. Licensees subject to 10 CFR Part 73 must also meet the reporting

requirements detailed in 10 CFR 73.71. The NRC evaluates all of the reported events, based on the criteria in 10 CFR 73.71 and Appendix G to 10 CFR Part 73. The NRC also maintains and relies on its safeguards inspection program to ensure the reliability of recorded and reported data.

VALIDATION:

Events assessed under this performance measure are those that threaten nuclear activities by deliberate acts, such as radiological sabotage, directed against facilities. If a licensee reports such an event, the information assessment team evaluates and validates the initial report and determines any further actions that may be necessary. Tracking breakdowns of physical security indicates whether the licensee is taking the necessary security precautions to protect the public, given the potential consequences of a nuclear accident attributable to sabotage or the inappropriate use of nuclear material either in this country or abroad.

Events collected under this performance measure may indicate a vulnerability to radiological sabotage, theft, diversion, or loss of special nuclear materials or radioactive waste. Such events could compromise public health and safety, the environment, and the common defense and security. The NRC relies on its safeguards inspection program to help validate the reliability of recorded data and determine whether a breakdown of a physical protection or material control and accounting system has actually resulted in a vulnerability.

■ Number of significant unauthorized disclosures (loss, theft, or deliberate acts) of classified or safeguards information is 0.

VERIFICATION:

With regard to AO Criterion I.C.5, any alleged or suspected violations by NRC licensees of the Atomic Energy Act, Espionage Act, or other Federal statutes related to classified or safeguards information must be reported to the NRC under the requirements of 10 CFR 95.57(a) (for classified information), 10 CFR Part 73 (for safeguards

information), and NRC orders (for safeguards information subject to modified handling requirements). However, for performance reporting, the NRC would only count those disclosures or compromises that actually cause damage to the national security or to public health and safety. Such events would be reported to the cognizant security agency (i.e., the security agency with jurisdiction) and the regional administrator of the appropriate NRC regional office, as listed in Appendix A, "U.S. Nuclear Regulatory Commission Offices and Classified Mailing Addresses," to 10 CFR Part 73. The regional administrator would then contact the Division of Security Operations at NRC headquarters, which would assess the violation and notify other NRC offices and other Government agencies, as appropriate. A determination would be made as to whether the compromise damaged the national security or public health and safety. The NRC would immediately investigate any unauthorized disclosures or compromises of classified or safeguards information that damaged the national security or public health and safety. In addition, NRC inspections will verify that licensees' routine handling of classified and safeguards information (including safeguards information subject to modified handling requirements) conforms to established security information management requirements.

Any alleged or suspected violations of this performance measure by NRC employees, contractors, or other personnel would be reported in accordance with NRC procedures to the Director of Division of Facilities and Security at NRC headquarters. The NRC maintains a strong system of controls over national security and safeguards information, including (1) annual required training for all employees, (2) safe and secure document storage, and (3) physical access control in the form of guards and badged access.

Validation:

Events collected under this performance measure are unauthorized disclosures of classified or safeguards information that damage the national security or public health and safety. Events of this magnitude are rare. If such an event occurs, the NRC would promptly investigate to

determine root causes, consequences, and actions to mitigate the situation and prevent recurrence. The NRC investigation teams also validate the materials event data to ensure that licensees are reporting and collecting the proper data.

ORGANIZATIONAL EXCELLENCE OBJECTIVE 1 – OPENNESS

Ensure openness in our regulatory process

Performance Measure:

- Percentage of selected openness output measures that achieve performance targets is equal to or greater than 88 percent.

Verification:

The NRC views nuclear regulation as the public's business. Nuclear regulation should be transacted openly and candidly to maintain the public's confidence. The goal to ensure openness explicitly recognizes that the public must be informed about, and have a reasonable opportunity to participate meaningfully in, the NRC's regulatory processes. In assessing how the NRC will gauge its openness with its stakeholders, the NRC will (1) provide accurate and timely information to the public about the uses and risks of radioactive materials; (2) enhance the awareness of the NRC's independent role in protecting public health and safety and the environment; (3) provide accurate and timely information about the safety performance of the licensees regulated by the NRC; (4) provide a fair and timely process to allow public involvement in NRC decisionmaking in matters not involving sensitive unclassified, safeguards, classified, or proprietary information; (5) provide a fair and timely process to allow authorized (appropriately cleared with a need to know) stakeholders to participate in NRC decisionmaking in matters involving sensitive unclassified, safeguards, classified, or proprietary information; and (6) obtain early public involvement on issues most likely to generate substantial interest and promote two-way communication to enhance public confidence in the NRC's regulatory processes.

VALIDATION:

The NRC will measure overall actual performance by determining the percentage of the associated output measures that delivered their intended openness outcome. At a minimum, to meet the overall target, the agency must meet 8 percent of the output measure targets.

The process of collecting the data and making sure the information is complete, accurate, and consistent will be the responsibility of the individual office director who will review and approve the data submitted by staff.

ORGANIZATIONAL EXCELLENCE
OBJECTIVE 2 – EFFECTIVENESS
Ensure that NRC actions are effective, efficient, realistic, and timely

Performance Measures:

- The percentage of selected processes that deliver the desired efficiency improvement is greater than 70 percent. (The goal is greater than 90 by 2008).

VERIFICATION:

Initiatives such as the Government Performance and Results Act challenge Federal agencies to become more effective and efficient and to justify their budget requests with demonstrated program results. The drive to improve performance in Government, coupled with increasing demands on the NRC's finite resources, clearly indicates a need for the agency to become more effective and efficient. The NRC has established a performance measure to improve efficiency, which supports the two primary goals of safety and security and also addresses management excellence.

On an annual basis, candidate processes would be selected as part of this performance measure. For the purposes of this measure, the desired efficiency improvement of a process is defined as a positive change in its cost, quality, productivity, or timeliness. A desired efficiency improvement would be expressed as resource savings or cost avoidance for the agency or as a positive benefit to external stakeholders with respect to effectiveness, efficiency, or realism.

Offices will use the following process to identify and report on desired efficiency improvements:

(1) Select and define a candidate process. Offices will identify processes at the beginning of each fiscal year that they will measure for desired efficiency improvement.

(2) Analyze process for areas in need of improvement. This could include cost reduction, quality, timeliness, or other unique factors that can be measured for desired efficiency improvement.

(3) Establish targets for efficiency improvements. Based on past experience and if previous trend data is available, offices will identify specific desired targets that they feel are challenging but achievable. The targets could involve improvements in cost, quality, productivity, or timeliness.

(4) Report progress annually. Offices will report the actual data at the end of each fiscal year and may adjust the target accordingly, based on the results from previous years.

VALIDATION:

Overall actual performance will be measured by determining the percentage of the processes selected annually that delivered their intended desired efficiency improvement. At a minimum, the agency must achieve its target in 70 percent of the selected processes.

The process of collecting the data and ensuring the information is complete, accurate, and consistent will be the responsibility of the individual Office Director who will review and approve the data submitted by staff.

- No more than one instance per program where licensing or regulatory activities unnecessarily impede the safe and beneficial uses of radioactive materials. *Target: Reactor Program = 2 (1 in each Tier II program) Materials/Waste Program = 5 (1 in each Tier II program)*

VERIFICATION AND VALIDATION:

This measure is intended to serve as a precursor to the strategic-level outcome of "no significant licensing or

regulatory impediments to the safe and beneficial uses of radioactive materials." The purpose of the measure is to provide an indication of overall agency performance with respect to the strategic objective of enabling the safe use of radioactive materials for beneficial civilian purposes.

The following table describes how the agency fulfills its role in enabling various phases of the business cycle.

Phase of Business Cycle	Intent of enabling in each category
Potential applicants	Provide an effective and efficient regulatory infrastructure so that this group is inclined to pursue licenses if they so choose. Ensure that the NRC is not a barrier to entry due to unnecessary regulatory burden.
Applicants	Provide stable and predictable processes so that applicants can enter the business in a timely fashion, only constrained by their ability to operate safely and securely (i.e., abide by NRC regulations).
Current licensees	Ensure that the regulation do not pose an unnecessary regulatory burden.

The key difference between this performance measure and the related strategic outcome is that the strategic outcome focuses on significant impediments, while the performance measure does not contain this qualifier. Thus, the performance measure is designed to capture lower-level instances where NRC programs may have unnecessarily created impediments. The following types of examples could count against this performance measure (and possibly against the strategic outcome as well, depending on severity):

■ missing a key timeliness measure (e.g., for fuel-cycle licensing actions or reactor power uprates) or milestone (e.g., termination of a license for complex decommissioning cases)

■ failing to adjust the regulatory framework to support new technologies or otherwise respond to significant changes in the regulatory environment

■ imposing an unnecessary regulatory burden on licensees or applicants to the extent that the NRC becomes a barrier to entry or sustainability

Efforts to risk inform regulatory programs, improve programmatic effectiveness and efficiency, and reduce unnecessary regulatory burden are all positive steps that can be taken to enable the safe use of radioactive materials.

Because the NRC does not have prior experience in applying this type of measure, the metric will likely require adjustment over the first few years. The intent is to set aggressive annual targets that reflect the agency's commitment to continuous improvement. Consequently, it should be expected that some impediments will occur at the performance level due to resource limitations, emergent high-priority demands, or other circumstances beyond the control of program managers. Exceptions reported under this measure are considered in the agency's assessment of the related strategic outcome.

ORGANIZATIONAL EXCELLENCE
OBJECTIVE 3 – OPERATIONAL EXCELLENCE

Ensure excellence in agency management to carry out the NRC's strategic objective

Performance Measures:

■ Percentage of selected NRC management programs reported by support offices to have delivered intended outcomes is equal to or greater than 80 percent.

VERIFICATION:

The NRC considered the management and support needed to achieve the agency's mission, preexisting management challenges, and other initiatives. This goal includes strategies for the management of human capital, infrastructure management, improved financial performance, expanded electronic government, budget and performance integration, and internal communications. The process of collecting the data and making sure the information is complete, accurate, and consistent will be the responsibility of the individual Office Director, who will review and approve the data submitted by staff.

VALIDATION:

Overall actual performance will be measured by determining the percentage of the four programs that delivered their intended management outcomes. At a minimum, to meet the overall target of 80 percent, all four programs must achieve an average score of 75 percent of the activity targets.

■ The percentage of selected processes reported by support offices that deliver desired efficiency improvement is equal to or greater than 90 percent. (Goal is greater than 90 percent by 2008.)

VERIFICATION:

Initiatives such as the Government Performance and Results Act are challenging Federal agencies to become more effective and efficient and to justify their budget requests with demonstrated program results. The drive to improve performance in Government, coupled with increasing demands on the NRC's finite resources, clearly indicates a need for the agency to become more effective and efficient. The NRC has established a performance measure to improve efficiency, which supports the two primary goals of safety and security, and also addresses management excellence.

On an annual basis, the agency will select candidate processes as part of this performance measure. For the purposes of this measure, the desired efficiency improvement of a process is defined as a positive change in its cost, quality, productivity, or timeliness. Desired efficiency improvement would be expressed as resource savings or cost avoidance for the agency or as a positive benefit to external stakeholders with respect to effectiveness, efficiency, or realism.

Support offices will use the following process to identify and report on desired efficiency improvements:

(1) Select and define a candidate process. Offices will identify processes at the beginning of each fiscal year that they will measure for desired efficiency improvement.

(2) Analyze process for areas in need of improvement. This could include cost reduction, quality, timeliness, or other unique factors as appropriate that can be measured for desired efficiency improvement.

(3) Establish targets for efficiency improvements. Based on past experience and if previous trend data is available, offices will identify specific desired targets that they feel are challenging but can be achieved. The target improvements could involve cost, quality, productivity, or timeliness.

(4) Report progress annually. Offices will report the actual data at the end of each fiscal year and may adjust the target accordingly, based on the results from previous years.

VALIDATION:

Overall actual performance will be measured by determining the percentage of the processes selected annually that delivered their intended desired efficiency improvement. At a minimum, 90 percent of the selected processes must have achieved their targets.

The process of collecting the data and ensuring the information is complete, accurate, and consistent will be the responsibility of the individual Office Director, who will review and approve the data submitted by staff.

The Brunswick nuclear power plant, named for the county in which it is located, covers 4.86 sq km (1,200 acres). The site is adjacent to the town of Southport, NC, and to wetlands and woodlands.

APPENDIX E
AGREEMENT STATES

(AS OF APRIL 2008)

U.S.NRC
United States Nuclear Regulatory Commission
Protecting People and the Environment

Photo Courtesy of the Entergy Corporation.

Grand Gulf nuclear power station uses a General Electric boiling-water reactor near Port Gibson, MS. The plant has a 156.5-meter (520-foot) cooling tower and is situated on a wooded site with two lakes.

AGREEMENT STATES (AS OF APRIL 2008)

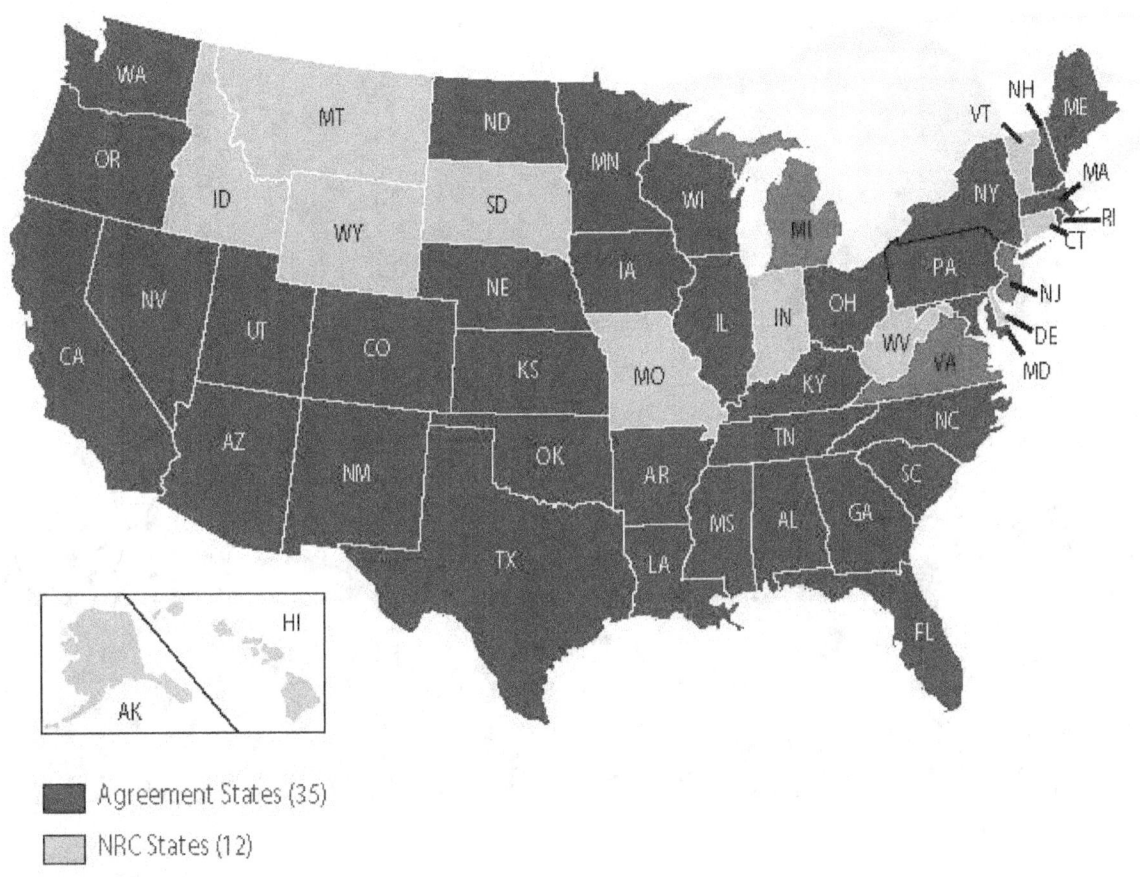

■ Agreement States (35)

☐ NRC States (12)

■ NRC States that have expressed
intent to sign Agreement (3)

Photo Courtesy of the NRC Photo Library.

The Kewaunee Power Station in Carlton, WI, 43 km (27 miles) southeast of Green Bay, WI. The Kewaunee Power Station was the fourth nuclear plant built in Wisconsin and the 44th built in the United States.

APPENDIX F
NRC ORGANIZATIONAL CHART

(AS OF NOVEMBER 2008)

U.S. NUCLEAR REGULATORY COMMISSION

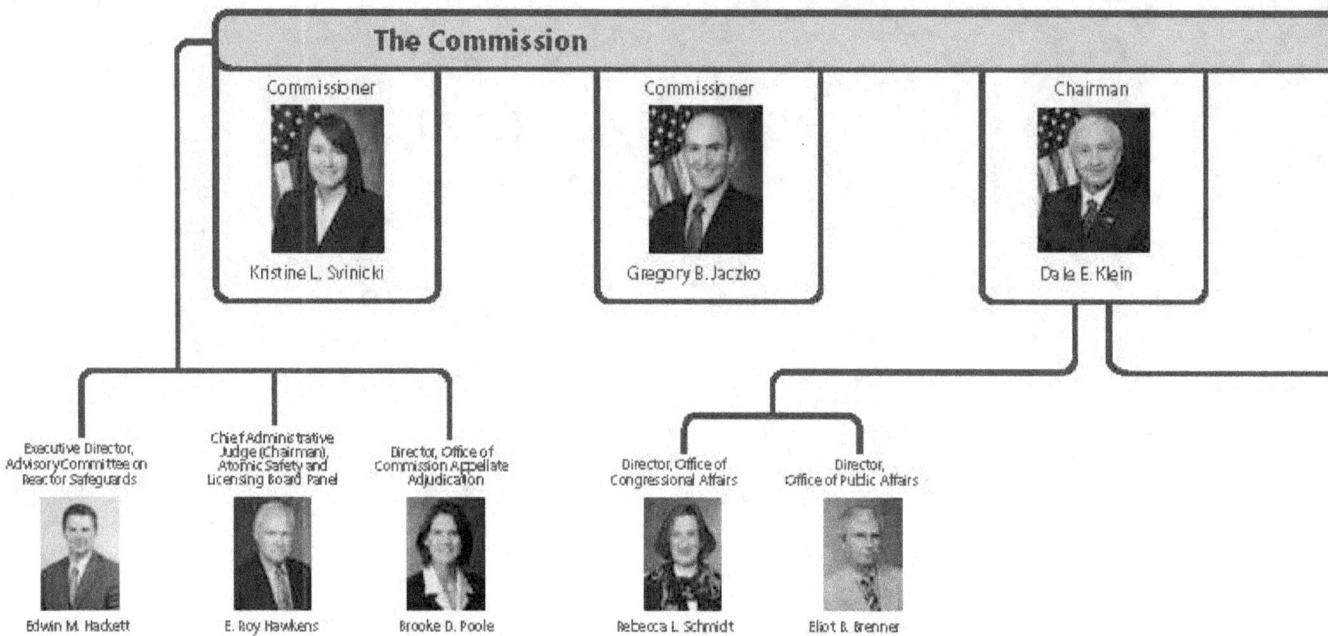

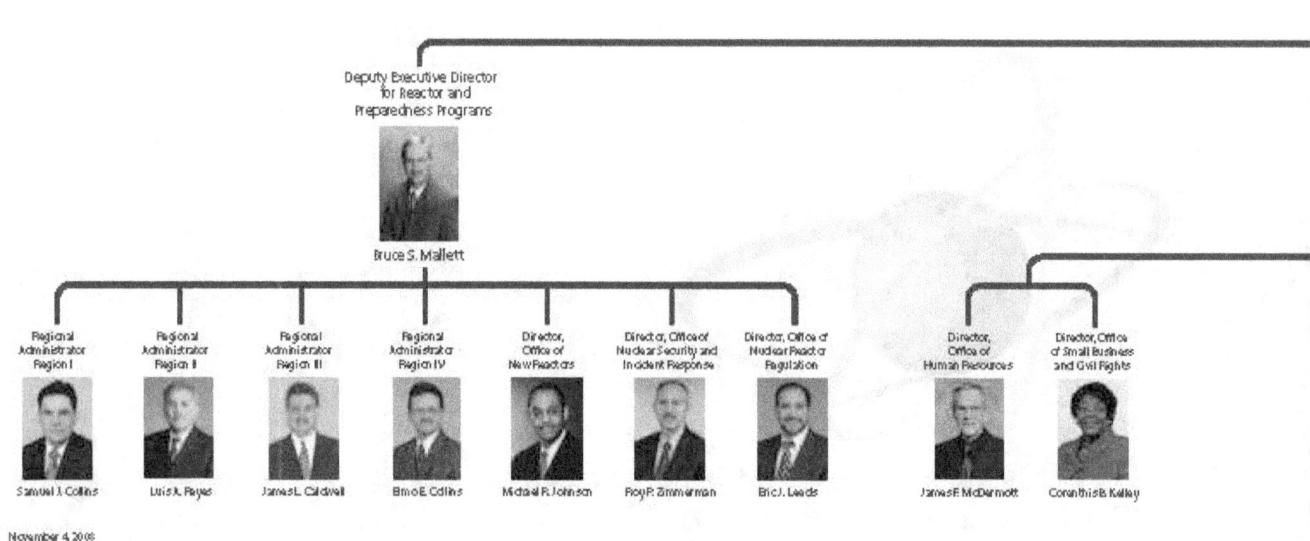

November 4, 2008

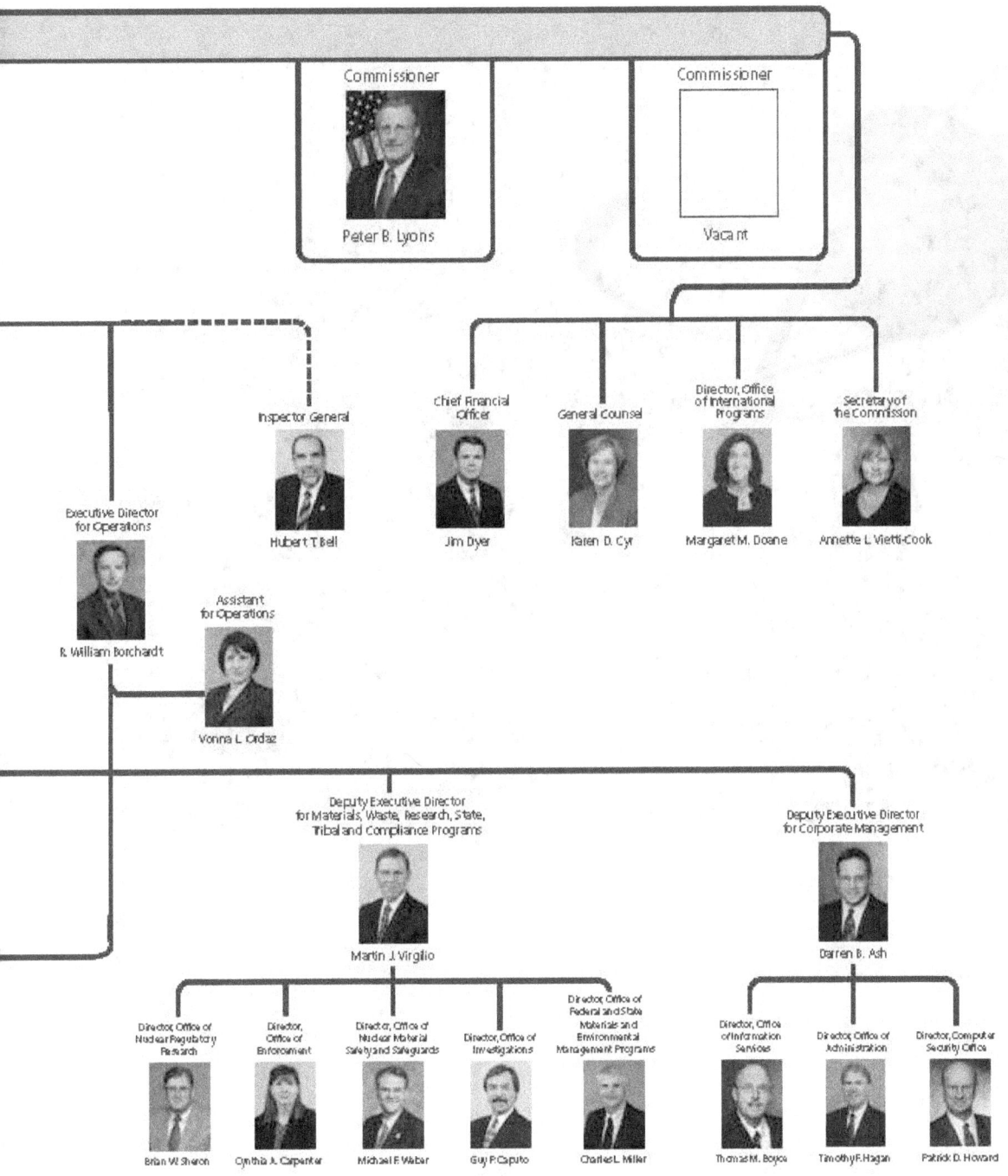

Commissioner
Peter B. Lyons

Commissioner
Vacant

Inspector General
Hubert T. Bell

Chief Financial Officer
Jim Dyer

General Counsel
Karen D. Cyr

Director, Office of International Programs
Margaret M. Doane

Secretary of the Commission
Annette L. Vietti-Cook

Executive Director for Operations
R. William Borchardt

Assistant for Operations
Vonna L. Ordaz

Deputy Executive Director for Materials, Waste, Research, State, Tribal and Compliance Programs
Martin J. Virgilio

Deputy Executive Director for Corporate Management
Darren B. Ash

Director, Office of Nuclear Regulatory Research
Brian W. Sheron

Director, Office of Enforcement
Cynthia A. Carpenter

Director, Office of Nuclear Material Safety and Safeguards
Michael F. Weber

Director, Office of Investigations
Guy P. Caputo

Director, Office of Federal and State Materials and Environmental Management Programs
Charles L. Miller

Director, Office of Information Services
Thomas M. Boyce

Director, Office of Administration
Timothy F. Hagan

Director, Computer Security Office
Patrick D. Howard

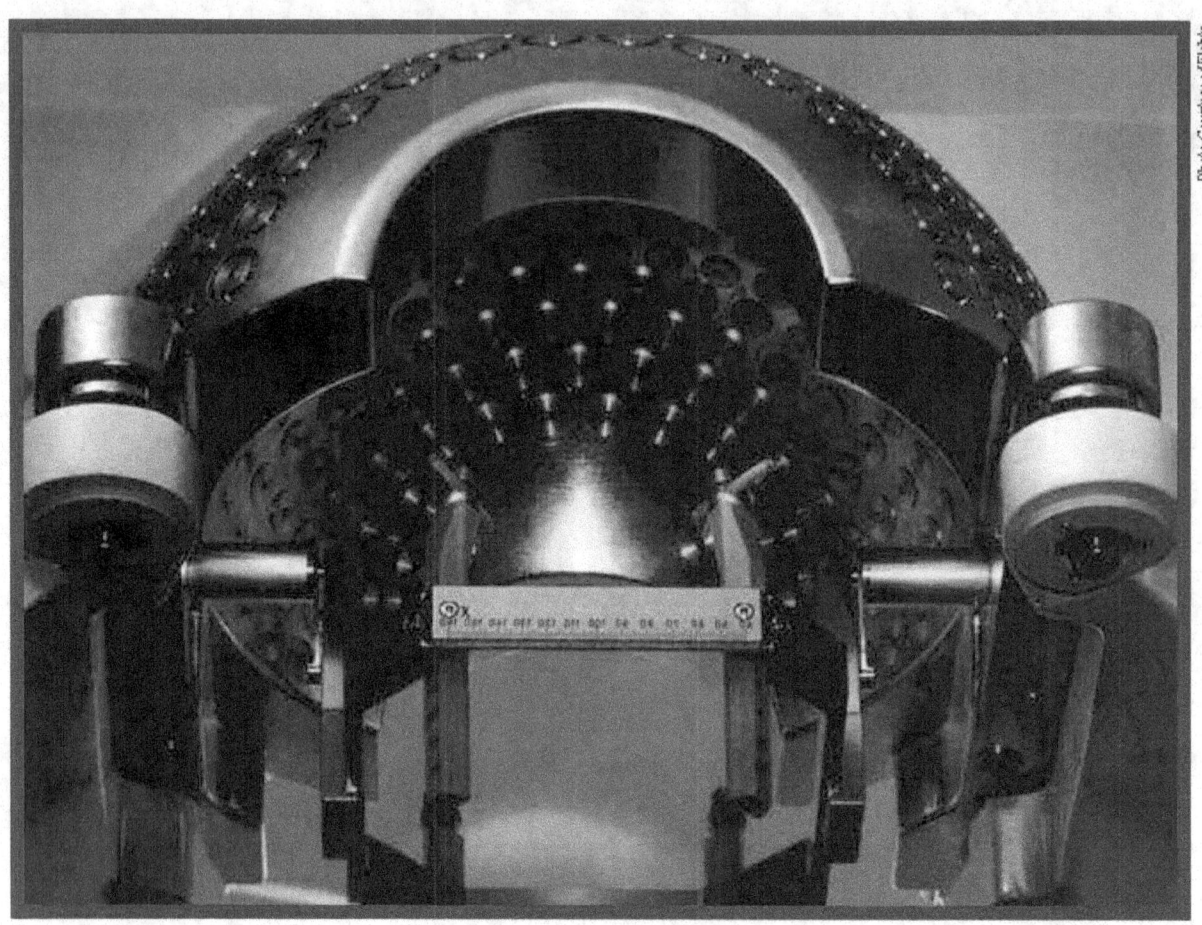

Gamma Knife® device used for treating brain tumors with focused radiation beams.

APPENDIX G
ACRONYMS AND ABBREVIATIONS

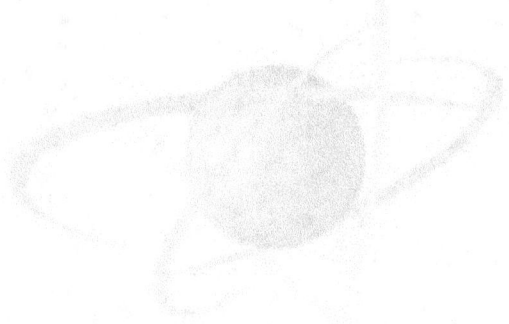

Acronym	
10 CFR	Title 10 of the *Code of Federal Regulations*
ACNW&M	Advisory Committee on Nuclear Waste and Materials
ADAMS	Agencywide Documents Access and Management System
AICOA	American Institute of Certified Public Accountants
ALARA	as low as reasonably achievable
ALC	agency location code
AO	abnormal occurrence
ASP	accident sequence precursor
C&A	certification and accreditation
CAROLFIRE	Cable Response to Live Fire
CCDP	conditional core damage probability
CFO	Chief Financial Officer
CFR	*Code of Federal Regulations*
COL	combined operating license
CRCPD	conference of radiation control program directors
CSO	Computer Security Office
CSRS	Civil Service Retirement System
CUI	controlled unclassified information
CWP	centralized work planning
CY	calendar year
DAA	designated approving authority
DBT	design basis threat
DFS	Division of Facilities and Security
DHS	U.S. Department of Homeland Security
DOE	U.S. Department of Energy
DOI-NBC	Department of the Interior National Business Center
DOL	U.S. Department of Labor
DOT	U.S. Department of Transportation
ECIC	Executive Committee on Internal Control

Acronym	
EDATS	Electronic Document and Action Tracking System
EDO	Executive Director for Operations
e-Gov	Federal Government's Electronic Government
EO	executive order
EPAct	Energy Policy Act of 2005
EPR	Evolutionary Power Reactor
EPRI	Electric Power Research Institute
ERIDS	Electronic Regulatory Information Distribution System
ESBWR	Economic Simplified Boiling-Water Reactor
ETUS	Enrichment Technology U.S., Inc.
FCFOP	Fuel Cycle Facility Oversight Program
FCNMED	Fuel Cycle Nuclear Material Event Database
FECA	Federal Employees Compensation Act
FERS	Federal Employees Retirement System
FFMIA	Federal Financial Management Improvement Act
FICA	Federal Insurance Contribution Act
FIPS	Federal Information Processing Standard
FISMA	Federal Information Security Management Act
FMFIA	Federal Managers Financial Integrity Act
FOIA	Freedom of Information Act
FPS	Federal Protective Service
FR	*Federal Register*
FTE	full-time equivalent
FY	fiscal year
GAAP	generally accepted accounting principles
GAO	U.S. Government Accountability Office

U.S.NRC
United States Nuclear Regulatory Commission
Protecting People and the Environment

Acronym	
GEM	graphical evaluation module
GLTS	General License Tracking System
GPRA	Government Performance and Results Act
GSA	General Services Administration
HHS	U.S. Department of Health and Human Services
HSPD	Homeland Security Presidential Directive
IAEA	International Atomic Energy Agency
IATO	interim approval to operate
IG	Inspector General
IMPEP	integrated materials performance evaluation program
Improvement Act	Federal Financial Management Improvement Act
INL	Idaho National Laboratory
Integrity Act	Federal Managers Financial Integrity Act
IPAC	Intragovernmental Payment and Collection System
IPR	intellectual property rights
IPSS	Integrated Personnel Security System
ISA	integrated safety analysis
ISG	interim staff guidance
ISO	International Standards Organization
IT	information technology
ITAAC	inspections, tests, analyses, and acceptance criteria
KM	knowledge management
LER	licensee event report
LERSearch	Licensee Event Report Search System
LES	Louisiana Energy Services
MC	NRC Manual Chapter
MC&A	material control and accounting

Acronym	
MD	management directive
MDEP	Multinational Design Evaluation Program
MOC	memorandum of cooperation
NEA	Nuclear Energy Agency
NGNP	next generation nuclear plant
NIST	National Institute of Standards and Technology
NMED	Nuclear Materials Event Database
NMMSS	Nuclear Materials Management and Safeguards System
NMSS	Office of Nuclear Material Safety and Safeguards
NNSA	National Nuclear Safety Administration of China
NRC	U.S. Nuclear Regulatory Commission
NRR	Office of Nuclear Reactor Regulation
NSIR	Office of Nuclear Security and Incident Response
NSTS	National Source Tracking System
NTEU	National Treasury Employees Union
NWF	Nuclear Waste Fund
OAR	official agency record
OBRA-90	The Omnibus Budget Reconciliation Act of 1990
OCM	Office of the Commission
OGC	Office of General Counsel
OHR	Office of Human Resources
OIG	Office of the Inspector General
OIS	Office of Information Services
OMB	Office of Management and Budget
OUO	official use only
PAR	Performance and Accountability Report

Acronym	
PART	Program Assessment Rating Tool
PATRAM 2007	The International Symposium on Packaging and Transportation of Radioactive Materials
PC	personal computer
PI	performance indicators
PII	personally identifiable information
PMM	project management methodology
POA&M	plan of action and milestones
PRA	probabilistic risk assessment
RDD	radiological dispersal device
RIS	regulatory issue summary
ROP	Reactor Oversight Process
SAPHIRE	Systems Analysis Program for Hands-On Integrated Reliability Evaluations
SCSS	Sequence Coding and Search System
SDP	significant determination process
SES	senior executive service
SFFAS	Statements of Federal Financial Accounting Standards
SGI	safeguards information
Silex	separation of isotopes by laser excitation
SNM	special nuclear material
SOARCA	State-of-the-Art Reactor Consequence Analyses
SPPP	Standard Practice Procedures Plan
SRS	Savannah River Site
SSP	(GLTA) System Security Plan
ST&E	security test and evaluation
SUNSI	sensitive unclassified, nonsafeguards information
T&L	time and labor

Acronym	
TAD	transportation, aging, and disposal
TSP	Thrift Savings Plan
UF_6	uranium hexafluoride
USAID	U.S. Agency for International Development
USAPWR	U.S. Advanced Pressurized-Water Reactor
USEC	United States Enrichment Corporation
USSGL	United States Standard General Ledger
V&V	verification and validation
VARANSAC	Vietnam Agency for Radiation and Nuclear Safety and Control

U.S.NRC
United States Nuclear Regulatory Commission
Protecting People and the Environment

NRC FORM 335 (9-2004) NRCMD 3.7	U.S. NUCLEAR REGULATORY COMMISSION	1. REPORT NUMBER (Assigned by NRC, Add Vol., Supp., Rev., and Addendum Numbers, If any.)
BIBLIOGRAPHIC DATA SHEET *(See Instructions on the reverse)*		NUREG-1542, Vol. 14

2. TITLE AND SUBTITLE	3. DATE REPORT PUBLISHED	
U.S. Nuclear Regulatory Commission Performance and Accountability Report FY 2008	MONTH	YEAR
	November	2008

4. FIN OR GRANT NUMBER

n/a

5. AUTHOR(S)	6. TYPE OF REPORT
Richard Rough, et. al	Annual

7. PERIOD COVERED *(Inclusive Dates)*

FY 2008

8. PERFORMING ORGANIZATION - NAME AND ADDRESS *(If NRC, provide Division, Office or Region, U.S. Nuclear Regulatory Commission, and mailing address; if contractor, provide name and mailing address)*

Resource Management and Support Staff
Office of the Chief Financial Officer
U.S. Nuclear Regulatory Commission
Washington, DC 20555-0001

9. SPONSORING ORGANIZATION - NAME AND ADDRESS *(If NRC, type "Same as above"; if contractor, provide NRC Division, Office or Region, U.S. Nuclear Regulatory Commission, and mailing address)*

Same as 8, above

10. SUPPLEMENTARY NOTES

11. ABSTRACT *(200 words or less)*

The FY 2008 Performance and Accountability Report provides performance results and audited financial statements that enable Congress, the President, and the public to assess the performance of the agency in achieving its mission and stewardship of its resources. The report contains a concise overview, management's discussion and analysis, as well as performance and financial sections. Additional details of performance results and program evaluations can be found in the appendices.

12. KEY WORDS/DESCRIPTORS *(List words or phrases that will assist researchers in locating the report)*	13. AVAILABILITY STATEMENT
Performance and Accountability Report FY 2008 PAR	unlimited
	14. SECURITY CLASSIFICATION
	(This Page) unclassified
	(This Report) unclassified
	15. NUMBER OF PAGES
	16. PRICE

NRC FORM 335 (9-2004)

PRINTED ON RECYCLED PAPER